D1443085

3 0900 00312 2943

MICHAEL LAINE is a member of the Department of English at the University of Toronto.

Among the services provided by the *Mill News Letter*, published in conjunction with the Collected Works of John Stuart Mill, has been the collection of bibliographical information about Mill. From 1965 to 1970 an alphabetical checklist compiled by Dudley L. Hascall and John M. Robson was published serially, and subsequent issues have contained lists of recent publications. Professor Laine has now revised, updated, and indexed these listings for publication in more permanent form.

The bibliography lists almost 2000 books and articles published to the end of 1978 dealing in a substantial way with Mill's thought and career. Annotation has been provided where the title of the book or article is not self-explanatory, and occasionally to indicate the direction of an argument or to quote a revealing or amusing passage. Cross-references note items that take up the same point or dispute it.

Three appendixes list light or satiric verse mentioning Mill, cartoons (both chiefly found during the parliamentary years), and portraits. Two indexes, a topical index and an index of persons cited, add to the usefulness of the volume.

Bibliography of Works on John Stuart Mill

MICHAEL LAINE

UNIVERSITY OF TORONTO PRESS

Toronto Buffalo London

© *University of Toronto Press 1982*
Toronto Buffalo London
Printed in Canada

ISBN 0-8020-2414-9

Canadian Cataloguing in Publication Data

Laine, Michael, 1932-
  Bibliography of works on John Stuart Mill
  Includes indexes.
  ISBN 0-8020-2414-9
  1. Mill, John Stuart, 1806-1873 – Bibliography.
  I. Title.
  Z8574.8.L34   016.192   C82-094625-7

Contents

Introduction

The first modern comprehensive checklist of works on John Stuart Mill was published in Japan by Keitaro Amano in 1964 as volume III, part 4 of his *Bibliography of the Classical Economists*. Amano's volume includes a bibliography of works by Mill and a record of their translations into foreign languages as well as writings about him. The section of writings on Mill, comprising less than half the volume, is arranged under subject headings. Unfortunately, a user may not always respond to Amano's divisions; should he not, he has no way of locating an article.

The present bibliography originates in the alphabetical checklist compiled by Dudley L. Hascall and John M. Robson and published serially in the *Mill News Letter* from 1965 to 1970. This list, although extraordinarily useful and comprehensive, includes many items which, although they may mention Mill, give him only passing attention and develop no arguments about his thought or his career. These have been excluded here, and useful items, omitted from the Hascall-Robson list and from Amano, have been added. At the time that the list was completed in 1970, Robson, as editor of the *News Letter*, wrote that he was considering its republication in more permanent form. During the publication of the list, and subsequently, the *Mill News Letter* has attempted to keep its readers apprised of new work in Mill studies through its column 'Recent Publications'; readers have been a great help to us in keeping up to date and in filling gaps. At the beginning of 1975 we felt that we were in possession of enough new material to make a complete revision of the list worthwhile. So the present bibliography is comprised of an extensively revised Hascall-Robson list to which has been added new material to the end of 1978.

Like all such checklists, this one is not designed to be complete. All entries in the Hascall-Robson list and those in 'Recent Publications' have been checked, and much material from other sources has been added. But, as will be obvious, work concerning Mill crosses many disciplines; almost every textbook in philosophy, economics, and political science at least mentions Mill, and most summarize his work and career. Such texts, although useful in themselves, often merely repeat received knowledge and therefore have been excluded except where especially interesting either because of their content or because of the prominence of their authors. Those works dealing with specific problems in philosophy, economics, or political science, as well as surveys of history and histories of literature merely mentioning Mill in passing, have been excluded. So have most dissertations, except those published dissertations that deal with topics not extensively treated elsewhere and those published in foreign languages which seem to direct us to a national preoccupation or interest. Only especially important or interesting reviews of Mill's work or those by especially prominent reviewers have been included, and there are no reviews of posthumous editions. Mill was Member of Parliament for Westminster from 1865 to 1868. During that time, he was mentioned in nearly every issue of every British journal and repeatedly in journals on this side of the Atlantic. It was decided that a complete list of such articles would be of little use and that only those of special interest should appear.

Since scholars and researchers will come to Mill with their own interests and prejudices and will wish to make their own decisions, annotation is light, and, for the most part, restricted to entries where the title of the book or article is not self-explanatory. Occasionally the direction of an argument or a revealing or an amusing passage is quoted. Articles taking up the same point or disputing it are cross-indexed.

As in the Hascall-Robson list, entries appearing in Germanic, Romance, and Scandinavian languages have been included, and its separate section of entries in Russian (transliterated) has been placed in alphabetical order in the text. For works in Japanese, Amano's bibliography is comprehensive to 1964, and the *Mill News Letter* will be found useful for titles after that date.

The bibliography closes with appendices listing light or satiric verse mentioning Mill, and cartoons (both chiefly found during the parliamentary years). There is also a list of portraits; modern reproductions of these have not been listed except when they are not easily accessible elsewhere.

The index, in its section on Mill himself, has been kept as general as possible so that fine discriminations concerning categories would be made by users and not for them. This section of the index is followed by one indexing those persons extensively treated in the entries. Where items might have been placed under one heading or another, I have tried not to make hard decisions and have indexed the item under each in the belief that this would aid rather than confuse a user. Verse, cartoons, and portraits have not been indexed.

Users of this bibliography will, of course, wish to consult *The Collected Works of John Stuart Mill* published by the University of Toronto Press under the editorship of John M. Robson. Introductions and Textual Introductions to these volumes have not been listed here.

Acknowledgements

I owe a great debt to Dudley L. Hascall who generously gave his work to John Robson and the Mill Project in 1965. I am also indebted to correspondents to the *Mill News Letter* who have kept us informed of current entries; Dennis Rohatyn and Claude Urey are owed special thanks as are my Japanese colleagues Gyozo Fukuhara, Shigekazu Yamashita, and Shiro Sugihara. J.B. Schneewind has been very helpful with advice as has Jack Stillinger. For the section on light verse I am in the greatest part indebted to Evelyn Pugh; James Scanlan found and transliterated the majority of the titles in Russian for the Hascall-Robson list.

I am also very grateful to personnel at the British Library, the British Library of Political and Economic Science, the Library of the University of London, the New York Public Library, the Rare Book Room at the University of Illinois (Urbana-Champaign), the Widener Library at Harvard, the Robarts Library and the Library of Victoria College at my own University. Librarians at all of these places have been extraordinarily patient and helpful. And no one can avoid a debt of gratitude to Walter Houghton and his colleagues for the *Wellesley Index*.

I must also thank members of the Mill Project: Bruce Kinzer and Marion Filipiuk have been helpful and kind as have Mary O'Connor, Maureen Clarke and Allison Taylor.

Judith LeGoff, who helped with research, deserves a great deal of credit; without her the list would be much less complete. Jean Houston read the MS for the University of Toronto Press; she caught errors and inconsistencies and improved it enormously. Rea Wilmshurst prepared the typescript; without her care and attention, it would be far less accurate. My thanks also to Judith Broughton, who read proof.

Finally I want to thank John Robson for sharing his knowledge and for his patience and support not only during the term of this project but throughout our association.

The research for this bibliography was supported by a grant from the Social Sciences and Humanities Research Council of Canada and to them I am very grateful.

BIBLIOGRAPHY OF WORKS ON JOHN STUART MILL

Bibliography

1 Anon. [Account of JSM's Death and Funeral], *Literary Guide and Rationalist Review*, 1 July 1907

2 —— *An Alphabetical List of the Philosophers and Discoverers of John Stuart Mill's System of Logic*. Oxford: Shrimpton, 1871

3 —— *An Answer to Mr J. Stuart Mill's 'Subjection of Women.' The Advance of Transcendentalism. Female Suffrage: An Answer to Mrs H. Fawcett on the Electoral Disabilities of Women*. The Grosvenor Papers, nos 1-3. London: Darton, 1869, 1870

4 —— 'The Austrian Economists and Their View of Value,' *Harvard Quarterly Journal of Economics*, 3 (1888), 1-31

5 —— 'Autobiography by John Stuart Mill,' *La Critique Philosophique*, 2:2 (1873), 227-33

6 —— 'The Autobiography of an Atheist,' *Scribner's Monthly*, 7 (1874), 600-11. (Review)

7 —— 'The Autobiography of Consciousness; or, The Experiences of an Indoor Servant,' *Fraser's Magazine*, 80 (1869), 119-28. (An account of the history of consciousness from Descartes to Mill)

8 —— 'Autobiography of John Stuart Mill,' *Christian Observer*, 74 (1874), 37-50. (Review)

9 —— 'Autobiography of John Stuart Mill,' *Popular Science Monthly*, 4 (1874), 376-7. (Review)

10 —— 'Autobiography of John Stuart Mill,' *Saturday Review*, 36 (1873), 570-1. Reprinted in *Eclectic Magazine*, ns 19 (1874), 55-9. (Review)

11 —— 'Beer and Bigotry,' *National Reformer*, 6 (1865), 469-70. (Westminster election)

12 —— *A Century of Books. How More than 100 Famous Books of the Past Century Were Judged by Contemporary Critics … in Reviews Gleaned from the Pages of the 'New York Times.'* New York, 1951

13 —— 'Ce qu'il y a de possible en fait d'attributs de la Divinité, selon Stuart Mill,' *La Critique Philosophique*, 4:1 (1875), 172-6

14 —— 'Courage in Belief,' *Christian Examiner*, 74 [5th ser, 12] (1863), 383-400. (Uses the *Logic* [5th ed.] and Spencer's *A System of Philosophy* to attack empiricism and to assert that 'belief is the lawful sovereign of the senses')

15 —— 'La Crise du développement mental de Stuart Mill d'après son Autobiographie,' *La Critique Philosophique*, 2:2 (1874), 385-94

16 —— 'The Death of Mr Mill,' *Pall Mall Gazette*, 10 May 1873, 1-2

17 —— 'Disraeli on Mill,' *Spectator*, 19 (1846), 444. (Describes Disraeli's use of *Some Unsettled Questions* in House of Commons debate 3 May 1846. Claims Disraeli misrepresented JSM in presenting him as an advocate of reciprocity.)

18 —— 'The Doctrine of Perception,' *National Quarterly Review*, 39 (1879), 151-61

19 —— 'L'Education de Stuart Mill, d'après son Autobiography,' *La Critique Philosophique*, 2:2 (1873), 321-31

20 —— 'Education, Personally Supervised,' *North American Review*, 184 (1907), 447-8

21 —— 'Emerson to John Stuart Mill,' *More Books*, 15 (1940), 436-7. (A letter of introduction, dated 6 May 1865, from Emerson to JSM concerning George Walker. Printed in full.)

22 —— 'England and Ireland,' *The Times*, 20 Feb. 1868, 10. (Review)

23 —— 'The Ethics of Utilitarianism,' *National Quarterly Review*, 39 (1878), 335-47

24 —— 'Examination of Mill's Philosophy of Necessary Truth and of Causation,' *New Englander*, 8 (1850), 161-86

25 —— 'Famous Autobiographies,' *Edinburgh Review*, 214 (1911), 331-56. (See also Mary Taylor)

26 —— 'Female Suffrage,' *Saturday Review*, 23 (1867), 385-6. (Critical comment on JSM's proposal to extend vote to women)

27 —— 'Female Suffrage,' *Saturday Review*, 23 (1867), 647-8. (JSM's amendment to the 2nd Reform Bill)

28 —— 'Fitzjames Stephen's Answer to Mill,' *Church Eclectic*, 2 (1874), 66-8. (Reprinted from *Literary Churchman*)

29 —— 'The Forthcoming Election in Westminster,' *National Reformer*, 6 (1865), 425

30 —— *Gneist und Stuart Mill. Alt-englische und neu-englische Staatsanschauungen. Eine politische Parallele.* Berlin: Adolf, 1869

31 —— 'Goethe and Mill: A Contrast,' *Westminster Review*, ns 46 (1874), 38-70

32 —— *The Gospel for the Nineteenth Century.* 4th ed. London: Longmans, Green, 1880. (1st ed., 1876, published as *Leaving Us an Example: Is It Living - and Why? An Enquiry Suggested by Certain Passages in John Stuart Mill's 'Essays on Religion.'* 2nd and subsequent eds as above.)

33 —— 'A Great and Good Man,' *Times Literary Supplement*, 16 Apr. 1964, 301-3. (Review of *The Earlier Letters of John Stuart Mill, 1812-1848.* Ed. Francis E. Mineka. *Collected Works*, XII & XIII. Toronto: University of Toronto Press, 1963)

34 —— *Hamilton versus Mill. A Thorough Discussion of Each Chapter in Mr John S. Mill's Examination of Hamilton's Logic and Philosophy Beginning with the Logic.* Pt I, Edinburgh: Maclachlan and Stewart, 1866; Pt II, London, 1867

35 —— 'Housing Drive Takes Toll of History: J.S. Mill's House at Avignon,' *The Times*, 31 Aug. 1960, 7

36 —— 'Inaugural Address,' *Westminster Review*, ns 31 (1867), 523-5. (Review)

37 —— *Is Theism Immoral? An Examination of Mr J.S. Mill's Arguments against Mansel's View of Religion.* Swansea: Rowse, 1877

38 —— 'John Stuart Mill,' *Appleton's Journal*, 3 (1870), 126-9

39 —— 'John Stuart Mill,' *British Quarterly Review*, 48 (1868), 1-58

40 —— 'John Stuart Mill,' *Church Herald*, 4 (1873)

41 —— 'John Stuart Mill,' *Harper's Magazine*, 47 (1873), 528. (Obit. with portrait)

42 —— 'John Stuart Mill,' *Harper's Weekly*, 9 (1865), 677. (Short summary of career complimenting JSM on his election. With portrait.)

43 —— 'John Stuart Mill,' *Harper's Weekly*, 17 (1873), 436. (Obit. with portrait)

44 —— 'John Stuart Mill,' *Illustrated London News*, 62 (1873), 456. (Obit. with portrait)

45 —— 'John Stuart Mill,' *Leisure Hour*, 23 (1874), 73-7

46 —— 'John Stuart Mill,' *Nation*, 91 (1910), 217-19

47 —— 'John Stuart Mill,' *Nation and Athenaeum*, 33 (1923), 111-12

48 —— 'John Stuart Mill,' *Nature*, 8 (1873), 47

49 —— 'John Stuart Mill,' *Revue Britannique*, 6 (1873), 238-40

50 —— 'John Stuart Mill,' *Western*, ns 3 (1877), 555-61

51 —— 'John Stuart Mill als Philosoph und Nationalökonom,' *Unsere Zeit*, NF, 1 Jg (1865), 919-39

52 —— 'John Stuart Mill als Politiker und Sozialist,' *Vorwörts*, 20 May 1906

53 —— 'John Stuart Mill and Tuition Grants,' *Educational Freedom*, 9 (1970-71), 35-6

54 —— 'John Stuart Mill: Ein Karaktäristik,' *Forkskaren*, Jg 15, no 3 (1907)

55 —— 'John Stuart Mill et ses doctrines,' *Revue Britannique*, 2 (1874), 65-97

56 —— 'John Stuart Mill, MP,' *Eclectic Magazine*, 67 (1866), 120-2. (With portrait. Brief laudatory biographical sketch on JSM's entry into Parliament, quotes 'Mr John Stuart Mill,' *Illustrated London News*, 48 [1866], 280-1.)

57 —— 'John Stuart Mill, son politiker och sozialist,' *Forkskaren*, Jg 13, no 3 (1907)

58 —— 'John Stuart Mill's Autobiography,' *New England*, 33 (1874), 193-5

59 —— 'John Stuart Mill's Essays,' *Leisure Hour*, 24 (1875), 117-19

60 —— 'John Stuart Mills politische Schriften,' *Preussische Jahrbücher*, 10 (1862), 152-69

61 —— 'J.S. Mill on Parliamentary Reform,' *National Reformer*, 1 (1860), 6

62 —— 'J.S. Mill's Autobiography,' *Victoria Magazine*, 22 (1873), 181-9

63 —— *J.S. Mill's Psychological Theory. By a Philosophical Conservative*. [London,] 1867

64 —— 'J. St. Mill, Ueber die Freiheit,' *Stimmen der Zeit*, Nov. 1859

65 —— *Leaving Us an Example: Is It Living - and Why? An Enquiry Suggested by Certain Passages in John Stuart Mill's 'Essays on Religion.'* (See Anon., *The Gospel for the Nineteenth Century*)

66 —— 'Letters of G. Bancroft, J.A. Froude, S.R. Gardiner, A.W. Kinglake, J.S. Mill, John Morley, J.E.T. Rogers and Others to Richard and George Bentley, 1835-89,' *Bodleian Library Record*, 2 (1948), 229. (Note of a recent acquisition of MSS)

67 —— 'The Malt Tax and the National Debt,' *Saturday Review*, 21 (1866), 459-60. (Criticism of JSM's speech)

68 —— 'Mill,' *Gunton's Magazine*, 15 (1898), 342-4

69 —— 'Mill, Education, and Science,' *Popular Science Monthly*, 4 (1874), 368-73

70 —— 'Mill et M. J. Morley. - Note sur l'introduction des possibilités dans les analyses de Stuart Mill,' *La Critique Philosophique*, 4:1 (1875), 317-19

71 —— 'Mill on Hamilton,' *North American Review*, 103 (1866), 250-60

72 —— 'Mill on Liberty,' *National Review*, 8 (1859), 393-424. Reprinted in *On Liberty*. Ed. David Spitz. New York: Norton, 1975, 123-42

73 —— 'Mill on Liberty,' *Universal Review*, 1 (1859), 224-44

74 —— 'Mill on Representative Government,' *North American Review*, 95 (1862), 228-55. Reprinted in Anon., *True and False Democracy*, which see

75 —— 'Mill, Spencer and Socialism,' *Independent*, 61 (1906), 525-6

76 —— 'Mill's Autobiography,' *British Quarterly Review*, 59 (1874), 195-215

77 —— 'Mill's Essays on Some Unsettled Questions of Political Economy,' *Spectator*, 17 (1844), 810-11

78 —— 'Mill's Life and Thought,' *Times Literary Supplement*, 7 May 1954, 291

79 —— 'Mill's Logic,' *British Critic*, 4th ser, 34 (1843), 349-427

80 —— 'Mill's Logic,' *Saturday Review*, 2 (1856), 735-6. (Review of 4th ed.; remarks on corrections)

81 —— 'Mill's Logic. The Theory of Proof - The Science of Evidence,' *United States Magazine and Democratic Review*, ns 15 (1844), 441-53. (Very favourable review of *A System of Logic*)

82 —— 'Mill's Manuscript of "Autobiography" in John Rylands Library,' *Manchester Guardian*, 19 Aug. 1959, 5

83 —— 'Mr John Stuart Mill,' *Athenaeum*, 17 May 1873, 632, 662

84 —— 'Mr John Stuart Mill,' *Illustrated London News*, 48 (1866), 280-1. (With portrait.)   Reprinted in *National Reformer*, 7 (1866), 195-6. (JSM's work and his suitability as an MP; engraved portrait from London Stereoscopic Co.'s photo)

85 —— 'Mr John Stuart Mill,' *Spectator*, 46 (1873), 631-2. Reprinted in *Every Saturday*, 3rd ser, 3 (1873), 668-70. (Obit.)

86 —— 'Mr John Stuart Mill for Westminster,' *National Reformer*, 6 (1865), 217

87 —— 'Mr John Stuart Mill on Marriage,' *Public Opinion*, 15 July 1865, 55-6. (Substantial reprinting of an anon. leader in the *Standard*, 10 July 1865, 5-6; see Anon., *Standard*)

88 —— 'Mr John Stuart Mill's Atheism,' *National Reformer*, 6 (1865), 389-90. (Refers to the controversy over JSM's remarks in *Sir William Hamilton's Philosophy*)

89 —— 'Mr J.S. Mill and His Supporters,' *Record*, 2 June 1865, 2. (Attacks JSM over religious views in *Sir William Hamilton's Philosophy*; comment and extract inserted 'at the request of a correspondent.'   See Anon., '*The Record* on the Westminster Election.')

90 —— 'Mr J.S. Mill and the Inductive Origin of First Principles,' *Journal of Sacred Literature*, 4th ser, 9 (1866), 1-35

91 —— 'Mr J.S. Mill's Religious Confession,' *Spectator*, 47 (1874), 1325-7. Reprinted in *Littell's Living Age*, 123 (1874), 508-12; *Eclectic Magazine*, ns 21 (1875), 108-11

92 —— 'Mr Mill,' *Saturday Review*, 20 (1865), 38-9. (Critical comment on JSM's election campaign)

93 —— 'Mr Mill,' *Saturday Review*, 35 (1873), 638-9. (Critical obituary)

94 —— 'Mr Mill and the Infallible,' *Saturday Review*, 26 (1868), 584-5. (Critical of JSM for recommending candidates, particularly Bradlaugh)

95 —— 'Mr Mill and the Ladies,' *Saturday Review*, 22 (1866), 73-4. (Against right of women to vote)

96 —— 'Mr Mill and the Land-Laws,' *Nation*, 16 (1873), 71-2

97 —— 'Mr Mill and Mrs M'Laren,' *Saturday Review*, 26 (1868), 815-16. (Reasons for JSM's defeat - Eyre, Bradlaugh, and women's suffrage)

98 —— 'Mr Mill as a Politician,' *Saturday Review*, 22 (1866), 167-9. (Criticism of JSM as too partisan)

99 —— 'Mr Mill in Parliament,' *National Reformer*, 7 (1866), 113-14. Reprinted from the *Star*.

100 —— 'Mr Mill in Parliament,' *Saturday Review*, 21 (1866), 225-6. (Criticism of his speeches)

101 —— 'Mr Mill on America,' *Saturday Review*, 15 (1863), 302-3. (Comment on letter of JSM's supporting North in war against slavery)

102 —— 'Mr Mill on Double Chambers,' *Spectator*, 34 (1861), 443-4. (Refers to Chap. 13, 'Of a Second Chamber,' of *Considerations on Representative Government*)

103 —— 'Mr Mill on Education,' *Saturday Review*, 23 (1867), 165-6. (Review of JSM's inaugural lecture at St Andrews)

104 —— 'Mr Mill on Endowments,' *Saturday Review*, 27 (1869), 468-9. (Review of JSM's essay in *Fortnightly Review*)

105 —— 'Mr Mill on England and Ireland,' *Saturday Review*, 25 (1868), 282-3. (Hostile review)

106 —— 'Mr Mill on Land Tenure,' *The Times*, 19 Mar. 1873, 6

107 —— 'Mr Mill on Landed Property,' *Saturday Review*, 35 (1873), 370-1. (Review of speech)

108 —— 'Mr Mill on Political Liberty,' *Saturday Review*, 7 (1859), 186-7, 213-14. (Review of *On Liberty*)

109 —— 'Mr Mill on Property in Land,' *Saturday Review*, 31 (1871), 617-18. (Critical of Land Tenure Reform Association)

110 —— 'Mr Mill on Representative Government,' *Saturday Review*, 11 (1861), 424-5

111 —— 'Mr Mill on Utilitarianism,' *Westminster Review*, ns 24 (1863), 45-67. (Review)

112 —— 'Mr Mill on Women's Suffrage,' *Saturday Review*, 31 (1871), 71-2. (Review of speech)

113 —— 'Mr Mill's Autobiography,' *Daily News*, 18 Oct. 1873, 2

114 —— 'Mr Mill's Essays,' *Saturday Review*, 8 (1859), 46-8, 76-8. (Review of *Dissertations and Discussions*)

115 —— 'Mr Mill's Indictment of Sir William Hamilton,' *Eclectic Review*, 9 (1865), 378-87

116 —— 'Mr Mill's Plan for London,' *Spectator*, 39 (1866), 292-3. (Favourable comment on JSM's Bill for the municipal reorganization of London)

117 —— 'Mr Mill's Plan of Reform,' *Spectator*, 38 (1865), 433-4. (Opposes JSM's reformist policies as given to the Westminster electors)

118 —— 'Mr Mill's Speech on Capital Punishment,' *Westminster Review*, ns 35 (1869), 429-36. ('The next best thing to having Mr Mill for a friend is to have him for an opponent. You may not learn from him the full strength of your own case, but you, at least, have all the difficulties to be encountered arrayed in the clearest and most forcible manner, without taint from sophism or exaggeration' [430]. Controverts JSM's argument [most respectfully].)

119 —— *Mr Mill's Subjection of Women, from a Woman's Point of View.* London, 1870

120 —— 'Mneniya Boklya o sochineniyakh Millya' ['Buckle's Opinions of Mill's Works'], *Otechestvennyye zapiski* [*Annals of the Fatherland*], 1, 2 (1865), 117-38, 716-41

121 —— 'Modern Ideals and the Liberty of the Press,' *Dublin Review*, ns 29 (1877), 191-222. (Review of, *inter alia*, *On Liberty* and Milton's *Areopagitica*)

122 —— 'M. Mill et le droit politique des femmes,' *Revue Britannique*, 1 (1869), 233-4

123 —— 'Musings without Method,' *Blackwood's*, 187 (1910), 881-92. (Includes a review of Elliot's edition of the *Letters* [886-9] - 'an arid book which gives the picture of an arid man')

124 —— 'Mysli Dzhona-Styuarta Millya o pozitivnoy filosofii Ogyusta Konta' ['John Stuart Mill's Thoughts on the Positive Philosophy of Auguste Comte'], *Otechestvennyye zapiski [Annals of the Fatherland]*, 7, 9 (1865), 304-17, 156-72

125 —— 'News of Week,' *Spectator*, 46 (1873), 589. (1st leader, short notice of JSM's death)

126 —— 'Notes and News,' *Bulletin of the John Rylands Library*, 42 (1960), 259-72. (Concerns the acquisition of the press-copy of the *Autobiography*)

127 —— *Observations on the Royal Commission. By Jamaica*. London: Hardwicke, 1866

128 —— *Odd Bricks from a Tumbledown Private Building: By a Retired Constructor*. London: Newby, 1866. (On *Sir William Hamilton's Philosophy*)

129 —— *Opinions on the Admission of Dissenters and on University Reform (Lord Palmerston, Lord John Russell, Sir William Hamilton, J.S. Mill, and Others)*. [London?] 1847

130 —— 'Parliament and Reform,' *Westminster Review*, ns 27 (1865), 503-33. (Includes review of JSM's *Representative Government*)

131 —— '*The Personal Life of George Grote*,' *Quarterly Review*, 135 (1873), 98-137. Extract reprinted in *The Times*, 17 July 1873, 6. (Review. 'I deeply regret the mischievous teaching of John Mill'; personal reminiscence by the reviewer [136]. Reviewer given as Adam Smith or Abraham Hayward in *Wellesley Index* - probably Hayward.)

132 —— 'La Personnalité divine et la création dans la pensée de Stuart Mill,' *La Critique Philosophique*, 4:1 (1875), 132-6

133 —— 'The Philosophy of John Stuart Mill,' *Theological Eclectic*, 4 (1868), 289

134 —— 'The Political Faith of John Stuart Mill,' *Current Literature*, 49 (1910), 60-2

135 —— 'Politics, Woman's Special Sphere,' *Everybody's Magazine*, 33 (1915), 9

136 —— *Polozhitel'naya logika Dzh. St. Millya, yeyo osnovnyye nachala*

i nauchnaya postanovka [*The Positive Logic of J.S. Mill, Its Basic Principles and Scientific Formulation*]. St Petersburg: Trunov, 1897

137 —— 'Positivism in England,' *Southern Review*, 5 (1869), 341-78. (Anti-positivist discussion stimulated by the work of Comte, Buckle, A.M. Morell, and JSM's *Logic*. 'Mr Mill's process must ever be precisely as preposterous as the attempt of a man to hang a chain upon nothing!')

138 —— 'La Question de l'immortalité dans la philosophie de Stuart Mill,' *La Critique Philosophique*, 4:1 (1875), 187-92

139 —— 'Recent Discussions Concerning Liberal Education,' *Biblical Repertory and Princeton Review*, ser 3, 39 (1867), 585-616. (Reviews Youmans' *The Culture Demanded by Modern Life* and JSM's *Inaugural Address*)

140 —— 'Recent Discussions on the Representations of Minorities,' *Biblical Repertory and Princeton Review*, ser 3, 41 (1869), 581-601. (Review of, *inter alia*, Thomas Hare, *The Election of Representatives, Parliamentary, and Municipal*, but more attention paid to JSM's account of proportional representation)

141 —— *Record*, 14 June 1865, 2. (Denounces JSM over religious views in *Sir William Hamilton's Philosophy* [Chap. 7], in which he attacks Mansel's arguments. See also next entry.)

142 —— '*The Record* on the Westminster Election,' *Spectator*, 38 (1865), 631-2. (Criticizes the *Record* and the *Morning Advertiser* for hunting down JSM for heterodoxy. The *Record* referred to him as 'the head of the "Satanic School" of English writers' ['Mr J.S. Mill and His Supporters,' *Record*, 2 June 1865, 2; 'The Religious Views of Mr Mill - Representation of Westminster,' *Morning Advertiser*, 3 June 1865, 5.])

143 —— 'The Recreation of John Stuart Mill,' *Saturday Review*, 101 (1906), 615-16. (Describes JSM's interest in botany)

144 —— 'Religion and Politics,' *National Reformer*, 6 (1865), 441-2. (Discusses controversy over JSM's remarks in *Sir William Hamilton's Philosophy*)

145 —— 'Religious Opinions of John Stuart Mill,' *Lutheran Quarterly*, 5 (1875), 279-92

146 —— 'The Religious Views of Mr Mill - Representation of Westminster,' *Morning Advertiser*, 3 June 1865, 5. (Attacks JSM over remarks in *Sir William Hamilton's Philosophy*)

147 —— *Remarks, with Reference to the Land-laws of England, on Some Passages in Mr John Stuart Mill's 'Principles of Political Economy,' and M. Louis Blanc's 'Letters on England.'* London, 1867

148 —— 'Representative Government,' *Spectator*, 34 (1861), 446-7. (Review)

149 —— 'La Révélation et les espérances chrétiennes dans la philosophie de Stuart Mill,' *La Critique Philosophique*, 4:1 (1875), 279-88

150 —— *A Review of Mr J.S. Mill's Essay 'On Liberty,' and an Investigation of His Claim to Be Considered One of the Leading Philosophers and Thinkers of the Age; Also a Refutation of His Two Statements: - I. That Christian Morality Teaches Us to Be Selfish. II. That the Working Classes of This Country Are Mostly Habitual Liars. By a Liberal.* London: Watson and Gardiner, 1867

151 —— 'The Saint of Rationalism,' *Current Literature*, 41 (1906), 74-6

152 —— 'Science of Political Economy,' *National Quarterly Review*, 34 (1877), 247-87

153 —— 'Social Freedom,' *Littell's Living Age*, 254 (1907), 323-36

154 —— 'Some Aspects of the Tariff Question,' *Harvard Quarterly Journal of Economics*, 3 (1889), 259-92

155 —— *Standard*, 10 July 1865, 5-6. (Adverse comment on the 'harmony' between JSM and Malthus regarding large families. Refers to Westminster campaign, and supports the Conservative candidate who at least 'has not come forward to advocate a dangerous and disgusting theory.' Substantially reprinted as 'Mr John Stuart Mill on Marriage,' *Public Opinion*, 15 July 1865, 55-6. See Anon., 'Mr John Stuart Mill on Marriage.')

156 —— 'The Subjection of Women,' *Lippincott's*, 5 (1870), 125-6. (Review)

157 —— 'The Subjection of Women,' *Saturday Review*, 27 (1869), 811-13. (Review)

158 —— 'The Testimony of John Stuart Mill to Mysticism,' *Outlook*, 95 (1910), 818-20

159 —— 'Three Essays on Religion,' *Daily Free Press*, 20 Oct. 1874. (Review)

160 —— 'Three Essays on Religion,' *Daily Telegraph*, 20 and 22 Oct. 1874. (Review)

161 —— 'Three Essays on Religion,' *Dublin Morning Mail*, 21 Oct. 1874. (Review)

162 —— 'Three Essays on Religion,' *Dublin Review*, ns 24 (1875), 223. (Review)

163 —— 'Three Essays on Religion,' *Morning Post*, 20 Oct. 1874. Reprinted from *Manchester Guardian*. (Review)

164 —— 'Three Essays on Religion,' *Morning Post*, 22 Oct. 1874. (Review)

165 —— 'Three Essays on Religion,' *Pall Mall Gazette*, 22 Oct. 1874, 10; 29 Oct. 1874, 9-10. (Review)

166 —— 'Three Essays on Religion,' *The Times*, 21 Oct. 1874. (Review)

167 —— 'Three Political Philosophers,' *Times Literary Supplement*, 29 Dec. 1950, 821-2. (Review of *Mill on Bentham and Coleridge*, ed. F.R. Leavis)

168 —— *True and False Democracy. Representation of All, and Representation of the Majority Only. A Brief Synopsis of Recent Publications on This Subject, by John Stuart Mill and Thomas Hare.* Boston: Prentiss, 1862. (See Anon., 'Mill on Representative Government,' above)

169 —— 'Utilitarianism,' *Times Literary Supplement*, 11 Nov. 1949, 733. (An article occasioned by Plamenatz's *Mill's 'Utilitarianism,'* which see)

170 —— 'Utilitarianism and the "Saturday Review,"' *Spectator*, 34 (1861), 1144-6

171 —— *Utilitarianism Explained and Exemplified in Moral and Political Government: Being a Reply to J.S. Mill's 'Utilitarianism.'* London: Longman, Green, Longman, Roberts, and Green, 1864. (Reviewed anonymously, *Westminster Review*, ns 25 [1864], 567-9)

172 —— 'A Visit to the Late Mr Mill's Grave,' *Daily News*, 29 July 1874, 5

173 —— 'The Westminster Election,' *National Reformer*, 6 (1865), 469. (Congratulates JSM on his victory)

174 —— *Who Is the 'Reformer' John Stuart Mill or John Bright?* London: Bosworth and Harrison, 1859

175 —— 'Woman's Duties and Rights,' *National Quarterly Review*, 28 (1874), 29-54

176 —— 'Women's Rights,' *Saturday Review*, 21 (1866), 715-16. (Concerning JSM's motion for a return of persons disfranchised because of sex)

177 —— 'The Wood and the Trees,' *Times Literary Supplement*, 10 Mar. 1961, 153. (A leading article on recent interpretations of *On Liberty*

178 A. 'Mr Mill and His Critics,' *Spectator*, 46 (1873), 1435. (Letter to editor)

179 A., J.P. 'William Maccall and John Stuart Mill,' *National Reformer*, 6 (1865), 549-50

180 [Abbot, Thomas K.] 'Logic of Induction - Mill,' *North British Review*, 28 (1858), 101-22

181 Abel, Henry George. 'John Stuart Mill and Socialism,' *Fortnightly Review*, ns 144 (1938), 343-8. (A partisan piece, presenting fragmentary quotations to support the claim that JSM was not, and could not ever have been, a socialist. Refutes statements made about JSM by Shaw in *An Intelligent Woman's Guide to Socialism*, which see.)

182 —— 'Mill and Socialism,' *Nation and Athenaeum*, 44 (1929), 613-14. (A letter to the editor objecting to Shaw's statement that 'John Stuart Mill from being an eminent Ricardian became an avowed Socialist')

183 Abraham, J.H. 'J.S. Mill and "Utilitarianism,"' *Listener*, 69 (1963), 1031-2

184 Abrams, M.H. *The Mirror and the Lamp: Romantic Theory and the Critical Tradition*. New York: Oxford University Press, 1953. (Discusses JSM's theory of poetry and art, 23-5. References *passim*.)

185 Acton, H.B. 'Comte's Positivism and the Science of Society,' *Philosophy*, 26 (1951), 291-310. (Comparisons with JSM)

186 ——, ed. Introduction. *Utilitarianism, On Liberty and Considerations on Representative Government. By John Stuart Mill*. Everyman's Library. London: Dent; New York: Dutton, 1972

187 Acton, John E.E. 'Mill on Liberty,' *Rambler*, ns 2 (1859, 1860), 62-75, 376-85. Reprinted in *Political Thought in Perspective*. Ed. W. Ebenstein. New York: McGraw-Hill, 1957, 501-23

188 Adams, K. 'How the Benthamites Became Democrats,' *Journal of Social Philosophy*, 7 (1942), 161-71

189 Adams, Lyell. 'John Stuart Mill,' *New Englander*, 36 (1877), 92-114, 425-44, 740-84. (The last instalment was published after Adams' death. An extensive sketch.)

190 Adamson, J.W. *English Education, 1789-1902*. Cambridge: Cambridge University Press, 1930. (302-9 on JSM)

191 Adamson, Robert. 'Professor Jevons on Mill's Experimental Methods,' *Mind*, 3 (1878), 415-17. (Discussion of Jevons' review of JSM's theory of induction in *Contemporary Review*, 31 [which see]. Defends JSM's method.)

192 Adelman, Paul. 'Frederic Harrison and the Positivist Attack on Orthodox Political Economy,' *History of Political Economy*, 3 (1971), 170-89

193 —— 'Frederic Harrison on Mill,' *Mill News Letter*, V, 2 (1970), 2-5

194 Adler, Mortimer J. *The Idea of Freedom*. Garden City, NY: Doubleday, 1958. (Citations to JSM listed in annotated index, 684)

195 Aiken, Henry David. 'Definitions, Factual Premises, and Ethical Conclusions,' *Philosophical Review*, 61 (1952), 331-48. Reprinted in his *Reason and Conduct*. New York: Knopf, 1962, 44-64; and in *Mill: Utilitarianism*. Ed. Samuel Gorovitz. Indianapolis and New York: Bobbs-Merrill, 1971, 138-50

196 —— 'Mill and the Justification of Social Freedom.' In *Liberty*. Ed. Carl J. Friedrich. *Nomos* (Yearbook of the American Society for Political and Legal Philosophy), IV. New York: Atherton; London: Prentice-Hall, 1962, 119-39

197 —— 'Utilitarianism and Liberty; John Stuart Mill's Defense of Freedom.' In his *Reason and Conduct*. New York: Knopf, 1962, 293-314.

198 ——, ed. *The Age of Ideology: The Nineteenth Century Philosophers*. Boston: Houghton-Mifflin, 1957. (Selections from and comment on JSM, 138-60. References *passim*.)

199 Albee, Ernest. *A History of English Utilitarianism*. London: Sonnenschein; New York: Macmillan, 1902. (Especially 191-267)

200 Alexander, Edward. 'Disinterested Virtue: Dickens and Mill in Agreement,' *Dickensian*, 65 (1969), 163-70. (A comparison of the critiques of orthodox utilitarianism in *Hard Times* and in JSM's writings, persuasively showing the similarities)

201 —— 'John Stuart Mill on Dogmatism, *Liberticide*, and Revolution,' *Victorian Newsletter*, 37 (1970), 12-18

16

202 —— *Matthew Arnold and John Stuart Mill*. New York: Columbia University Press, 1965

203 —— 'Mill's Marginal Notes on Carlyle's "Hudson's Statue,"' *English Language Notes*, 7 (1969), 120-3. (Description of JSM's notes in Somerville copy of *Latter-Day Pamphlets*)

204 —— 'Mill's Theory of Culture: The Wedding of Literature and Democracy,' *University of Toronto Quarterly*, 35 (1965), 75-88

205 —— 'The Principles of Permanence and Progression in the Thought of J.S. Mill.' In *James and John Stuart Mill: Papers of the Centenary Conference*. Ed. John M. Robson and Michael Laine. Toronto: University of Toronto Press, 1976, 126-42

206 ——, ed. Introduction. *John Stuart Mill: Literary Essays*. Indianapolis: Bobbs-Merrill, 1967

207 Alexander, Patrick Proctor. *Mill and Carlyle: An Examination of Mr John Stuart Mill's Doctrine of Causation in Relation to Moral Freedom. With an Occasional Discourse on Sauerteig, by Smelfungus*. Edinburgh: Nimmo, 1866

208 —— *Moral Causation; or, Notes on Mr Mill's Notes to the Chapter on 'Freedom,' in the Third Edition of His 'Examination of Sir W. Hamilton's Philosophy.'* Edinburgh: Nimmo, 1868. 2nd ed., revised and extended. Edinburgh, London: Blackwood, 1875. (Alexander criticized JSM's chapter on 'Freedom' in *Mill and Carlyle*. Mill replied; here Alexander answers his reply.)

209 Allan, Robert. *L'Affaire Stuart Mill*. [Avignon: privately printed,] nd. (Deals with the destruction of JSM's house in 1961)

210 Allen, Derek P.H. 'The Utilitarianism of Marx and Engels,' *American Philosophical Review*, 10 (1973), 189-99

211 Allentuck, Marcia. 'An Unpublished Letter from John Stuart Mill to Joshua Toulmin Smith in the Lilly Library,' *Mill News Letter*, XII, 1 (1977), 2-3

212 —— 'An Unremarked Yiddish Translation of Mill's *On Liberty*,' *Mill News Letter*, V, 1 (1969), 10

213 Althaus, Friedrich. *Englische Charakterbilder*. 2 vols. Berlin: Decker, 1869

214 —— 'John Stuart Mill,' *Unsere Zeit*, NF, Jg 10 (1874)

215 Amano, Keitaro. 'A Bibliography of John Stuart Mill,' *Keizai Ronshu*

[*The Economic Review of Kansai University*], 6 (1956), 621-61. (See also next entry)

216 —— *John Stuart Mill, Bibliography of the Classical Economists.* Vol. III, Pt 4. Tokyo: Science Council of Japan, 1964

217 Ames, Van Meter. 'Kant and Mill Visit an Old Lady,' *Open Court*, 42 (1928), 528-36. (A heuristic question is here posed to illustrate the differences between Kant's and JSM's ethical theories)

218 [Amos, Sheldon.] '*The Subjection of Women*,' *Westminster Review*, ns 37 (1870), 63-89. (Review)

219 Anderson, John Parker. 'Bibliography.' Appended to W.L. Courtney's *Life of John Stuart Mill*. London: Walter Scott, 1889. (Comprehensive bibliography to 1889)

220 Anderson, William. 'John Stuart Mill and the Model City Charter,' *National Municipal Review*, 11 (1922), 321-6. ('Mill, writing more than a generation before our Committee on a Municipal Program reported the Model Charter, advanced the same principles which we now advocate.' [Headnote, 321.] Compares *Considerations on Representative Government* with *Model Charter*.)

221 Annan, Noel. 'John Stuart Mill.' In *The English Mind*. Ed. Hugh Sykes Davies and George Watson. Cambridge: Cambridge University Press, 1964, 219-39. Reprinted in *Mill: A Collection of Critical Essays*. Ed. J.B. Schneewind. Garden City, NY: Doubleday, 1968, 22-45

222 —— 'J.S. Mill and Intellectual Liberty,' *Listener*, 53 (1950), 727-8. (We 'are usually thought ... to regard' *On Liberty* 'as full of noble sentiment but also of bad philosophy. This is true' [727]. Liberty 'as a philosophic principle in Mill's sense has vanished' [728].)

223 —— 'Landmarks of Political Thought: *On Liberty*,' *Listener*, 43 (1960), 171-2. (Centennial review)

224 Annas, Julia. 'Mill and the Subjection of Women,' *Philosophy*, 52 (1977), 179-94

225 Anoyaut, Marcel. *L'Etat progressif et l'état stationnaire de la richesse nationale chez A. Smith and St. Mill*. Paris: Croville-Morant, 1907. (Published dissertation)

226 Anschutz, Richard Paul. 'John Stuart Mill.' In *Encyclopaedia Britannica*. Chicago: Encyclopaedia Britannica, 1962, XV, 490-3

227 —— 'John Stuart Mill.' In the *New Encyclopedia Britannica*. Chicago: Benton, 1974, xxx, 197-200

228 —— 'J.S. Mill, Carlyle, and Mrs Taylor,' *Political Science*, 7 (1955), 65-75

229 —— 'J.S. Mill: Philosopher of Victorianism.' In *1840 and After*. Ed. Arthur Sewell. Auckland: University College, 1939, 125-37

230 —— 'The Logic of J.S. Mill,' *Mind*, 58 (1949), 277-305. Reprinted in *Mill: A Collection of Critical Essays*. Ed. J.B. Schneewind. Garden City, NY: Doubleday, 1968, 46-83

231 —— *The Philosophy of J.S. Mill*. Oxford: Clarendon Press, 1953

232 [Anthony, Charles, Jr.] *The Social and Political Dependence of Women*. London: Longmans, Green, 1867; Boston: Spencer, 1868. 1st ed. anon. (Refers as much to *Enfranchisement of Women* as to JSM's *Subjection of Women*)

233 'Antichrist.' *The Jesus Christ of John Stuart Mill*. London: Edward Truelove, 1875

234 Antonovich, Maksim Alekseyevich. 'Dobrosovestnyye mysliteli i nedobrosovestnyye zhurnalisty' ['Conscientious Thinkers and Unconscientious Journalists'], *Sovremennik* [*The Contemporary*], no 2 (1865). (A critical analysis of the 1865 Russian edition of *Principles of Political Economy*)

235 Apchié, Madeleine. *Les Sources françaises de certains aspects de la pensée économique de John Stuart Mill*. Paris: Hartmann, 1931

236 Appadorai, Angadipuram. *Revision of Democracy*. London: Milford, 1940. (References to JSM throughout this pamphlet)

237 Appleman, Philip, William A. Madden, and Michael Wolff, eds. *1859: Entering an Age of Crisis*. Bloomington: Indiana University Press, 1959. (Bibliographical references in notes, 291-314. Many references to JSM; includes R.B. McCallum, 'The Individual in the Mass: Mill on Liberty and the Franchise,' 147-61, which see.)

238 Arata, Fidia. *La logica de J. Stuart Mill et la problematica etica-sociale*. Milan: Marzonati, 1964

239 Archambault, Paul. *Stuart Mill. Choix de textes et étude du système philosophique*. Paris: Louis-Michaud, [1912]

240 Arias, Gino. 'Il pensiero economico di Giovanni Stuart Mill,' *Annali di Economia*, 2 (1925), 107-65

241 Armstrong, Richard Acland. *Latter-day Teachers: Six Lectures.*
London: Paul, 1881. (JSM, Arnold, Parker, Tyndall, Farrar)

242 [Arnold, Thomas, Jr.] 'Mill *On Liberty,*' *Rambler*, os 25
(1859-60), 62-75, 376-85. Reprinted in *Political Thought in
Perspective.* Ed. William Ebenstein. New York: McGraw-Hill, 1957,
502-23. (Signed 'A.' Ebenstein mistakenly attributes to Lord Acton.)

243 Ashley, Myron Lucius. 'The Nature of Hypothesis.' In *Studies in
Logical Theory.* Ed. John Dewey. Chicago: University of Chicago Press,
1903, 142-83. (JSM's doctrine of the hypothesis is treated on 160-8)

244 Ashley, W.J. 'The Present Position of Political Economy in England.' In
*Die Entwicklung der deutschen Volkswirtschaftslehre im neunzehnten
Jahrhundert.* 2 vols. Leipzig: Dunker and Humboldt, 1908, I, xv,
1-26. (On JSM's economics and inductive method, 5-10)

245 ——, ed. *Principles of Political Economy with Some of Their
Applications to Social Philosophy. By John Stuart Mill.* London, New
York: Longmans, Green, 1909. (With introduction, notes, bibliographical
appendix, by W.J. Ashley. Index by Miss M.A. Ellis. Text is that of the
7th ed. All significant changes, additions, and deletions from the 1st
to the 7th editions are indicated in notes.)

246 Ashworth, M. 'The Marriage of John Stuart Mill,' *Englishwoman*, 30
(1916), 159-72

247 Aster, Ernst von. 'James und John Stuart Mill, Bain, Hamilton,' and
'Die Entwicklung der Ethic- und Moralphilosophie (Bentham und Mill).'
In his *Geschichte der englischen Philosophie.* Bielefeld and Leipzig:
Velhagen and Klasing, 1927, 139-60, 160-76, and *passim*

248 Atkinson, R.F. 'J.S. Mill's "Proof" of the Principle of Utility,'
Philosophy, 32 (1957), 158-67

249 [Atwater, L.H.] 'McCosh on J.S. Mill and Fundamental Truth,' *Biblical
Repertory and Princeton Review*, 38 (1866), 416-24. (Review article,
hostile to JSM, friendly to McCosh's *Examination of Mr J.S. Mill's
Philosophy*)

250 August, Eugene R. *John Stuart Mill: A Mind at Large.* New York:
Scribner's, 1975

251 —— 'Mill as Sage: The Essay on Bentham,' *PMLA*, 89 (1974), 142-53

252 —— 'Mill's *Autobiography* as Philosophic *Commedia*,'
Victorian Poetry, 11 (1973), 143-62

279 Balmforth, Ramsden. 'John Stuart Mill and Political Education, 1806-1873.' In his *Some Social and Political Pioneers of the Nineteenth Century*. London: Sonnenschein, 1900, 112-32

280 Bambrough, Renford. 'Plato's Welfare State,' *Listener*, 67 (1962), 164. (Compares *On Liberty* with the *Laws* and the *Republic*)

281 Barber, William J. 'The Economics of Affluence,' *South Atlantic Quarterly*, 60 (1961), 249-61. (Comparison of *Principles of Political Economy* with J.K. Galbraith's *The Affluent Society*)

282 —— 'The Revisionism of John Stuart Mill.' In his *A History of Economic Thought*. Harmondsworth: Penguin, 1967, 94-106

283 Barr, N.C. 'Mill and Comte.' In *Philosophical Essays in Honour of James Edwin Creighton*. Ed. G.H. Sabine. New York: Macmillan, 1917, 78-94

284 Barth, Paul. 'Zu J. St. Mills 100. Geburtstage,' *Vierteljahrsschrift für wissenschaftliche Philosophie und Soziologie*, 30 (1906), 203-12

285 Barton, Mary N. 'Rare Books and Other Bibliographical Resources in Baltimore Libraries,' *Papers of the Bibliographical Society of America*, 55 (1961), 1-16. (Five volumes of JSM correspondence in Johns Hopkins University Library - no description)

286 Bascom, John. 'Utilitarianism,' *Bibliotheca Sacra*, 23 (1866), 435-52

287 Bastable, Charles Francis. 'On Some Applications of the Theory of International Trade,' *Quarterly Journal of Economics*, 4 (1889), 1-17. (Exposition of Ricardian theory with particular reference to JSM)

288 Baudin, Louis. 'John Stuart Mill: la codification de l'individualisme.' In his *Précis d'histoire des doctrines économiques*. 5th ed. Paris: Montchrestien, 1949, 144-59

289 Baudrillart, Henri Joseph Léon. 'J.S. Mill.' In his *Publicistes modernes*. Paris: Didier, 1862, 455-540

290 Baumgardt, David. *Bentham and the Ethics of Today*. Princeton: Princeton University Press, 1952. (Numerous references to JSM)

291 —— 'Bentham's "Censorial" Method,' *Journal of the History of Ideas*, 6 (1945), 456-67. (Maintains that JSM and other commentators underestimated Bentham's critical radicalism)

292 Baumgarten, Murray. 'The Ideas of History of Thomas Carlyle and John Stuart Mill: A Summary Statement,' *Mill News Letter*, III, 1 (1967), 8-9

293 —— 'Mill, Carlyle, and the Question of Influence,' *Mill News Letter*, X, 1 (1975), 4-9

294 Bay, Christian. *The Structure of Freedom*. Stanford: Stanford University Press, 1958. Reprinted New York: Atheneum, 1965. (36-47 refer specifically to *Utilitarianism* and *On Liberty*)

295 Bearce, George Donham. 'John Stuart Mill.' In his *British Attitudes toward India, 1784-1858*. [London:] Oxford University Press, 1961, 277-95

296 —— 'John Stuart Mill and India,' *Journal of the Bombay Branch of the Royal Asiatic Society*, 27 (1954), 67-80

297 Beard, C.A. 'The Idea of Let Us Alone,' *Virginia Quarterly Review*, 15 (1939), 500-14

298 Beattie, F.R. *An Examination of the Utilitarian Theory of Morals*. Brantford: Sutherland, 1885

299 Becher, Siegfried. *Erkenntnistheoretische Untersuchungen zu Stuart Mills Theorie der Kausalität*. Halle a. S.: Niemeyer, 1906

300 Becker, Hermann. 'J. St. Mill.' In his *Zur Entwicklung der englischen Freihandelstheorie*. Jena: Fischer, 1922, 89-104

301 Becker, Lydia E. *Liberty, Equality, Fraternity: A Reply to Mr Fitzjames Stephen's Strictures on Mr J.S. Mill's Subjection of Women*. Manchester: Ireland, 1874. Reprinted from the *Women's Suffrage Journal*

302 Beer, Max. *A History of British Socialism*. 2 vols. London: Bell, 1920, II, 175-91

303 Beggs, Thomas. *The Deterrent Influence of Capital Punishment: Being a Reply to the Speech of J.S. Mill, Esq, MP, Delivered by Him in the House of Commons on the 21st of April, 1868*. London: Tweedie, 1868. 2nd ed., revised, 1868

304 [Bellot, H.H.L.] 'Contemporary Literature: Philosophy and Theology,' *Westminster Review*, 150 (1898), 107-8

305 Benn, Alfred William. *The History of English Rationalism in the Nineteenth Century*. 2 vols. London: Longmans, Green, 1906, I, 421-50

306 Benn, S.I., and R.S. Peters. 'The Philosophical Problem of Liberty.' In their *Social Principles of the Democratic State*. London: Allen and

Unwin, 1959, 220-4. Reprinted as *The Principles of Political Thought*. New York: Free Press, 1965, 257-62; and in *Limits of Liberty: Studies of Mill's 'On Liberty.'* Ed. Peter Radcliff. Belmont: Wadsworth, 1966, 82-6

307 Bennett, James R. 'Mill, Francis W. Newman, Socialism: Mill's Two Argumentative Voices,' *Mill News Letter*, II, 1 (1966), 2-7

308 Berlin, Isaiah. *John Stuart Mill and the Ends of Life*. London: Council of Christians and Jews, l960. Reprinted in his *Four Essays on Liberty*. London: Oxford University Press, 1969, 173-206. (The Robert Waly Cohen Memorial Lecture delivered in County Hall, London, 1959. See also Rohatyn.)

309 —— 'The Notion of "Negative" Freedom.' In his *Two Concepts of Liberty*. Oxford: Clarendon Press, 1958, 9-16. Reprinted in his *Four Essays on Liberty*. London: Oxford University Press, 1969, 122-31. (*Two Concepts of Liberty* was his inaugural lecture delivered before the University of Oxford)

310 Bernard, Michel. *Introduction à une sociologie des doctrines économiques: des physiocrates à Stuart Mill*. Société, sociaux et idéologies. Sér 1. Etudes no 7. Series in Economic History. Paris: Mouton, 1963

311 Bicknell, Percy F. 'An Apostle of Clear Thinking,' *Dial*, 40 (1906), 285-7

312 —— 'John Stuart Mill,' *Popular Science Monthly*, 69 (1906), 451-7

313 Billings, John R. 'J.S. Mill's Quantity-Quality Distinction,' *Mill News Letter*, VII, 1 (1971), 6-16

314 Binkley, Robert C. 'Mill's Liberty Today,' *Foreign Affairs*, 16 (1938), 563-73

315 Birks, Thomas Rawson. *Modern Utilitarianism; or, The Systems of Paley and Mill Examined and Compared*. London: Macmillan, 1874

316 Blachford, Frederic. 'The Reality of Duty as Illustrated by the Autobiography of J.S. Mill,' *Contemporary Review*, 28 (1876), 508-36

317 Black, R.D. Collison. 'Economic Policy in Ireland and India in the Time of J.S. Mill,' *Economic History Review*, 2nd ser, 21 (1968), 321-36

318 —— *Economic Thought and the Irish Question, 1817-1870*. Cambridge: Cambridge University Press, 1960. (References *passim*)

319 —— 'Jevons and Cairnes,' *Economica*, 27 (1960), 214-32

320 Blackie, John Stuart. *Four Phases of Morals: Socrates, Aristotle, Christianity, Utilitarianism*. Edinburgh: Edmonston and Douglas, 1871

321 Blackwood, Frederick Temple Hamilton Temple [Marquis of Dufferin and Ava]. *Mr Mill's Plan for the Pacification of Ireland Examined*. London: Murray, 1868

322 Bladen, Vincent W. 'The Centenary of Marx and Mill,' *Journal of Economic History*, 8 (Supplement, 1948), 32-41

323 —— *From Adam Smith to Maynard Keynes: The Heritage of Political Economy*. Toronto: University of Toronto Press, 1974. (Contains a general chapter on JSM and a chapter on *The Principles of Political Economy*)

324 —— 'John Stuart Mill's *Principles*: A Centenary Estimate,' *American Economic Review* (Papers and Proceedings), 39 (1949), 1-12

325 —— 'Mill to Marshall: The Conversion of the Economists,' *Journal of Economic History*, 1 (Supplement, 1941), 17-29

326 Blake, Ralph, *et al. Theories of Scientific Method: The Renaissance through the Nineteenth Century*. Seattle: University of Washington Press, 1960. Reprinted 1966. (Chap. 8 on JSM, Whewell and Mansel; Chap. 9, 'John Stuart Mill's System of Logic')

327 Blakely, R.J. 'Adult Education - Stalk or Flower?' *National Education Association Journal*, 42 (1953), 232-3

328 Blaug, Mark. *Economic Theory in Retrospect*. London: Heinemann, 1964. (References *passim*)

329 —— 'The Empirical Content of Ricardian Economics,' *Journal of Political Economy*, 64 (1956), 41-58. (Separation of Ricardian theory from empirical evidence. Several references to JSM.)

330 —— 'The Half-way House of John Stuart Mill.' In his *Ricardian Economics*. New Haven: Yale University Press, 1958, 162-92

331 Bleckly, Henry. *A Colloquy on the Utilitarian Theory of Morals Presented in Mr W.E.H. Lecky's 'History of European Morals from Augustus to Charlemagne.'* London: Simkin, Marshall, 1873

332 Bledsoe, A.J. 'John Stuart Mill and Dr Lieber on Liberty,' *Southern Review*, 2 (1867), 52-86

333 —— 'What Is Liberty?' *Southern Review*, 5 (1869), 249-75. (Tries

to use JSM's remarks about slavery in certain circumstances as a means toward freedom as a justification for slavery)

334 Blegvad, Mogens. 'Mill, Moore, and the Naturalistic Fallacy.' In *Philosophical Essays Dedicated to Gunnar Aspelin*. Lund, 1963

335 Blind, Karl. 'Stuart Mill über Irland,' *Die Gegenwart*, 21 (1882)

336 Bliss, W.D.P., ed. *Socialism by John Stuart Mill*. New York: Humbolt, 1891. (A wide selection from JSM's work with a short introduction by Bliss arguing that JSM was a socialist)

337 Blyth, Edmund Kell. *Life of William Ellis*. London: Kegan Paul, Trench, 1889. (References to JSM, especially in the 1820s. Ellis, an educational reformer, was a member of the Utilitarian Society, and joint author, with JSM, of a review of McCulloch's *Political Economy* [*Westminster Review*, 4 (1825), 88-92].)

338 Boatner, Janet W. 'John Stuart Mill: Causes and Effects of His Mental Crisis,' *Psychiatric Quarterly Supplement*, 41 (1967), 294-306

339 Boegholt, Carl Moeller. 'Examination of Cohen and Nagel's Reply to Mill in Chapter Fourteen of Their Book "An Introduction to Logic and Scientific Method,"' *Journal of Philosophy*, 33 (1936), 514-23

340 Bogen, Daniel, and D.M. Farrell. 'Freedom and Happiness in Mill's Defence of Liberty,' *Philosophical Quarterly*, 28 (1978), 325-38

341 Bogomolov, A. *Anglo-amerikanskaya burzhuaznaya filosofiya* [*Anglo-American Bourgeois Philosophy*]. Moscow, 1964, 30-7

342 Bolton, M.P.W. *Inquisitio Philosophica: An Examination of the Principles of Kant and Hamilton*. London: Chapman and Hall, 1866. (Includes a consideration, generally sympathetic to JSM, of some of the issues raised in his *Examination of Sir William Hamilton's Philosophy*)

343 Bonafous, Marie. 'La Maison de John Stuart Mill à Avignon,' *Reflets Méditerranéens*, no 28 (1961), [np]. (With photograph of the house. See also *ibid.*, no 24 [1960].)

344 Bonar, James. 'The Economics of John Stuart Mill,' *Journal of Political Economy*, 19 (1911), 717-25

345 —— 'John Stuart Mill.' In his *Philosophy and Political Economy: In Some of Their Historical Relations*. London: Swan Sonnenschein; New York: Macmillan, 1893, 237-65. (Chiefly summary)

346 —— *John Stuart Mill on the Protection of Infant Industries*. London:
The Cobden Club, 1911. (A selection of letters with a short introduction
by Bonar and a preface by Hugh Elliot)

347 —— *The Tables Turned: A Lecture and Dialogue on Adam Smith and the
Classical Economists*. London: King, 1926. (Few references to JSM
but see next entry)

348 —— *The Tables Turned*. London: Macmillan, 1931. (Includes previous
entry, largely rewritten, and, *inter alia*, a chapter in dialogue,
'John Stuart Mill, the Reformer,' 79-132, reprinted from *Indian
Journal of Economics*, 10 (1930), 761-805)

349 Bonatelli, F. 'Intorno al sistema di logica di J.S. Mill,' *Rivista
bolognese di scienze, lettere, arti e scuole*, 1:2 (1867), 416-43, 565-602

350 Borchard, Ruth. *John Stuart Mill: The Man*. London: Watts, 1957

351 —— 'Mill: The Man and the Thinker,' *Contemporary Review*, 185
(1954), 99-103

352 Bosanquet, Bernard. *The Philosophical Theory of the State*. London:
Macmillan, 1899. (Especially Chap. 3, 'The Paradox of Self-Government')

353 Bourne, Henry Richard Fox. 'John Stuart Mill: A Sketch of His Life,'
Examiner, 17 May 1873, 502-6. Reprinted as 'John Stuart Mill: His
Education and Marriage,' *Popular Science Monthly*, 3 (1873), 368-71;
and in his *John Stuart Mill: Notices of His Life and Works*. London:
Dallow, 1873, 5-29; see also next entry)

354 ——, ed. *John Stuart Mill: Notices of His Life and Works*. London:
Dallow, 1873. Reprinted as *John Stuart Mill: His Life and Works*. New
York: Holt; Boston: Osgood, 1873. (Twelve memorial sketches, reprinted
from the *Examiner*, by Fox Bourne, W.T. Thornton, Herbert Spencer,
Henry Trimen, W. Minto, J.H. Levy, W.A. Hunter, J.E. Cairnes, Henry
Fawcett, Millicent Fawcett, and Frederic Harrison, which see)

355 Bousquet, G.-H. 'Stuart Mill.' In his *Essai sur l'évolution de la
pensée économique*. Paris: Giard, 1927, 90-8

356 Bouton, Clark W. 'John Stuart Mill: On Liberty and History,' *Western
Political Quarterly*, 18 (1968), 569-78

357 Bowen, Francis. 'J.S. Mill on the Theory of Causation,' *North American
Review*, 78 (1854), 82-105

358 —— 'Mr Mill and His Critics,' *American Presbyterian Review*, 18
(1869), 351-75, 427-50

359 Bowle, John. 'The Liberal Compromise: De Tocqueville, John Stuart Mill.'
     In his *Politics and Opinion in the Nineteenth Century*. London: Cape,
     1954, 180-208

360 Bowne, Borden Parker. 'Moral Intuition vs Utilitarianism,' *New
     Englander*, 32 (1873), 217-42

361 —— *The Principles of Ethics*. New York: Harper, 1892. (Few
     references to JSM but general discussion of Utilitarian principles.
     See Chap. 3 and Conclusion.)

362 Boyd, William Falconer. *John Stuart Mills Utilitarismus im Vergleich
     mit dem seiner Vorgänger*. Borna-Leipzig: Noske, 1906. (Dissertation,
     Tübingen, 1906)

363 Brace, Charles L. 'A Reminiscence of John Stuart Mill,' *Victoria
     Magazine*, 21 (1873), 265-70

364 Bradlaugh, Charles. 'J.S. Mill.' In his *Five Dead Men Whom I Knew When
     Living: Robert Owen, Joseph Mazzini, Charles Sumner, J.S. Mill & Ledru
     Rollin*. London: Freethought Publishing, 1882, 14-18

365 Bradley, F.H. *Ethical Studies*. London: King, 1876. 2nd ed. rev.,
     Oxford: Clarendon Press, 1927. (Especially Chap. 3. See also Smith and
     Sosa.)

366 —— *The Principles of Logic*. London: Kegan Paul, Trench, 1883.
     2nd ed. rev., London: Oxford University Press, 1922. (A discussion of
     JSM particularly concerned with Association of Ideas, Inductive
     Method and Inference. Bk II, Pt II, i-iii; Bk III, Pt I, ii.)

367 Brandes, Georg. 'John Stuart Mill.' In his *Moderne Geister*.
     Frankfurt: Literarische Anstalb, 1882, 133-60. Trans. R.B. Anderson in
     Eminent Authors. New York: Crowell, 1886, 123-46; also published as
     Creative Spirits of the Nineteenth Century. London: T. Fisher Unwin,
     1924, 184-204. Trans. as 'Dzhon Styuart Mill' ['John Stuart Mill'], in
     Severny vestnik [*Northern Herald*], 8 (1887), Pt 2, 32-47

368 Brazer, J. 'Mill's System of Logic,' *North American Review*, 61
     (1845), 349-83

369 Brebner, John Bartlet. 'Laissez-Faire and State Intervention in
     Nineteenth-Century Britain,' *Journal of Economic History*, 8
     (Supplement, 1948), 59-73. Reprinted in *Essays in Economic History*.
     Ed. E.M. Carus-Wilson. Vol. III. London: Arnold, 1962, 252-62

370 Brecht, Arnold. 'Liberty and Truth: The Responsibility of Science.'

In *Liberty*. Ed. Carl J. Friedrich. *Nomos* (Yearbook of the American Society for Political and Legal Philosophy), IV. New York: Atherton; London: Prentice-Hall, 1962, 243-61

371 Bregmann, F.W.E.J. *Über den Utilitarianismus*. Marburg: Elwert, 1883. (See also Gizycki)

372 Brewster, D. *The Radical Party: Its Principles, Objects, & Leaders - Cobden, Bright, & Mill*. Manchester: Heywood, 1867

373 Bridges, John Henry. *The Unity of Comte's Life and Doctrine. A Reply to Strictures on Comte's Later Writings, Addressed to John Stuart Mill*. London: Trübner, 1866

374 Brinton, Clarence Crane. *English Political Thought in the Nineteenth Century*. London: Benn, 1933, 89-103

375 Britton, Karl W. *John Stuart Mill*. Baltimore and Harmondsworth: Penguin, 1953. 2nd ed. corrected, New York: Dover, 1969

376 —— 'John Stuart Mill,' *Wijsgerig perspectief op maatschappij en wetenscap*, 13e jaargang: no 5 (1972-73), 209-17

377 —— 'John Stuart Mill.' In *The Concise Encyclopaedia of Western Philosophy and Philosophers*. Ed. James Opie Urmson. London: Hutchinson, 1960, 267-72

378 —— 'John Stuart Mill on Christianity.' In *James and John Stuart Mill: Papers of the Centenary Conference*. Ed. John M. Robson and Michael Laine. Toronto: University of Toronto Press, 1976, 21-34

379 —— 'John Stuart Mill: The Ordeal of an Intellectual,' *Cambridge Journal*, 2 (1948), 96-105

380 —— 'J.S. Mill: A Debating Speech on Wordsworth, 1829,' *Cambridge Review*, 79 (1958), 418-23

381 —— 'J.S. Mill and the Cambridge Union Society,' *Cambridge Review*, 76 (1955), 92-5

382 —— 'The Nature of Arithmetic: A Reconsideration of Mill's Views,' *Proceedings of the Aristotelian Society*, 48 (1947-48), 1-12

383 —— 'Perpetuating a Mistake about Mill's Three Essays on Religion,' *Mill News Letter*, V, 2 (1970), 6-7

384 —— 'Utilitarianism.' In *The Concise Encyclopaedia of Western Philosophy and Philosophers*. Ed. James Opie Urmson. London: Hutchinson, 1960, 383-401

385 —— 'Utilitarianism: The Appeal to a First Principle,' *Proceedings of the Aristotelian Society*, 60 (1959-60), 141-54

386 ——, and John M. Robson. 'Mill's Debating Speeches,' *Mill News Letter*, I, 1 (1965), 2-6

387 Broad, C.D. *Five Types of Ethical Theory*. London: Routledge and Kegan Paul; New York: Harcourt Brace, 1930. Frequently republished. (References to JSM in chap. on Sidgwick, 143-256, also 258)

388 Brochard, Victor. 'La Logique de J. Stuart Mill,' *Revue Philosophique*, 12 (1881), 449-78, 592-614

389 Brock, Dan W. 'Recent Work in Utilitarianism,' *American Philosophical Quarterly*, 10 (1973), 241-76. (Critical review and bibliography 1961-71)

390 Bronaugh, R.N. 'The Utility of Quality: An Understanding of Mill,' *Canadian Journal of Philosophy*, 4 (1974), 317-25

391 Bronfenbrenner, Martin. 'Poetry, Pushpin, and Utility,' *Economic Inquiry*, 15 (1977), 95-110

392 Brown, D.G. 'John Rawls: John Mill,' *Dialogue*, 12 (1973), 477-9

393 —— 'Mill on Harm to Others' Interests,' *Political Studies*, 26 (1978), 395-9

394 —— 'Mill on Liberty and Morality,' *Philosophical Review*, 81 (1972), 133-58

395 —— 'Mill's Act-Utilitarianism,' *Philosophical Quarterly*, 24 (1974), 67-8

396 —— 'What Is Mill's Principle of Utility?' *Canadian Journal of Philosophy*, 3 (1973), 1-12

397 Brown, E. Phelps. 'Prospects of Labour,' *Economica*, ns 16 (1949), 1-10. (Deals with the ideas of Marshall and of JSM as found in the *Principles of Political Economy* concerning the future of the labouring classes)

398 Brown, Francis J. Commentary on Abram L. Harris' 'Mill on Freedom and Voluntary Association,' *Review of Social Economy*, 18 (1960), 41-4

399 Brown, J.A. 'The Religious Opinions of John Stuart Mill,' *Lutheran Quarterly*, ns 5 (1875), 279-92

400 Brown, Stuart M., Jr. 'Duty and the Production of Good,' *Philosophical*

Review, 61 (1952), 298-311. Reprinted in *Mill: Utilitarianism*.
Ed. S. Gorovitz. Indianapolis and New York: Bobbs-Merrill, 1971, 129-37

401   Browne, Albert G. 'Mill's Autobiography,' *Atlantic*, 33 (1874), 489-91.
(Part of general review article)

402   Browne, Matthew. See William Brighty Rands

403   Browne, Walter Raleigh. *The Autobiography of John Stuart Mill: A
Lecture*. London: Hodder and Stoughton, 1874. (Examined with a
Christian bias. Both James Mill and JSM in error because they deny
freedom of the will.)

404   —— 'Mill's Autobiography,' *Christian Evidence Journal* (1874), 2-5

405   Buchdahl, Gerd. 'Inductivist *versus* Deductivist Approaches in the
Philosophy of Science as Illustrated by Some Controversies between
Whewell and Mill,' *Monist*, 55 (1971), 343-67

406   Buckle, Henry Thomas. 'Mill on Liberty,' *Fraser's Magazine*, 59
(1859), 508-42. Reprinted in his *Essays*. New York: Appleton, 1863;
and in *Miscellaneous and Posthumous Works*. Ed. Helen Taylor. 3
vols. London: Longmans, 1872, I, 20-70. Trans. in *Etudy*
[Essays]. Ed. P.N. Tkachov. St Petersburg: Yu. Lukanin, 1867

407   Buckley, Jerome Hamilton. 'The Revolt from "Rationalism" in the
Seventies and Some of Its Literary Consequences.' In *Booker Memorial
Studies: Eight Essays on Victorian Literature in Memory of John Manning
Booker (1881-1948)*. Ed. Hill Shine. Chapel Hill: University of North
Carolina Press, 1950, 122-32. (JSM considered as a major Victorian
'rationalist')

408   —— *The Victorian Temper*. Cambridge: Harvard University Press,
1951. Reprinted New York: Vintage Books, 1964

409   Bunge, Nikolay Khristianovich. 'Styuart Mill', kak ekonomist' ['Stuart
Mill as an Economist'], *Zhurnal ministerstva narodnovo
prosveshcheniya [Journal of the Ministry of Public Education]*, 140
(1868), 1-100. Reprinted in his *Ocherki politicheskoy-ekonomicheskoy
literatury [Essays in the Literature of Political Economy]*. St
Petersburg: Kirshbaum, 1895. Trans. as 'John Stuart Mill envisagé comme
économiste.' In his *Esquisses de littérature politico-économique*.
Geneva: Georg, 1900

410   Burns, J.H. 'J.S. Mill and Democracy, 1929-61,' *Political Studies*, 5
(1957), 158-75, 281-94. Reprinted in *Mill: A Collection of Critical
Essays*. Ed. J.B. Schneewind. Garden City, NY: Doubleday, 1968,
280-328

411 —— 'J.S. Mill and the Term "Social Science,"' *Journal of the History of Ideas*, 20 (1959), 431-2

412 —— 'The Light of Reason: Philosophical History in the Two Mills.' In *James and John Stuart Mill: Papers of the Centenary Conference*. Ed. John M. Robson and Michael Laine. Toronto: University of Toronto Press, 1976, 3-20

413 —— 'Utilitarianism and Democracy,' *Philosophical Quarterly*, 9 (1959), 168-71. Reprinted in *Mill: Utilitarianism*. Ed. S. Gorovitz. Indianapolis and New York: Bobbs-Merrill, 1971, 269-72

414 —— 'Was Mill a Democrat?' *History Today*, 8 (1958), 283-4

415 Burr, Anna Robeson. 'John Stuart Mill, "Autobiography."' In *Encyclopedia Americana*. New York: Americana, 1957, XIX, 113

416 Burston, Wyndham Hedley. *James Mill on Philosophy and Education*. London: Athlone, 1973. (Includes study of JSM's education)

417 —— 'The Utilitarians and the Monitorial System of Teaching.' In *The Year Book of Education: 1957*. University of London Institute of Education and Teachers College, Columbia University, New York; London: Evans, 383-404. (Chiefly refers to James Mill)

418 ——, ed. *James Mill on Education*. Cambridge: Cambridge University Press, 1969. (Edition of *Education* and *Schools for All* with introduction which contains references to JSM)

419 Bury, J.B. *A History of Freedom of Thought*. New York: Holt, 1913. (References *passim*)

420 Buzzetti, Dino. 'Sulla teoria della connotazione di John Stuart Mill,' *Rivista di filosofia*, 5 (1976), 265-88

421 C., W. *Wealth: Definitions by Ruskin and Mill Compared: A Paper Read before the Ruskin Society of Glasgow on 23rd January, 1882, by a Member*. Glasgow: Wilson and McCormick, 1882

422 Cabot, James E. 'Mill's Three Essays on Religion,' *North American Review*, 120 (1875), 461-9

423 Cada, Frantisek. *Mill: Pojema a obor logiky*. Prague, 1892

424 —— *Noeticka zahada u Herbarta a Stuarta Milla*. Rozpravey České Akademie Císaře Františka Josefa, 1:3:5. Prague, 1894. Trans. German, Prague, 1895

425 Cadiou, R. 'La Philosophie de John Stuart Mill,' *Revue Philosophique*, 139 (1949), 423-40

426 Cadman, Samuel Parkes. *Charles Darwin and Other English Thinkers, with Reference to Their Religious and Ethical Value*. Boston: Pilgrim Press, 1911, 89-139

427 Cairnes, John Elliot. *The Character and Logical Method of Political Economy*. Dublin: William McGee, 1869. (Refers to JSM *passim* especially on Theory of Rent)

428 —— 'John Stuart Mill: His Work in Political Economy,' *Examiner*, 17 May 1873, 513-14. Reprinted in *Popular Science Monthly*, 3 (1873), 381-4; in Alexander Bain's *John Stuart Mill*. London: Longmans, Green, 1882, 197-201; and in *John Stuart Mill: Notices of His Life and Works*. Ed. H.R. Fox Bourne. London: Dallow, 1873, 65-73

429 —— *Some Leading Principles of Political Economy Newly Expounded*. London: Macmillan, 1874. (Cites JSM's *Principles of Political Economy, passim*, and states in 'Preface' that it is in agreement with his assumptions and final conclusions, along with those of Smith, Malthus, and Ricardo, but would criticize the '*axiomata media*')

430 —— *University Education in Ireland: A Letter to J.S. Mill, Esq, MP*. London: Macmillan, 1866

431 Cairns, Huntington, Allen Tate and Mark Van Doren. 'John Stuart Mill - Autobiography.' In their *Invitation to Learning*. New York: Random House, 1941, 108-18. (Edited transcript of Radio Broadcast)

432 Calderwood, Henry. *Handbook of Moral Philosophy*. London: Macmillan, 1872

433 —— 'The Sensational Philosophy - Mr J.S. Mill and Dr M'Cosh,' *British and Foreign Evangelical Review*, 15 (1866), 396-412

434 [Call, Wather Mark Wilks.] 'John Stuart Mill's Three Essays on Religion,' *Westminster Review*, ns 47 (1875), 1-28

435 Cannan, Edwin. *A History of the Theories of Production and Distribution in English Political Economy, from 1776 to 1848*. London: Percival, 1893

436 Cannegieter, Tjeerd. *De Nuttigheidsleer van John Stuart Mill en Prof. Van der Wijck*. Groningen: Noordhoff, 1876

437 Capaldi, Nicholas. 'Censorship and Social Stability in J.S. Mill,' *Mill News Letter*, IX, 1 (1973), 12-16

438 —— 'Mill's Forgotten Science of Ethology,' *Social Theory and Practice*, 2 (1973), 409-20

439 Capes, John Moore. 'The *Autobiography* of John Stuart Mill,' *Contemporary Review*, 23 (1873), 53-65. Reprinted in *Church Eclectic*, 1 (1874), 371-6

440 Carey, George W., and Willmoore Kendall. 'The "Roster Device": J.S. Mill and Contemporary Elitism.' (See Willmoore Kendall)

441 Carlile, William W. 'The Humist Doctrine of Causation,' *Philosophical Review*, 5 (1896), 113-34. (Criticism of JSM's theory of causation)

442 Carlyle, Thomas. *Letters of Thomas Carlyle to John Stuart Mill, John Sterling and Robert Browning*. Ed. Alexander Carlyle. London: T. Fisher Unwin, 1923

443 Carr, Robert. 'The Religious Thought of John Stuart Mill: A Study in Reluctant Scepticism,' *Journal of the History of Ideas*, 23 (1962), 475-95

444 Carr, Wendell Robert. 'James Mill's Politics: A Final Word,' *Historical Journal*, 13 (1972), 315-20. (A reply to Wm. Thomas, 'James Mill's Politics: A Rejoinder')

445 —— 'James Mill's Politics Reconsidered,' *Historical Journal*, 14 (1971), 553-80. (A criticism of Wm. Thomas, 'James Mill's Politics: The "Essay on Government" and the Movement for Reform')

446 Carrau, Ludovic. 'Le Dualisme de St. Mill,' *Revue Philosophique*, 8 (1879), 139-56

447 —— 'Stuart Mill.' In his *La Morale utilitaire; exposition et critique des doctrines qui fondent la morale sur l'idée du bonheur*. Paris: Didier, 1875, 227-68

448 Carré, Meyrick Heath. *Phases of Thought in England*. Oxford: Clarendon, 1949. Reprinted Westport: Greenwood, 1972. (Survey, emphasizes *Logic*, especially 312-16)

449 Carruthers, John. *Communal and Commercial Economy: Some Elementary Theories of the Political Economy of Communal and of Commercial Societies; Together with an Examination of the Correlated Theorems of the Pseudo-Science of Wealth as Taught by Ricardo and Mill*. London: Stanford, 1883

450 [Carus, P.] 'Nature and Morality: An Examination of the Ethical Views of John Stuart Mill,' *Open Court*, 6 (1892), 3186-9, 3201-3, 3210-11. (Signed P.C.)

451 Casellato, Sante. *G. Stuart Mill e l'utilitarismo inglese*. Padua: Casa Editrice Dotti; Antonio Milani, 1951

452   Castell, Alburey. *Mill's Logic of the Moral Sciences: A Study of the Impact of Newtonism on Early Nineteenth Century Social Thought*. Chicago: University of Chicago Libraries, 1936. (Dissertation, Chicago, 1936)

453   Catherwood, Benjamin Franklin. 'John Stuart Mill.' In his *Basic Theories of Distribution*. New York: Barnes and Noble, 1939, 177-236

454   Catlin, George. 'The Later Utilitarians: James and John Stuart Mill.' In his *History of the Political Philosophers*. New York: McGraw-Hill, 1939, 390-403

455   Cavenagh, Francis Alexander, ed. *James and John Stuart Mill on Education*. Cambridge: Cambridge University Press, 1931. Reprinted New York: Harper, 1969. (Selections with introduction)

456   [Cazelles, Emile.] 'John Stuart Mill: l'homme politique,' *La Démocratie du Midi*, 28 May 1873, 3. (Signed E.C.)

457   [——] 'John Stuart Mill: l'influence général de Mill,' *La Démocratie du Midi*, 24 May 1873, 3. (Signed E.C.)

458   [——] 'John Stuart Mill: le philosophe,' *La Démocratie du Midi*, 25 May 1873, 3. (Signed E.C.)

459   [——] 'John Stuart Mill: le réformateur,' *La Démocratie du Midi*, 28 May, 30 May, 4 June 1873, 3. (Signed E.C.)

460   Cecil, Robert. 'Democracy on Trial,' *Quarterly Review*, 110 (1861), 247-88. (Review of *Considerations on Representative Government*)

461   Chadwick, Edwin. *University of London Election. Address to the Members of Convocation, and a Letter from John Stuart Mill, Esq, MP*. London: Swift, 1867

462   Chamberlin, William Henry. 'John Stuart Mill: Independent Radical,' *Saturday Review*, 20 May 1967, 30-1. (Brief popular account of JSM's career)

463   Chapin, A.L. 'Autobiography of John Stuart Mill,' *New Englander*, 33 (1874), 605-22. (Review)

464   Chapman, Edward Mortimer. *English Literature and Religion, 1800-1900*. London: Constable, 1910, 318-27

465   Charactacus. 'Political Letters, II: The National Debt,' *National Reformer*, 7 (1866), 374-5. (About JSM's speech on Malt Tax)

466   —— 'Political Letters, VI: The Rights of Women,' *National Reformer*, 7 (1866), 393-4. (About JSM's petition of 7 June 1866)

467 Charles-Roux, J. *J.H. Fabre en Avignon*. Paris: Lemerre, 1913. (Fabre was supervisor of the Requien Collection of natural history in the Abbaye St Martial, Avignon)

468 Chernyshevsky, Nikolay Gavrilovich. *Dopolneniya i primechaniya na pervuyu knigu politicheskoy ekonomii Dzhona Styuarta Millya* [*Supplements and Notes to the First Book of John Stuart Mill's Political Economy*]. Geneva: Elpiden, 1869

469 —— *L'Economie politique jugée par la science: Critique des principes d'économie politique de John Stuart Mill*. Vol. I. Trans. from Russian. Brussels: Brismée, 1874

470 —— 'Ocherki iz politicheskoy ekonomii (po Millyu)' ['Essays on Political Economy (According to Mill)'], *Sovremennik* [*The Contemporary*] (1861), no 6, 477-549; no 7, 119-84; no 8, 397-443; no 9, 183-254; no 10, 519-75; no 12, 521-97. Reprinted in collected editions of Chernyshevsky's works in Geneva in 1870 and in Russia in 1905, 1935-37, and 1949

471 Chouville, L. 'Un Article de J. Stuart Mill sur Vigny,' *French Quarterly*, 1 (1919), 19-24

472 Christensen, Parley A. 'On Liberty in Our Time: Milton and Mill,' *Western Humanities Review*, 6 (1952), 110-18

473 Christie, William Dougal. *John Stuart Mill and Mr Abraham Hayward, QC: A Reply about Mill to a Letter to the Rev.Stopford Brooke, Privately Circulated and Actually Published*. London: King, 1873. Also published, without correspondence, as *Reply to Mr Abraham Hayward*

474 —— 'Mr John Stuart Mill for Westminster,' *Macmillan's Magazine*, 12 (1865), 92-6

475 [Church, R.W.] 'Mill, *On Liberty*,' *Bentley's Quarterly Review*, 2 (1860), 434-73

476 Clark, George A. 'Mill's "Notorious Analogy,"' *Journal of Philosophy*, 56 (1959), 652-6. (Defends JSM in his 'naturalistic fallacy')

477 Clark, Pamela M. 'Some Difficulties in Utilitarianism,' *Philosophy*, 29 (1954), 244-52

478 Clarke, Martin Lowther. *George Grote: A Biography*. London: Athlone Press, 1962

479 Clive, John. 'The Edinburgh Review: The Life and Death of a Periodical.' In *Essays in the History of Publishing in Celebration of the 250th*

Anniversary of the House of Longman, 1724-1974. Ed. Asa Briggs. London: Longman, 1974, 115-40

480 —— 'More or Less Eminent Victorians: Some Trends in Recent Victorian Biography,' *Victorian Studies*, 2 (1958), 5-28

481 Clough, J.S. *On Mill's Position as a Moralist.* Cambridge, 1884. (Pamphlet)

482 Cobbe, Frances Power. *The Hopes of the Human Race, Hereafter and Here: Essays on the Life after Death. With an Introduction Having Special Reference to Mr Mill's Essay on Religion.* London: Williams and Norgate, 1880. (1st ed. 1874)

483 —— 'The Subjection of Women,' *Theological Review*, 6 (1869), 355-75

484 Cockshut, A.O.J. 'John Stuart Mill: The Half Circle.' In his *The Unbelievers: English Agnostic Thought, 1840-1890.* London: Collins, 1964, 19-30

485 Cohen, L. Jonathan. 'The Inductive Logic of Progressive Problem Shifts,' *Revue Internationale de Philosophie*, 25, fasc. 1-2 (1971), 62-77. (Criticism of JSM's methods of induction)

486 Cohen, Marshall. *The Philosophy of John Stuart Mill.* New York: Random House, 1961. Reprinted London: Modern Library – Wildwood House, 1973

487 Cohen, Morris Raphael, and Ernest Nagel. *An Introduction to Logic and Scientific Method.* New York: Harcourt, Brace, 1934, 177-81. (See also Cohen's *A Preface to Logic.* New York: Holt, 1944; and Boegholt, above)

488 Cole, Henry. *Fifty Years of Public Work.* Edited and completed by A.S. and H.L. Cole. 2 vols. London: Bell, 1884

489 Cole, Margaret. 'John Stuart Mill.' In her *The Makers of the Labour Movement.* London: Longmans, 1948, 106-26

490 Collini, Stefan. 'Liberalism and the Legacy of Mill,' *Historical Journal*, 20 (1977), 237-54. (Review article dealing with Alan Ryan's *J.S. Mill*, Gertrude Himmelfarb's *On Liberty and Liberalism*, and Willard Wolfe's *From Radicalism to Socialism*)

491 Collins, James. 'Interpretation: The Interweave of Problems,' *New Literary History*, 4 (1973), 389-403. (Suggestions for a development in interrelational reading of Mill [*sic*])

492 Collins, Phillip. 'When Morals Lay in Lumps,' *Listener*, 90 (1973), 213-15. (Article on phrenology discusses JSM)

493 Comte, Auguste. *Lettres d'Auguste Comte à John Stuart Mill, 1841-1846*. Paris: Leroux, 1877

494 Conway, Moncure Daniel. 'The Great Westminster Canvass,' *Harper's*, 31 (1865), 733-45. (Detailed and friendly description of JSM's election)

495 —— *In Memoriam: A Memorial Discourse in Honour of John Stuart Mill, May 25th, 1873*. London: Austin, 1873

496 —— 'John Stuart Mill,' *Harper's*, 47 (1873), 528-34. (Obit. and personal reminiscences)

497 Cooney, Seamus. ' "The Heart of That Mystery": A Note on John Stuart Mill's Theory of Poetry,' *Victorian Newsletter*, 21 (1962), 20-3

498 —— 'Mill, Poets, and Other Men,' *Victorian Newsletter*, 17 (1960), 23-4

499 Cooper, Neil. 'Mill's "Proof" of the Principle of Utility,' *Mind*, 78 (1969), 278-9

500 Copi, Irving M. 'Causal Connections: Mill's Method of Experimental Inquiry.' In his *Introduction to Logic*. 2nd ed. New York: Macmillan, 1961, 355-415

501 Coplestone, Frederick A. 'The Utilitarian Movement (2): J.S. Mill: Logic and Empiricism.' In his *A History of Philosophy*. 9 vols. Rev. ed. London: Burns and Oates, 1951- , Vol. VII: *Bentham to Russell*, 25-92. Reprinted Garden City, NY: Doubleday, Image Books, 1967, 42-112

502 Corry, B.A. *Money, Saving and Investment in English Economics, 1800-1850*. London: Macmillan, 1962. (References *passim*)

503 —— 'The Theory of the Economic Effects of Government Expenditure on English Classical Economy,' *Economica*, ns 25 (1958), 34-48. (A short note which includes discussion of JSM's 1824 review of William Blake's *Observations on the Effects Produced by the Expenditure of Governments during the Restriction of Cash Payments*)

504 Coss, John Jacob, ed. *Autobiography of John Stuart Mill*. New York: Columbia University Press, 1924. (The Columbia MS with a short Preface by Coss)

505 Costigan, Giovanni. *Makers of Modern England*. New York: Macmillan, 1966. (Popular biography of Bentham, JSM, Webbs, etc.)

506 Courcelle-Seneuil, J.-G. 'L'Oeuvre de John Stuart Mill,' *Journal des Economistes*, 31 (1873), 5-13

507 Courtney, William Leonard. *Life of John Stuart Mill*. London: Scott, 1889

508 —— *The Metaphysics of John Stuart Mill*. London: Kegan Paul, 1879. (See also Robertson, 'Courtney's Metaphysics')

509 [Cowell, Herbert.] 'John Stuart Mill, *Autobiography*,' *Blackwood's Magazine*, 115 (1874), 75-93

510 —— 'Liberty, Equality, Fraternity,' *Blackwood's Magazine*, 114 (1873), 347-62. (A reference to [in a sense a review of] Fitzjames Stephen's attack; strongly opposes sexual equality)

511 Cowley, Malcolm. 'An Afterword on the Modern Mind.' In *Books That Changed Our Minds*. Ed. Malcolm Cowley and Bernard Smith. New York: Doubleday, Doran, 1940, 245-55. Reprinted Freeport: Books for Libraries, 1970. (Mentions *On Liberty* and *Considerations on Representative Government*)

512 —— 'The End of the Reasoning Man,' *New Republic*, 100 (1939), 237-40. (Reconsideration of *On Liberty*)

513 Cowling, Maurice. *Mill and Liberalism*. Cambridge: Cambridge University Press, 1963. 77-105 reprinted in *Mill: A Collection of Critical Essays*. Ed. J.B. Schneewind. Garden City, NY: Doubleday, 1968, 329-54; and in *On Liberty*. Ed. David Spitz. New York: Norton, 1975, 167-77

514 ——, introd. *Selected Writings of John Stuart Mill*. New York: New American Library, 1968

515 Cox, Catharine Morris. *The Early Mental Traits of Three Hundred Geniuses*. Palo Alto, Calif.: Stanford University Press, 1926, 707-10

516 Crane, C.B. 'John Stuart Mill and Christianity,' *Baptist Quarterly*, 8 (1874), 348-62

517 Cranston, Maurice. *Freedom*. New York: Longmans, Green, 1953

518 —— *John Stuart Mill*. London: Longmans, Green, 1958. Writers and Their Work, no 99. Published for the British Council and the National Book League. (Pamphlet) Reprinted in *British Writers and Their*

Work, no 2. Ed. Bonamy Dobrée. Lincoln: University of Nebraska Press, 1963, 5-36

519 —— 'J.S. Mill Exonerated: Illiberal Tract Proved Spurious,' *Manchester Guardian*, 9 June 1956, 6. (Review of Rees's *Mill and His Early Critics*, with additional information)

520 —— 'J.S. Mill as a Political Philosopher,' *History Today*, 8 (1958), 38-46

521 —— 'Mill on Liberty: A Revaluation,' *Listener*, 57 (1957), 58-9

522 —— 'Mr and Mrs Mill on Liberty,' *Listener*, 62 (1959), 385-6

523 Crawford, J. Forsyth. *The Relation of Inference to Fact in Mill's Logic*. Philosophic Studies, Dept of Philosophy, University of Chicago, 5. Chicago: University of Chicago Press, 1916

524 Croce, Benedetto. 'The Roots of Liberty.' In *Freedom: Its Meaning*. Ed. Ruth Nada Anshen. New York: Harcourt, Brace, 1940, 24-41. Reprinted London: Allen and Unwin, 1942

525 Crook, David Paul. *American Democracy in English Politics, 1815-50*. Oxford: Clarendon Press, 1965

526 Crossman, R.H.S. *Government and the Governed: A History of Political Ideas and Political Practice*. London: Christophers, 1939, 159-65

527 —— 'Walter Bagehot,' *Encounter*, 20 (1963), 42-55. (Includes comparison of Bagehot and JSM)

528 Crozier, John Beattie. 'John Stuart Mill.' In his *The Wheel of Wealth*. London: Longmans, Green, 1906, 345-62

529 Cumming, Ian. *A Manufactured Man: The Education of John Stuart Mill*. University of Auckland, Bulletin no 55, Educational Series no 2. Auckland: University of Auckland, 1960

530 Cumming, Robert D. *Human Nature and History: A Study of Liberal Political Thought*. 2 vols. Chicago: University of Chicago Press, 1969

531 —— 'Mill's History of His Ideas,' *Journal of the History of Ideas*, 25 (1964), 235-56

532 Cummings, C.A. 'The Later Writings of John Stuart Mill,' *Christian Examiner*, 74 (1863), 1-43. (Review of *On Liberty*, *Considerations on Representative Government*, *Dissertations and Discussions*, and 'The Contest in America')

533 Cunningham, John. 'Mill's *Examination of Sir William Hamilton's Philosophy*,' *Edinburgh Review*, 124 (1866), 120-50. (Review)

534 Cupples, Brian. 'A Defence of the Received Interpretation of J.S. Mill,' *Australasian Journal of Philosophy*, 50 (1972), 131-7

535 D., W.G. 'Mr J.S. Mill and the Inductive Origin of First Principles,' *Journal of Sacred Literature*, ns 9 (1866), 1-35

536 Dahl, Norman O. 'Is Mill's Hedonism Inconsistent?' *Studies in Ethics*, American Philosophical Quarterly Monograph Series, 7 (1973), 37-54

537 Daniels, Winthrop More. 'A Letter to John Stuart Mill,' *Atlantic Monthly*, 86 (1900), 664-71. (Reassessment of JSM's work)

538 Davenport, H.J. 'John Stuart Mill.' In his *Value and Distribution*. Chicago: University of Chicago Press, 1908, 53-61

539 Davidson, William Leslie. *Political Thought in England: The Utilitarians from Bentham to J.S. Mill*. London: Williams and Norgate, 1915

540 Davies, Rev J. Llewellyn. 'Professor Grote on Utilitarianism,' *Contemporary Review*, 15 (1870), 80-96

541 —— 'Universal Morality and the Christian Theory of Duty,' *Fortnightly Review*, 6 (1869), 1-12

542 Davies, J. Ronnie, and Francis J. Casey, Jr. 'Keynes's Misquotation of Mill,' *Economic Journal*, 87 (1977), 329-30

543 Davin, N.F. 'John Stuart Mill,' *Canadian Monthly*, 3 (1873), 512-19. (Obit.)

544 Davy, Georges. 'L'Explication sociologique et le recours à l'histoire, d'après Comte, Mill et Durkheim,' *Revue de Métaphysique et de Morale*, 54 (1949), 330-62

545 Day, John Patrick. 'John Stuart Mill.' In *A Critical History of Western Philosophy*. Ed. D.J. O'Connor. New York: Free Press; London: Collier-Macmillan, 1964, 341-64. Concluding paragraph reprinted as 'On Proving Utilitarianism.' In *Mill: A Collection of Critical Essays*. Ed. J.B. Schneewind. Garden City, NY: Doubleday, 1968, 204-5

546 —— 'Mill on Matter,' *Philosophy*, 38 (1963), 52-60. Reprinted in *Mill: A Collection of Critical Essays*. Ed. J.B. Schneewind. Garden City, NY: Doubleday, 1968, 132-44

547 —— 'On Liberty and the Real Will,' *Philosophy*, 45 (1970), 177-92

548 —— 'Threats, Offers, Law, Opinion and Liberty,' *American Philosophical Quarterly*, 14 (1977), 252-72

549 DeFord, Miriam Allen. 'John Stuart Mill.' In *British Authors of the Nineteenth Century*. Ed. Stanley Jasspoon Kunitz. New York: Wilson, 1936, 434-6

550 Degenfeld-Schonburg, Ferdinand Graf von. *Die Lohntheorie von Adam Smith, Ricardo, John Stuart Mill und Marx*. Munich: Duncker and Humboldt, 1914. (Dissertation, Berlin, 1914)

551 De Marchi, Neil B. 'Mill and Cairnes and the Emergence of Marginalism in England,' *History of Political Economy*, 4 (1972), 334-63

552 De Morgan, Sophia Elizabeth. *Memoir of Augustus De Morgan*. London: Longmans, Green, 1882. (Includes letters to JSM)

553 De Ruggiero, Guido. *The History of European Liberalism*. Trans. R.G. Collingwood. London: Oxford University Press, 1927, 103-57

554 Desai, S.S.M. 'John Stuart Mill (1806-1873).' In his *Economic Doctrines*. Bombay: Jamnadas, 1956, 274-300

555 De Selincourt, Aubrey. 'John Stuart Mill.' In his *Six Great Thinkers*. London: Hamilton, 1958, 153-80. (The others are Socrates, Augustine, Bacon, Rousseau and Coleridge)

556 Deuchar, Robert. *Review of 'An Examination of Hamiltonian Philosophy. By J.S. Mill, MP.'* Including Strictures on Dr Mansel and Dr Candlish's *Modern Theology*. Edinburgh: Thin, 1865

557 [Devas, Charles Stanton.] 'Christian Charity and Political Economy - Part II,' *Dublin Review*, ns 30 (1878), 89-110. (Review of, *inter alia, Principles of Political Economy*)

558 Devaux, Philippe. *L'Utilitarisme*. Brussels: La Renaissance du Livre, 1955. (Extracts and commentary on Bentham, James Mill, and JSM)

559 De Vere, Aubrey. 'Principles of Political Economy,' *Edinburgh Review*, 91 (1850), 1-62. (Review)

560 Devlin, Patrick. *The Enforcement of Morals*. London: Oxford University Press, 1965. 1-25 reprinted as 'Morals and the Criminal Law.' In *On Liberty*. Ed. David Spitz. New York: Norton, 1975, 177-90

561 Dhar, T.N. 'On the Possibility of Optimum (Unique) Equilibrium in Mill's Reciprocal Demand,' *Indian Journal of Economics*, 39 (1959), 383-97

562 Dicey, Albert Venn. 'John Stuart Mill,' *Nation*, 34 (1882), 403-4, 482-4. (Review of Bain's biography)

563 —— *Law and Public Opinion in England during the Nineteenth Century*. London: Macmillan, 1905. 2nd ed. corrected with New Introduction, 1914. (See especially Lecture XII)

564 —— *Letters to a Friend on Votes for Women*. London: Murray, 1909

565 —— 'Mill's *Autobiography*,' *Nation*, 18 (1874), 26-8, 43-4

566 —— 'Mill's Essays on Religion,' *Nation*, 20 (1875), 98-100

567 Dickinson, Zenas Clark. 'Utilitarian Psychology: The Two Mills and Bain.' In his *Economic Motives: A Study in the Psychological Foundation of Economic Theory*. Cambridge: Harvard University Press, 1922, 67-80

568 Dickson, William Martin. *The Absolute Equality of All Men before the Law, the Only True Basis of Reconstruction. With an Appendix, Containing John Stuart Mill's Letter on Reconstruction, and the Correspondence Herewith Connected*. Cincinatti: Clarke, 1865

569 Di Demetrio di Russia, Demetrio Maria. *Il principio di Mill e la sua rilevanza logica per le dottrine economiche*. Rome: Academia di San Cirillo, 1975. (Pamphlet)

570 Diffenbaugh, Guy Linton. 'Mrs Taylor Seen through Other Eyes than John Stuart Mill's,' *Sewanee Review*, 31 (1923), 198-204. (Carlyle, Bain, Morley)

571 Dilke, Charles W. 'John Stuart Mill, 1869-1873,' *Cosmopolis*, 6 (1897), 629-41. (Argues that JSM moved towards socialism in his last years)

572 Dinwiddy, J.R. 'Bentham's Transition to Radicalism,' *Journal of the History of Ideas*, 36 (1975), 683-700

573 Dobb, Maurice. *Political Economy and Capitalism: Some Essays in Economic Tradition*. New York: International Publishers, 1945

574 Dockrill, David W. 'The Limits of Thought and Regulative Truths,' *Journal of Theological Studies*, ns 21 (1970), 370-87. (Deals with the JSM-Mansel controversy over *Sir William Hamilton's Philosophy*)

575 Donagan, Alan. 'Victorian Philosophical Prose: J.S. Mill and F.H. Bradley.' In *The Art of Victorian Prose*. Ed. George Levine and William Madden. New York: Oxford University Press, 1968, 53-72. Reprinted in *English Literature and British Philosophy*. Ed. S.P. Rosenbaum. Chicago and London: University of Chicago Press, 1971, 208-28

576 Donisthorpe, Wadsworth. *Individualism: A System of Politics*. London: Macmillan, 1889

577 Douglas, Charles Mackinnon. *The Ethics of John Stuart Mill*. Edinburgh: Blackwood, 1897

578 —— *John Stuart Mill: A Study of His Philosophy*. Edinburgh: Blackwood, 1895

579 Dower, Robert S. 'John Stuart Mill and the Philosophical Radicals.' In *The Social and Political Ideas of Some Representative Thinkers of the Age of Reaction and Reconstruction, 1815-65*. Ed. F.J.C. Hearnshaw. London: Harrap, 1932, 113-15

580 Downie, R. 'Mill on Pleasure and Self-Development,' *Philosophical Quarterly*, 16 (1966), 69-71

581 The Drifters. 'In the Driftway,' *Nation*, 139 (1934), 709. (Gossip column on JSM's education)

582 Drummond, J., and C.B. Upton. *Life and Letters of James Martineau*. 2 vols. London: Nisbet, 1902. (Includes letters from JSM)

583 Drysdale, Charles Robert. *The Population Question According to T.R. Malthus and J.S. Mill, Giving the Malthusian Theory of Overpopulation*. London: Standring, 1892

584 [Drysdale, George.] *Logic and Utility ... The Tests of Truth and Falsehood, and of Right and Wrong: Being an Outline of Logic, the Science of Reasoning, and of the Utilitarian or Happiness Theory of Morals*. London: Truelove, 1866. (Signed G.R.)

585 Duffy, Charles Gavan. *Conversations with Carlyle*. London, New York: Scribner, 1892, 166-71

586 —— *My Life in Two Hemispheres*. 2 vols. London: Unwin, 1898. (Includes letters from JSM)

587 Dugas, Ludovic. 'Réaction contre une éducation exclusivement intellectuelle: John Stuart Mill.' In his *Penseurs libres et liberté de pensée*. Paris: Alcan, 1914, 40-71. (Deals primarily with JSM's reaction to his education; compares him to Comte in this respect)

588 Dumas, Alfred. 'Stuart Mill et Mistral,' *Mémoires de l'Académie de Vaucluse*, 2e sér, 27 (1927), 63-71. (Deals with JSM's correspondence with Mistral on the subject of feminism)

589 Dunbar, Charles F. 'The Reaction in Political Economy,' *Quarterly*

Journal of Economics, 1 (1886), 1-27. Reprinted in his *Economic Essays*. Ed. O.M.W. Sprague. New York and London: Macmillan, 1904, 30-51. (Summary of methods and beliefs of the classical school and of the reaction against it)

590 Duncan, David. *The Life and Letters of Herbert Spencer*. London: Methuen, 1908. (Includes letters from JSM)

591 Duncan, Elmer. 'Has Anybody Committed the Naturalistic Fallacy?' *Southern Journal of Philosophy*, 8 (1970), 49-55

592 Duncan, Graeme. 'John Stuart Mill and Democracy,' *Politics*, 4 (1969), 67-83

593 —— *Marx and Mill*. Cambridge: Cambridge University Press, 1973

594 Durham, John. 'The Influence of John Stuart Mill's Mental Crisis on His Thought,' *American Imago*, 20 (1963), 369-84

595 Dworkin, Gerald B. 'Marx and Mill: A Dialogue,' *Philosophy and Phenomenological Research*, 26 (1966), 403-14

596 —— 'Paternalism,' *Monist*, 56 (1972), 64-84. (Critical of JSM's view that society is never justified in using compulsion toward an individual for his own good)

597 Dworkin, Ronald. 'Lord Devlin and the Enforcement of Morals,' *Yale Law Journal*, 75 (1966), 986-1005. (See also Devlin)

598 Ebel, Henry. '"The Primaeval Fountain of Human Nature": Mill, Carlyle, and the French Revolution,' *Victorian Newsletter*, 30 (1966), 13-18

599 Ebenstein, William. 'John Stuart Mill: Political and Economic Liberty.' In *Liberty*. Ed. Carl J. Friedrich. *Nomos* (Yearbook of the American Society for Political and Legal Philosophy), IV. New York: Atherton; London: Prentice-Hall, 1962, 89-109

600 Eccarius, J. Georg. *Eines Arbeiters Widerlegung der national-ökonomischen Lehren J.S. Mills*. Berlin: Eichhoff, 1869

601 Edgeworth, F.Y. 'John Stuart Mill.' In *Palgrave's Dictionary of Political Economy*. 3 vols. London and New York: Macmillan, 1894-99, II, 756-63

602 —— 'The Theory of International Values,' *Economic Journal*, 4 (1894), 35-50, 424-43, 606-38. Reprinted in his *Papers Relating to Political Economy*. London: Macmillan, 1925, 3-60. (Other papers in collection also refer to JSM)

603 Edwards, Matilda Barbara Betham. *Reminiscences*. London: Redway, 1898. (Contains description of JSM at a Women's Suffrage meeting)

604 Edwards, Thomas. *The Relativity, the Unconditioned, Belief and Knowledge: Being Some Remarks on John Stuart Mill's 'Examination of Sir William Hamilton's Philosophy.'* Calcutta: Thacker, Spirik, 1878

605 Eichthal, Eugène d', ed. 'Letters of John Stuart Mill to Gustave d'Eichthal,' *Cosmopolis*, 6 (1897), 21-38, 348-66; 9 (1898), 368-81, 780-90. Reprinted as *Correspondance inédite avec Gustave d'Eichthal, 1828-42, 1864-71*. Ed. E. d'Eichthal. Paris: Alcan, 1898

606 Ekelund, Robert B., Jr. 'A Short-Run Classical Model of Capital and Wages: Mill's Recantation of the Wages Fund,' *Oxford Economic Papers*, ns 28 (1976), 66-85

607 ——, and Emilie S. Olsen. 'Comte, Mill and Cairnes: The Positivist Empiricist Interlude in Late Classical Economics,' *Journal of Economic Issues*, 7 (1973), 383-416

608 ——, and Robert D. Tollison. 'J.S. Mill's New Political Economy: Another View,' *Economic Inquiry*, 16 (1978), 587-92

609 ——, and Robert D. Tollison. 'The New Political Economy of J.S. Mill,' *Canadian Journal of Economics*, 9 (1976), 213-31

610 Ellegard, Alvar. 'Darwinian Theory and Nineteenth-Century Philosophies of Science,' *Journal of the History of Ideas*, 18 (1957), 362-93. (Discusses the compatibility of the themes of Whewell and JSM with Darwinism)

611 Ellery, John Blaise. *John Stuart Mill*. New York: Twayne, 1964

612 Ellis, Ethel E. *Memoir of William Ellis and an Account of His Conduct-Teaching*. London: Longmans, Green, 1888. (Letter from JSM, 114)

613 Ellis, Miriam A. 'Variations in the Editions of J.S. Mill's *Principles of Political Economy*,' *Economic Journal*, 16 (1906), 291-302

614 [Ellis, William?] 'The Autobiography of John Stuart Mill,' *The Times*, 4 Nov. 1873, 7; 10 Nov. 1873, 6

615 —— 'Causes of Poverty,' *Westminster Review*, 50 (1848), 62-76. (Compares JSM's opinions in *Principles of Political Economy* favourably to those of Thiers made in a speech discussing the French Revolution of 1848. Signed W.E.)

616 —— 'The Founder of Social Science,' *The Times*, 12 Nov. 1873, 5. (Letter)

617 Ely, Richard T. 'John Stuart Mill,' *Progress*, 4 (1899), 740-2

618 Emerson, G.H. 'Mill's Examination of Hamilton,' *Universalist Quarterly Review*, 23 (1866), 79-94. (Review article)

619 [Empson, William.] 'Bentham's *Rationale of Evidence*,' *Edinburgh Review*, 48 (1828), 457-520. (Critical of JSM's editorship, 462n-6n)

620 English, William Watson. *An Essay on Moral Philosophy, and Its Relations to Science and the Bible; with a Few Criticisms on Some Statements of Professor Tyndall, the Duke of Argyll, in His 'Reign of Law,' and J.S. Mill in His Essay 'On Liberty.'* London, 1869. Reprinted from the *Journal of Transactions of the Victoria Institute in London*.

621 Espinasse, Francis. *Literary Recollections and Sketches*. London: Hodder and Stoughton, 1893, 125-7, 218, 253-4, 400-1

622 Evans, E.P. 'Mill's Inaugural Address,' *North American Review*, 105 (1857), 291-5

623 Everett, Edwin Mallard. *The Party of Humanity: The Fortnightly Review and Its Contributors, 1865-1874*. Chapel Hill: University of North Carolina Press, 1939

624 Ezorsky, Gertrude, ed. *Philosophical Perspectives on Punishment*. Albany: State University of New York Press, 1973. (JSM on capital punishment and work by Bentham included among forty-two essays on punishment)

625 Fabbricatti, C.A. *Positivismo? John Stuart Mill*. Florence: Lumachi, 1910

626 Faguet, Emile. 'Auguste Comte et Stuart Mill,' *Revue Bleue*, 14 (1899), 438-42

627 Fahri, Findikaglu. *Stuart Mill vi Tüskiryediki Teserlesi*. Istanbul: Association des Resherches [*sic*] Culturelles et Sociologiques de Turquie, 1963, A, 49. (In Turkish)

628 Fain, John Tyree. 'Ruskin and Mill,' *Modern Language Quarterly*, 12 (1951), 150-4

629 —— 'Ruskin and the Orthodox Political Economists,' *Southern Economic Journal*, 10 (1943), 1-13

630 Falco, Salvatore Esposito de. 'Il quarto teoreme di G.S. Mill sul capitale,' *Giornale degli economisti*, 46 (1931), 285-90

631 Fallis, Sheila Robinson. 'John Robson's "Impossible Task,"' *University of Toronto Bulletin*, 9 Apr. 1976, 4. (Deals briefly with the editing of *Collected Works*)

632 Faure, Fernand. 'Stuart Mill.' In *Nouveau Dictionnaire d'économie politique*. Ed. Léon Say and Joseph Chailley. Paris: Guillaumin, 1892, II

633 Fawcett, Henry. *Free Trade and Protection*. 4th ed. London: Macmillan, 1882. (Disagrees with JSM's opinion on protection in the colonies)

634 —— 'John Stuart Mill: His Influence at the Universities,' *Examiner*, 17 May 1873, 514-15. Reprinted in *Popular Science Monthly*, 3 (1873), 384-6; and in *John Stuart Mill: Notices of His Life and Works*. Ed. H.R. Fox Bourne. London: Dallow, 1873, 74-80

635 [——] 'Mr Mill's Treatise *On Representative Government*,' *Macmillan's Magazine*, 4 (1861), 97-103

636 Fawcett, Millicent Garrett. 'John Stuart Mill: His Influence as a Practical Politician,' *Examiner*, 17 May 1873, 515-17. Reprinted in *John Stuart Mill: Notices of His Life and Works*. Ed. H.R. Fox Bourne. London: Dallow, 1873, 81-7

637 —— *Life of Molesworth*. London: Macmillan, 1901. (Molesworth, the Colonial Reformer, was early associated with the Philosophical Radicals and was the 'angel' for the *London Review*)

638 ——, introd. *J.S. Mill, On Liberty, Representative Government, The Subjection of Women*. Oxford: Oxford University Press, World's Classics, 1912

639 Feinberg, Joel. 'Legal Paternalism,' *Canadian Journal of Philosophy*, 1 (1971), 105–24. (Critique of JSM's prohibition of paternalism)

640 Feltes, N.N. '"Bentham" and "Coleridge": Mill's "Completing Counterparts,"' *Mill News Letter*, II, 2 (1967), 2–6

641 Ferri, F. *'L'utilitarismo' di Stuart Mill*. Milan, 1892

642 Fetter, Frank Whitson. 'The Influence of Economists in Parliament on British Legislation from Ricardo to John Stuart Mill,' *Journal of Political Economy*, 83 (1975), 1051–64

643 Feuer, Lewis Samuel. 'John Stuart Mill and Marxian Socialism,' *Journal*

of the History of Ideas, 10 (1949), 297–303. (Schapiro's comment follows, *ibid.*, 303–4)

644 —— 'John Stuart Mill as a Sociologist: The Unwritten Ethology.' In *James and John Stuart Mill: Papers of the Centenary Conference*. Ed. John M. Robson and Michael Laine. Toronto: University of Toronto Press, 1976, 86–110

645 —— *Psychoanalysis and Ethics*. Springfield: Thomas, 1955, 49-62. (Remarks on JSM's utilitarianism and on the mental crisis)

646 Fielding, K.J. 'Mill and Gradgrind,' *Nineteenth Century Fiction*, 11 (1956), 148-51

647 Filipiuk, Marion. 'Tocqueville in Translation in Mill's Reviews of *Democracy in America*,' *Mill News Letter*, XIII, 1 (1978), 10-17

648 Finance, Joseph de. *Essai sur l'agir humain*. Analecta Gregoriana 126, Series Facultatis Philosophicae sectio A n 8. Rome: Presses de l'Université Gregorienne, 1962. (Passing reference to JSM)

649 Finlason, William Francis. *A History of the Jamaica Case*. 2nd ed. London: Chapman and Hall, 1869

650 Fiske, John. 'Dissertations and Discussions: Political, Philosophical, and Historical,' *North American Review*, 106 (1868), 300-3

651 —— 'The Positive Philosophy of Auguste Comte by J.S. Mill,' *North American Review*, 102 (1866), 275-80. Reprinted in his *Darwinism and Other Essays*. New ed., rev. and enl. Boston and New York: Houghton Mifflin, 1885, 131-42

652 —— 'Principles of Political Economy,' *North American Review*, 98 (1864), 270-3

653 Fitzhugh, George. 'The English Reviews,' *DeBow's Review*, 28 (1860), 392-405. (Takes issue with review of *On Liberty*. Refers to 'Spiritual Freedom' in *Westminster Review*, ns 16 [1859] , 392-426.)

654 —— 'John Stuart Mill on Political Economy,' *DeBow's Review*, After the War ser, 3 (1867), 52-6. (Ridicules JSM; best political economists are horse jockeys and negro market women)

655 —— 'Slavery and Political Economy,' *DeBow's Review*, 21 (1856), 331-49, 443-67. (Takes issue with review of *Political Economy* in 'Slavery and Freedom,' *Southern Quarterly Review*, 1 [1856], 62-95. Unwilling to accept JSM as prophet of political economy.)

656 Fleming, Donald. 'Charles Darwin, the Anaesthetic Man,' *Victorian Studies*, 4 (1961), 219-36. (Discusses Darwin's abandonment of religion and denial of the arts; compares JSM's 'mental crisis' and cites Dickens's *Hard Times*)

657 Fletcher, Ronald, ed. *John Stuart Mill: A Logical Critique of Sociology*. London: Michael Joseph, 1971. (A selection of JSM's work bearing on the social sciences with an introductory essay by Fletcher)

658 Flower, Elizabeth F. 'Mill and Some Present Concerns about Ethical Judgments.' In *Liberty*. Ed. Carl J. Friedrich. *Nomos* (Yearbook of the American Society for Political and Legal Philosophy), IV. New York: Atherton; London: Prentice-Hall, 1962, 140-61

659 Flower, R. 'The Autographed MS of Mill's Logic,' *British Museum Quarterly*, 3 (1928),76-7

660 Flugel, John Carl. 'Systematic Psychology - J.S. Mill, Bain, Lotze.' In his *A Hundred Years of Psychology*. London: Duckworth, 1933, 76-87

661 Folghera, J.-D. 'Le Syllogisme: Stuart Mill et M. Rabier,' *Revue Thomiste*, 5 (1897), 371-82

662 Fonblanque, Edward Barrington de. *The Life and Labours of Albany Fonblanque*. London: Bentley, 1874. (Letters from JSM)

663 Fontpertius, A.F. de. 'Un Ecrit posthume de John Stuart Mill sur le socialisme,' *Journal des Economistes*, 7 (1879), 19-42

664 Foote, George William. *What Was Christ? A Reply to John Stuart Mill*. London: Progressive Publishing, 1887

665 Ford, George H. 'The Governor Eyre Case in England,' *University of Toronto Quarterly*, 17 (1948), 219-33

666 Ford, Trowbridge. 'Bagehot and Mill as Theorists of Comparative Politics,' *Comparative Politics*, 2 (1970), 309-24

667 Fosdick, Dorothy. *What Is Liberty?* New York: Harper and Brothers, 1939. (A few short citations)

668 ——, introd. *On Social Freedom. By John Stuart Mill*. New York: Columbia University Press, 1941. (Essay of questionable authorship reprinted from *Oxford and Cambridge Review*, 1 [1907] , 57-83. See Rees, *Mill and His Early Critics*; and Cranston, 'J.S. Mill Exonerated.')

669 Fothergill, Samuel. *Liberty, Liquor, Licence, and Prohibition. In Answer to the Argument of John Stuart Mill in His Work 'On Liberty.'* Swindon: Piper, 1865

670 Fouillée, A. 'Les Etudes récentes sur la propriété,' *Revue des Deux Mondes*, 63 (1884), 759-90. (Includes review of JSM's 'Chapters on Socialism')

671 Foulk, Gary L. 'Kendall's Criticism of J.S. Mill,' *Personalist*, 51 (1970), 314-23. (See Kendall, 'The Open Society and Its Enemies')

672 Fournier, G. 'Influence de Coleridge sur Stuart Mill dans le problème de la liberté et de la nécessité,' *Revue de Philosophie*, 21 (1921), 134-51

673 Fox, Caroline. *Memories of Old Friends, Being Extracts from the Journals and Letters of Caroline Fox, from 1835 to 1871.* Ed. H.N. Pym. 2nd ed. 2 vols. London: Smith, Elder, 1882. (Records meetings with JSM in 1840 and after, and includes letters from him)

674 Fox, L.A. 'Utilitarianism,' *Lutheran Quarterly*, ns 18 (1888), 54-71

675 Franchini, Silvia. 'La questione femminile nel pensiero di John Stuart Mill,' *Movimento operaio e socialista*, 17 (1971), 331-74; 18 (1972), 243-78

676 Frankena, W.K. 'The Naturalistic Fallacy,' *Mind*, ns 48 (1939), 464-77

677 Franklin, F., and C.L. 'Mill's Natural Kinds,' *Mind*, 13 (1888), 83-5. (See Towry and Monck)

678 [Fraser, Alexander Campbell.] 'Biographical Notice of J.S. Mill. By Professor Fraser,' *Proceedings of the Royal Society of Edinburgh*, Session 1873-74, 259-73

679 —— 'Mr Mill's *Examination of Sir William Hamilton's Philosophy*,' *North British Review*, ns 4 (1865), 1-58

680 Fredman, L.E., and B.L.J. Gordon. 'John Stuart Mill and Socialism,' *Mill News Letter*, III, 1 (1967), 3-7

681 Freed, Lan. 'Principia Ethica,' *New Statesman*, 49 (1955), 536. (Letter in reply to Stuart Hampshire's reassessment of Moore, which see)

682 Freeden, Michael. *The New Liberalism.* Oxford: Clarendon Press, 1978. (Frequent references to JSM *passim*)

683 Frege, Gottlob. *Die Grundlagen der Arithmetik.* Breslau: Koebner,

1884. Trans. J.L. Austin as *The Foundations of Arithmetic*. Oxford: Blackwell, 1950

684 Fresco, M.F. 'John Stuart Mill, een genuanceerd utilist,' *Wijsgerig perspectief op maatschappij en wetenschap*, 13e jaargang, no 5 (1972-73), 241-63

685 Friedman, Richard B. 'An Introduction to Mill's Theory of Authority.' In *Mill: A Collection of Critical Essays*. Ed. J.B. Schneewind. Garden City, NY: Doubleday, 1968, 379-425

686 —— 'A New Exploration of Mill's Essay *On Liberty*,' *Political Studies*, 14 (1966), 281-304

687 Friedman, William H. 'Some Issues Raised by the Deductive Logic of John Stuart Mill,' *Mill News Letter*, VI, 2 (1971), 21-2

688 Friedrich, Carl J., ed. *Liberty*. *Nomos* (Yearbook of the American Society for Political and Legal Philosophy), IV. New York: Atherton; London: Prentice-Hall, 1962. (Prompted by centenary of *On Liberty*, contains many articles relating to JSM. See Henry Aiken, Arnold Brecht, William Ebenstein, Elizabeth F. Flower, Andrew Hacker, Harry W. Jones, Frank H. Knight, Leonard Krieger, Albert A. Mavrinac, Margaret Spahr, David Spitz.)

689 Froude, James Anthony. *Thomas Carlyle: A History of the First Forty Years of His Life, 1795-1835*. 2 vols. London, 1882

690 —— *Thomas Carlyle: A History of His Life in London, 1834-1881*. 2 vols. London, 1884

691 Frye, Northrop. 'The Problem of Spiritual Authority in the Nineteenth Century.' In *Literary Views: Critical and Historical Essays*. Ed. Charles Carroll Camden. Chicago: University of Chicago Press, 1964, 145-58. Reprinted in *Backgrounds to Victorian Literature*. Ed. Richard A. Levine. San Francisco: Chandler, 1967, 120-36; and in Frye's *The Stubborn Structure*. Ithaca: Cornell University Press, 1970, 241-56. (Discusses, briefly, Hegelian elements in JSM's thought; cites *On Liberty*)

692 Fryer, Peter. *The Birth Controllers*. London: Secker and Warburg, 1965. (Describes JSM's distribution of birth-control pamphlets)

693 Fukuhara, G. 'John Stuart Mill and the Backward Countries,' *Bulletin of University of Osaka Prefecture*, Series D (Economy, Commerce and Law), 3 (1959), 64-75

694 —— 'John Stuart Mill and Socialism,' *Bulletin of University of Osaka Prefecture*, Series D (Economy, Commerce and Law), 1 (1957), 53-76

695 —— 'John Stuart Mill on Production and Distribution Policy, in Relation to the Classical Economists,' *Bulletin of University of Osaka Prefecture*, Series D (Economy, Commerce and Law), 2 (1958), 76-88

696 —— 'N.W. Senior and J.S. Mill,' *Bulletin of University of Osaka Prefecture*, Series D (Economy, Commerce and Law), 11 (1967), 43-58

697 —— 'On the Position and Structure of John Stuart Mill's Political Economy,' *Bulletin of University of Osaka Prefecture*, Series D (Economy, Commerce and Law), 4 (1960), 39-50

698 —— 'Some Additional Considerations on John Stuart Mill's Socialism,' *Bulletin of University of Osaka Prefecture*, Series D (Economy, Commerce and Law), 6 (1962), 30-46

699 Fullinwider, Robert K. 'On Mill's Analogy between Visible and Desirable,' *Southern Journal of Philosophy*, 10 (1972), 17-22

700 Funck-Brentano, Théophile. *Les Sophistes grecs et les sophistes contemporains*. Paris: Plon, 1879

701 Galasso, Antonio. *Della conciliazione dell'egoismo coll'altruismo secondo J.S. Mill*. Naples, 1883. From vol. 18 of *Atti del'Accademia di Scienze morali e politiche*. (Published lecture)

702 Garnett, R. *Life of Thomas Carlyle*. London: Scott, 1887

703 —— *Life of W.J. Fox*. London: Lane, 1910. (Includes letters from JSM)

704 Gast, Henri. *La Religion dans Stuart Mill*. Montauban, 1882

705 Gazin, Ferdinand Charles Alfred. 'Les Enseignements pédagogiques de Stuart Mill,' *Revue Pédagogique*, ns 80 (1922), 125-38, 168-78, 253-66

706 Gehrig, Hans. 'John Stuart Mill als Sozialpolitiker,' *Jahrbücher für Nationalökonomie und Statistik*, 3rd ser, 47 (1914), 176-201

707 George, Henry. *Progress and Poverty*. San Francisco: Clinton, Author's ed., 1879; New York: Appleton, 1880. Frequently reprinted. (Numerous references to *Principles of Political Economy*)

708 —— *The Science of Political Economy*. New York and London: Continental Publishing, 1897. Ed. and expanded by Henry George, Jr.

New York: Doubleday and McClure, 1898. (Numerous references to *Principles of Political Economy*)

709 Gertsen, Aleksandr Ivanovich. See Herzen

710 Giannotti, José Arthur. *John Stuart Mill: o psicologismo e a fundamentacao da logica*. Sao Paulo: Faculdade de Filosofia, Ciencias e Letras Universidade de Sao Paulo, 1964. Boletem 269, Cadeira de Filosofia 5

711 —— 'Stuart Mill et la critica da evidencia Cartesiana,' *Anais do III Congresso Nacional de Filosofia*. Sao Paulo: Instituto Brasileiro de Filosofia, 1960, 307-11

712 Gide, Charles. 'L'Apogée et le déclin de l'école classique. Stuart Mill.' In his and Charles Rist's *Histoire des doctrines économiques depuis les physiocrates jusqu'à nos jours*. Paris: Sirey, 1909. Trans. R. Richards as *A History of Economic Doctrines*. London: Harrap, 1915; 2nd ed., 1948

713 —— *Principes d'économie politique*. Paris: La Rose et Forcel, 1884. Frequently reprinted. Trans. Edward P. Jacobsen as *Principles of Political Economy*. Boston: Heath, 1891

714 Gilden, Hilail. 'Mill's *On Liberty*.' In *Ancients and Moderns: Essays on the Tradition of Political Philosophy in Honor of Leo Strauss*. Ed. J. Cropsey. New York: Basic Books, 1964, 288-303

715 Gilman, Benjamin Ives. 'What Is Liberty when Two or More Persons Are Concerned?' *International Journal of Ethics*, 32 (1922), 124-8

716 Gilson, Etienne. *The Unity of Philosophical Experience*. New York: Scribner, 1937. (JSM seen briefly in relation to Comte)

717 Giulietti, Giovanni. *La dottrina dell'induzione nel 'Sistema' di Giovanni Stuart Mill*. Verona: Linotipia veronese Ghidini & Fiorini, [1958?]

718 Gizycki, G. von. 'Ueber den Utilitarismus,' *Vierteljahrsschrift für wissenschaftliche Philosophie*, 8 (1884), 265-91. (See also F.W.E.J. Bregmann)

719 Gnocchi-Viani, Osvaldo. Preface to *Sul socialismo*. Milan: Bignami, 1880

720 Godkin, E.L. 'Aristocratic Opinions of Democracy,' *North American Review*, 100 (1865), 194-232. (Review essay on Tocqueville's *Democracy in America* and JSM's *Dissertations and Discussions*, especially article on 'Democracy in America')

721 —— 'Mr J.S. Mill on the Irish Difficulty,' *Nation*, 6 (1868), 205-6

722 —— 'Mr Mill's Plea for Women,' *Nation*, 9 (1869), 72-3

723 —— 'Political Philosophers in the Legislature,' *Nation*, 7 (1868), 519

724 —— 'The Tyranny of the Majority,' *North American Review*, 104 (1867), 204-30. (JSM frequently and favourably mentioned)

725 [——, and C. Wright.] 'John Stuart Mill,' *Nation*, 16 (1873), 350-1. (Obit.)

726 Goggia, P.E. *La mente di Mill. Saggio di logica positiva applicata specialmente alla storia.* Livorno: Vigo, 1869

727 Gomperz, H. ' "Cuius regio illius opinio": Considerations on the Present Crisis of the Tolerance Idea,' *International Journal of Ethics*, 46 (1936), 292-307. (A reflection of the year 1936 referring to *On Liberty*)

728 Gomperz, Theodor. *Briefe und Aufzeichnungen.* Ed. Heinrich Gomperz. Vienna: Gerold, 1936, I. (Subsequent volumes were never published)

729 —— *John Stuart Mill. Ein Nachruf.* Vienna: Konegen, 1889

730 —— 'Zur Erinnerungen an John Stuart Mill.' In his *Essays und Erinnerungen.* Stuttgart and Leipzig: Deutsche Verlags-Anstalt, 1905

731 Gonnard, René. 'Stuart Mill et sa théorie de l'état stationnaire,' *Questions Pratiques*, 19 (1923), 12-20

732 Gordeon, B.L.G., and L.E. Fredman. 'John Stuart Mill and Socialism,' *Mill News Letter*, III, 1 (1967), 3-7

733 Gordon, D.R. 'The Unschooled Philosopher: An Unlikely Impression of John Stuart Mill.' In *The Victorians and Social Protest.* Ed. J. Butt and I.F. Clarke. London: David and Charles, Archon Books, 1973, 102-32

734 Gordon, Scott. 'Mill, Population, and Liberty,' *Mill News Letter*, IV, 2 (1969), 14-17

735 —— 'The Quality of Pleasure: Mill & Edgeworth,' *Mill News Letter*, VII, 2 (1972), 18-20

736 —— 'The Quality Problem in Utilitarianism,' *Mill News Letter*, X, 1 (1975), 9-13

737 Gorodtsev, Pavel Dmitriyevich. *Pozitivizm i khristianstvo: Religiozno-filosofskiya vozzreniya Dzhona Styuarts Millya i ikh otnosheniye k khristianstvu [Positivism and Christianity: The*

Religio-Philosophical Views of John Stuart Mill and Their Relation to Christianity]. St Petersburg: S. Dobrod'yev, 1881

738 Gorovitz, Samuel, ed. *Mill: Utilitarianism*. Indianapolis and New York: Bobbs-Merrill, 1971. (Includes, *inter alia*, articles by: H.D. Aiken, S.M. Brown Jr, J.H. Burns, E.W. Hall, Jonathan Harrison, R.F. Harrod, Norman Kretzmann, J.D. Mabbott, Maurice Mandelbaum, Joseph Margolis, A.I. Melden, H.J. McCloskey (2), H.A. Prichard, John Rawls (2), J.J.C. Smart, C.L. Ten, J.O. Urmson, which see)

739 Gotthelft, Frieda Esther. 'Die sozialpolitschen Wandlungen von John Stuart Mill,' *Schmollers Jahrbuch für Gesetzgebung, Verwaltung und Volkswirtschaft*, 41 (1917), 1755-1833

740 Gouhier, Henri. *La Jeunesse d'Auguste Comte et la formation du positivism*. 3 vols. Paris: Vrin, 1933-41

741 Gouraud, Charles. 'Tendances de l'économie politique en France et en Angleterre,' *Revue des Deux Mondes*, ns 14 (1852), 256-86

742 Govil, O.P. 'A Note on Mill and Browning's *Pauline*,' *Victorian Poetry*, 4 (1966), 287-91

743 Grabowsky, Adolf. 'John Stuart Mills Lebensgang.' In *Die Freiheit*. Trans. Adolf Grabowsky with Introduction and commentary. Zurich: Pan, 1945. Reprinted Darmstadt: Wissenschaftliche Buchgesellschaft, 1970, 266-83

744 Graff, J.A. 'Mill's Quantity-Quality Distinction: A Defence,' *Mill News Letter*, VII, 2 (1972), 14-18

745 Graham, Frank D. 'The Theory of International Values Re-examined,' *Quarterly Journal of Economics*, 38 (1923), 54-86

746 Graham, William. 'J.S. Mill: I - The Science of Society; II - On Representative Government.' In his *English Political Philosophy from Hobbes to Maine*. London: Arnold, 1899, 271-347

747 —— *Socialism: New and Old*. London: Kegan Paul, Trench, Trübner, 1890

748 Grant, Judith Skelton. 'Glimpses of J.S. Mill's Views in 1843,' *Mill News Letter*, XIII, 2 (1978), 2-7

749 Graubard, Stephen R. 'Le Pouvoir de la parole dans l'Angleterre victorienne,' *Critique*, 14 (1958), 605-21. (Review of Packe on JSM, Annan on Leslie Stephen, Faber on Jewett and Magnus on Gladstone)

750 Gray, J.N. 'John Stuart Mill and the Future of Liberalism,' *Contemporary Review*, 229 (1976), 138-45

751 Graziani, Augusto. *Ricardo e J.S. Mill*. Bari: Laterza, 1921

752 Greaves, Ida. 'The Character of British Colonial Trade,' *Journal of Political Economy*, 62 (1954), 1-11. (Application of JSM's definition of colonial trade to modern conditions)

753 Greeley, Horace. 'Mill on Protection,' *New York Tribune*, 13 Feb. 1871, 4. (See also his 'Mill's Logic,' 15 Feb., 4; and 'Intentions in Statesmanship,' 17 Feb., 4)

754 —— [Untitled editorial,] *New York Tribune*, 20 Nov. 1871, 4. (Attacks JSM's views on free trade)

755 Green, Phillip. 'Again, Tolerance, Democracy, Pluralism,' *Dissent*, 145 (1967), 368-73. (Continues the discussion engendered by Wolff *et al.*, *A Critique of Pure Tolerance*, with comments by Green and Spitz. See Spitz, Wolff, below.)

756 Green, Thomas Hill. *Lectures on the Principles of Political Obligation*. London: Longmans, 1912

757 —— 'The Logic of J.S. Mill.' In his *Works*. Ed. R.L. Nettleship. 3 vols. London: Longmans, Green, 1886, II, 195-306

758 —— *Prolegomena to Ethics*. Ed. A.C. Bradley. Oxford: Clarendon Press, 1883, 168-78

759 Greenberg, R.A. 'Mill on Bagehot and Reform,' *Notes and Queries*, 203 (1958), 83-4

760 Gregory, D.A. 'J.S. Mill and the Destruction of Theism,' *Princeton Review*, ns 2 (1878), 409-48

761 Greniewski, Henryk. *Elementy logiki indukcji* [*Elements of the Logic of Induction*]. Warsaw: Panstwowe Wydawnictwo Naukowe, 1955

762 —— 'Milla kanon zmian towarzyszacych' ['On Mill's Method of Concomitant Variations'], *Studia Logica*, 5 (1957), 109-27. (Polish with brief summaries in Russian and English. See also 'Dyskusja' ['Discussion'], *ibid.*, 134-5. This and item above summarized in English by Zbigniew Czerwinski, *Journal of Symbolic Logic*, 23 [1958],77-9.)

763 Greville, Charles. *The Greville Memoirs: 1814-1860*. Ed. Lytton Strachey and Roger Fulford. London: Macmillan, 1938

764 Gribble, Francis. 'John Stuart Mill,' *Fortnightly Review*, 86 (1906), 344-54

765 Grierson, Sir Herbert. 'The University and Liberal Education.' In his *Essays and Addresses*. London: Chatto and Windus, 1940, 187-209. (Discusses the *Inaugural Address*)

766 Griffin, Andrew. 'The Interior Garden and John Stuart Mill.' In *Nature and the Victorian Imagination*. Ed. U.C. Knoepflmacher, and G.B. Tennyson. Berkeley, Los Angeles and London: University of California Press, 1977, 171-86

767 Griffin, Nicholas. 'A Note on Mr Cooper's Reconstruction of Mill's "Proof,"' *Mind*, 81 (1972), 142-3. (See Cooper)

768 Griffin, William Hall, and Harry Christopher Minchin. *The Life of Robert Browning*. London: Methuen, 1910. (Discusses JSM's criticism of *Pauline*)

769 Griffin-Collard, Evelyne. *Egalité et justice dans l'utilitarisme: Bentham, J.S. Mill, H. Sidgwick. L'Egalité*, Vol. II. Brussels: Bruylant, 1974

770 —— 'Le Principe d'utilité et l'égalité: Bentham et J.S. Mill,' *L'Egalité. Revue Internationale de Philosophie*, 25, fasc. 3 (1971), 312-30

771 Griffith, Grosvenor Talbot. *Population Problems of the Age of Malthus*. Cambridge: Cambridge University Press, 1926

772 [Grote, George.] 'John Stuart Mill on the Philosophy of Sir William Hamilton,' *Westminster Review*, ns 29 (1866), 1-39. Reprinted in his *Minor Works*. Ed. Alexander Bain. London: Murray, 1873, 277-330. Also published as a pamphlet, *Review of the Work of Mr John Stuart Mill, Entitled, 'Examination of Sir W. Hamilton's Philosophy.'* London, 1867

773 —— 'John Stuart Mill's Political Economy,' *Spectator*, 21 (1848), 467-9. (Review)

774 Grote, Harriet. *The Personal Life of George Grote*. London: Murray, 1873

775 —— *The Philosophical Radicals of 1832*. London: Savill, 1866

776 Grote, John. *An Examination of the Utilitarian Philosophy*. Ed. Joseph Bickerath Mayor. Cambridge: Deighton, Bell, 1870

777 —— *Exploratio Philosophica: Rough Notes on Modern Intellectual Science*. Pt I. Cambridge: Deighton, Bell; London: Bell and Daldy, 1865. Reprinted Cambridge: Cambridge University Press, 1900. (Refers to *Examination of Sir William Hamilton's Philosophy*) Pt II, ed. Joseph B. Mayor. Cambridge: Cambridge University Press, 1900. (Especially vii-ix on the *Logic*)

778 Grube, John. '*On Liberty* as a Work of Art,' *Mill News Letter*, V, 1 (1969), 2-6

779 Guilietti, Giovanni. *La dottrina dell'induzione nel sistema di Giovanni Stuart Mill*. Verona: Ghidini, 1958

780 Guillaume, Edward H. 'Mr John Stuart Mill,' *National Reformer*, 6 (1865), 337-8. (Approval of JSM's candidacy)

781 Guskar, Hermann. 'Der Utilitarismus bei Mill und Spencer in kritischen Beleuchtung; eine Grundlegung für die Ethik,' *Archiv für Systematische Philosophie*, 15 (1909), 1-22

782 [Guy, Robert Ephrem.] 'Calderwood and Mill upon Hamilton,' *Dublin Review*, ns 5 (1865), 474-504. (Signed 'R.E.G.')

783 [——] 'Dr McCosh's *Intuitions of the Mind* and *Examination of Mill's Philosophy*,' *Dublin Review*, ns 8 (1867), 172-92. (Signed 'R.E.G.')

784 Guyau, Jean-Marie. *La Morale anglaise contemporaine*. Paris: Libraire Germen Baillière, 1879. 2nd ed. rev., Paris: Alcan, 1885

785 Hacker, Andrew. 'Freedom and Power: Common Men and Uncommon Men.' In *Liberty*. Ed. Carl J. Friedrich. *Nomos* (Yearbook of the American Society for Political and Legal Philosophy), IV. New York: Atherton; London: Prentice-Hall, 1962, 308-33

786 —— 'John Stuart Mill.' In his *Political Theory: Philosophy, Ideology, Science*. New York: Macmillan, 1961, 571-609

787 Hafer, R.W. See E.G. West

788 Hagberg, Knut. *Personalities and Powers*. Trans. Elizabeth Sprigge and Claude Napier. London: John Lane, 1930, 191-200. (Originally in Swedish, *Medmanniskor*)

789 Hagen, John, and Albert J. Fyfe. 'J.S. Mill,' *Book Collector*, 9 (1960), 202-3. (Appeal for information on unpublished works of JSM with a view to publication of an annotated edition)

790   Hainds, John Robert. 'John Stuart Mill and the Saint-Simonians,' *Journal of the History of Ideas*, 7 (1946), 103-12. (Reply to Hill Shine, 'J.S. Mill and an Open Letter to the Saint-Simonian Society in 1832,' *ibid.*, 6 [1945], 102-8)

791   —— 'J.S. Mill's *Examiner* Articles on Art,' *Journal of the History of Ideas*, 11 (1950), 215-34

792   Haines, Lewis F. 'Mill and "Pauline": The "Review" That "Retarded" Browning's Fame,' *Modern Language Notes*, 59 (1944), 410-12

793   —— 'Reade, Mill, and Zola: A Study of the Character and Intention of Charles Reade's Realistic Method,' *Studies in Philology*, 40 (1943), 463-80

794   Hale, E.E. 'John Stuart Mill,' *Old and New*, 9 (1874), 128-35. (Review of *Autobiography*)

795   —— 'Stuart Mill's History of Rome,' *Old and New*, 9 (1874), 135-8. (Extracts from Alfred Mills's *Pictures of Roman History in Miniature* [London: Printed for Darton Harvey and Darton; and J. Harris, 1809] which Hale wrongly claims to be the juvenile history referred to in *Autobiography*, suggesting Alfred Mills might be a pseudonym for JSM. Hale refers to a later edition.)

796   Hales, G.T. 'The Letters of John Stuart Mill,' *British Museum Quarterly*, 9 (1934), 40-2

797   Halévy, Elie. *La Formation du radicalisme philosophique*. 3 vols. Paris: Alcan, 1901-04. Trans. as *The Growth of Philosophic Radicalism*. London: Faber and Gwyer, 1928; Faber and Faber, 1952

798   —— *Histoire du peuple anglaise au XIXe siècle*. 6 vols. Paris: Hachette, 1912-46. Trans E.I. Watkin and D.A. Barker. London: T. Fisher Unwin, 1924-48. Frequently reprinted London: Ernest Benn with a supplementary section by R.B. McCallum, 'From 1852 to 1895,' Vol. IV

799   Hall, Everett W. 'The "Proof" of Utility in Bentham and Mill,' *Ethics*, 60 (1949), 1-18. Reprinted in *Mill: A Collection of Critical Essays*. Ed. J.B. Schneewind. Garden City, NY: Doubleday, 1968, 145-78; and in *Mill: Utilitarianism*. Ed. S. Gorovitz. Indianapolis and New York: Bobbs-Merrill, 1971, 99-116. (See also Rohatyn)

800   Hall, Roland. 'The Diction of John Stuart Mill,' *Notes and Queries*, 209 (1964), 29-34, 102-7, 183-8, 218-23, 307-12, 379-85, 423-9; 210 (1965), 51-6, 188-94, 246-54, 419-25

801 —— 'Further Addenda to "The Diction of John Stuart Mill,"' *Notes and Queries*, 215 (1970), 10-11

802 —— 'Still More Addenda to "The Diction of John Stuart Mill,"' *Notes and Queries*, 215 (1970), 368-9

803 —— 'A Virtually Untapped Source for Dictionary Quotations,' *Notes and Queries*, 204 (1959), 333-5. (Using Elliot's ed. of *Letters*, lists many uses of words which antedate those cited by the editors of the *OED Supplement* [1933])

804 Halliday, R.J. *John Stuart Mill*. Political Thinkers' series, no 4. London: Allen and Unwin, 1976

805 —— 'John Stuart Mill's Idea of Politics,' *Political Studies*, 18 (1970), 461-77

806 —— 'Some Recent Interpretations of John Stuart Mill,' *Philosophy*, 43 (1968), 1-17. Reprinted in *Mill: A Collection of Critical Essays*. Ed. J.B. Schneewind. Garden City, NY: Doubleday, 1968, 354-78. (Chiefly criticism of Cowling and Rees, which see)

807 Hallowell, John H. 'Utilitarianism - John Stuart Mill.' In his *Main Currents in Modern Political Thought*. New York: Holt, 1950, 217-34

808 Hamburger, Joseph. *Intellectuals in Politics: John Stuart Mill and the Philosophic Radicals*. New Haven and London: Yale University Press, 1965

809 —— '*James and John Stuart Mill: Father and Son in the Nineteenth Century*. By Bruce Mazlish,' *History and Theory*, 15 (1976), 328-41. (Review essay)

810 —— 'Mill and Tocqueville on Liberty.' In *James and John Stuart Mill: Papers of the Centenary Conference*. Ed. John M. Robson and Michael Laine. Toronto: University of Toronto Press, 1976, 111-25

811 —— 'The Writings of John Stuart Mill and His Father James Mill in the Archives of the India Office,' *American Philosophical Society Yearbook 1957*, 324-6. (Report on research)

812 Hamilton, Mary Agnes. *John Stuart Mill*. London: Hamish Hamilton, 1933

813 Hamilton, Walton H. 'John Stuart Mill.' In *Encyclopaedia of the Social Sciences*. 15 vols. New York: Macmillan, 1935, X, 481-3

814 Hammond, Albert Lamphier. 'Euthyphro, Mill, and Mr Lewis,' *Journal of Philosophy*, 49 (1952), 377-92

815 Hampshire, Stuart. *Morality and Pessimism*. Cambridge: Cambridge University Press, 1972. Reprinted, revised, in *New York Review of Books*, 25 Jan. 1973, 26-33. (An anti-utilitarian critique. The Leslie Stephen Lecture.)

816 —— 'Principia Ethica,' *New Statesman*, 49 (1955), 475-6, 579-80. (A reassessment of Moore's work which prompted a reply by Lan Freed [which see] regarding Hampshire's supposed support of Moore against JSM and Hampshire's further reply)

817 Hancock, Roger. 'Ethics and History in Kant and Mill,' *Ethics*, 68 (1957), 56-60

818 —— 'Mill, Saints and Heroes,' *Mill News Letter*, X, 1 (1975), 13-15

819 Haney, Lewis Henry. 'Rent and Price: "Alternative Use" and "Scarcity Value,"' *Quarterly Journal of Economics*, 25 (1910), 119-38. (An examination of cases in which, according to JSM, prices are in part determined by rent payments)

820 Hanschmann, Alexander Bruno. *Bernard Palissy der Künstler, Naturforscher und Schriftsteller als Vater der induktiven Wissenschaftsmethode des Bacon von Verulam. Mit der Darstellung der Induktionstheorie Francis Bacons und John Stuart Mills*. Leipzig: Weicher, 1903

821 Hansen, S. 'Versuch einer Kritik des Mill'schen Subjectivismus,' *Vierteljahrsschrift für wissenschaftliche Philosophie*, 13 (1889), 373-91

822 [Hare, Thomas.] 'John Stuart Mill,' *Westminster Review*, ns 45 (1874), 122-59

823 Harley, Clifford. 'Swedenborg and J.S. Mill,' *New-Church Magazine*, 41 (1921), 209-18

824 Harris, Abram L. 'John Stuart Mill: Government and Economy,' *Social Science Review*, 37 (1963), 134-53

825 —— 'John Stuart Mill: Liberalism, Socialism, and Laissez-Faire.' In his *Economics and Social Reform*. New York: Harper, 1958, 24-118

826 —— 'J.S. Mill on Monopoly and Socialism: A Note,' *Journal of Political Economy*, 67 (1959), 604-11

827 —— 'J.S. Mill: Servant of the East India Company,' *Canadian Journal of Economics and Political Science*, 30 (1964), 185-202

828 —— 'J.S. Mill's Theory of Progress,' *Ethics*, 66 (1956), 157-75

829 —— 'Mill on Freedom and Voluntary Association,' *Review of Social Economy*, 18 (1960), 27-41. (Commentary by Francis J. Brown appended, 41-4)

830 Harris, Henry Wilson. *Caroline Fox*. London: Constable, 1944

831 Harris, Robert T. 'Nature: Emerson and Mill,' *Western Humanities Review*, 6 (1952), 1-13

832 Harris, Wendell V. 'The Warp of Mill's "Fabric" of Thought,' *Victorian Newsletter*, 37 (1970), 1-7

833 Harris, William. *The History of the Radical Party in Parliament*. London: Kegan Paul, 1885

834 Harrison, Frederic. *Autobiographic Memoirs*. 2 vols. London, 1911

835 —— 'John Stuart Mill,' *Nineteenth Century*, 40 (1896), 487-508. French trans. L. Baraduc, *Revue Occidentale*, 2e sér, 17 (1898), 149-68, 342-62. Reprinted in his *Tennyson, Ruskin, Mill and Other Literary Estimates*. London: Macmillan, 1899, 285-322

836 —— 'John Stuart Mill: His Relation to Positivism,' *Examiner*, 17 May 1873, 517. Reprinted in *John Stuart Mill: Notices of His Life and Works*. Ed. H.R. Fox Bourne. London: Dallow, 1873, 88-90. (Part of a lecture on political institutions delivered at the Positivist School, 11 May 1873)

837 —— *On Society*. London: Macmillan, 1918. Reprinted Freeport, NY: Books for Libraries, 1971. (Two lectures on Comte and Mill, 203-58)

838 —— 'The Religion of Inhumanity,' *Fortnightly Review*, ns 13 (1873), 677-99. (Review of *Liberty, Equality, Fraternity* by Fitzjames Stephen. Brief reference to JSM.)

839 Harrison, Jonathan. 'The Expedient, the Right and the Just in Mill's Utilitarianism,' *Canadian Journal of Philosophy*, Suppl. vol. no 1, Pt 1 (1974), 93-107

840 —— 'Utilitarianism, Universalization, and Our Duty to Be Just,' *Proceedings of the Aristotelian Society*, 53 (1952-53), 105-34. Reprinted in *Mill: Utilitarianism*. Ed. S. Gorovitz. Indianapolis and New York: Bobbs-Merrill, 1971, 151-67

841 Harrod, R.F. 'Utilitarianism Revised,' *Mind*, 45 (1936), 137-56. Reprinted in *Mill: Utilitarianism*. Ed. S. Gorovitz. Indianapolis and New York: Bobbs-Merrill, 1971, 73-87

842 Hart, H.L.A. 'Immorality and Treason,' *Listener*, 62 (1959), 162-3. Reprinted, slightly abridged, in *On Liberty*. Ed. David Spitz. New York: Norton, 1975, 246-52

843 —— *Law, Liberty and Morality*. London: London University Press; Stanford: Stanford University Press, 1963. 25-34 reprinted in *Limits of Liberty: Studies of Mill's 'On Liberty.'* Ed. Peter Radcliffe. Belmont: Wadsworth, 1966, 58-63. (Cites JSM's *On Liberty* against Fitzjames Stephen and Lord Devlin. See also Pierce)

844 ——, and A.M. Honoré. *Causation in the Law*. Oxford: Clarendon Press, 1959

845 Harvey, Nigel. 'Phrenology,' *Listener*, 90 (1973), 283. (Letter to the editor on JSM and phrenology. See Collins.)

846 Haryrlesky, Thomas. 'The Money Supply Theory of J.S. Mill,' *South African Journal of Economics*, 40 (1972), 72-6

847 Havard, William C. *Henry Sidgwick and Later Utilitarian Political Philosophy*. Gainesville: University of Florida Press, 1959

848 Haven, Joseph. 'Mill versus Hamilton,' *Bibliotheca Sacra*, 25 (1868), 501-35

849 Hawley, Frederick Barnard. *Capital and Population: A Study of the Economic Effects of Their Relations to Each Other*. New York: Appleton, 1882

850 Hawtin, Gillian. 'The Case of Thomas Pooley, Cornish Well Sinker, 1657,' *Notes and Queries*, 21 (1974), 18-24. (A full analysis of the prosecution of Pooley for blasphemous libel. The case is referred to by JSM in *On Liberty*, Chap. 2.)

851 Hayek, Frederick A. von. *The Counter Revolution of Science: Studies on the Abuse of Reason*. Glencoe, Ill.: Free Press, 1952, Pts II, III

852 —— *Individualism and Economic Order*. Chicago: University of Chicago Press, 1948

853 —— 'John Rae and John Stuart Mill: A Correspondence,' *Economica*, ns 10 (1943), 253-5

854 —— *John Stuart Mill and Harriet Taylor: Their Friendship and Subsequent Marriage*. London: Routledge and Kegan Paul; Chicago: University of Chicago Press, 1951. (American edition has subtitle, corrected by errata slip, as *Correspondence and Subsequent Marriage*)

855 —— 'J.S. Mill's Correspondence,' *Times Literary Supplement*, 13 Feb. 1943, 84

856 —— 'Letters of J.S. Mill,' *Notes and Queries*, 184 (1943), 242-4

857 —— 'Portraits of J.S. Mill,' *Times Literary Supplement*, 11 Nov. 1949, 733. (Letter)

858 ——, ed. 'J.S. Mill's Notes on Nassau Senior's Political Economy,' *Economica*, ns 12 (1945), 134-9

859 ——, ed. 'On Marriage and Divorce: Being the Reflections of John Stuart Mill and Harriet Taylor,' *Midway*, 16 (1963), 100-26. Reprinted from his *John Stuart Mill and Harriet Taylor*

860 ——, ed. *The Spirit of the Age. By John Stuart Mill*. Chicago: University of Chicago Press, 1942

861 Hayes, William. *Remarks, with Reference to the Land-laws of England, on some Passages in Mr John Stuart Mill's Principles of Political Economy, and M. Louis Blanc's Letters on England*. London, 1867

862 [Hayward, Abraham.] 'John Stuart Mill,' *Fraser's Magazine*, ns 8 (1873), 663-81. (Review article of the *Autobiography*, written shortly after JSM's death; vitriolic. 'Both Rousseau and Mill were fanatics in the cause of progress, and both, from mistaken philanthropy, did an infinity of harm' [664]. Hayward is enraged about JSM's early stand on birth control.)

863 [——] 'John Stuart Mill,' *The Times*, 10 May 1873, 5. (Obit.)

864 [——] 'Mill's *Autobiography*,' *The Times*, 4 Nov. 1873, 7; 10 Nov. 1873, 6. (Review)

865 [——] 'Parliamentary Reform and the Government,' *Fraser's Magazine*, 73 (1866), 683-704. (Contains an account of the Parliamentary duels between JSM and Robert Lowe over reform in 1866)

866 Hazard, Rowland G. *Two Letters on Causation and Freedom in Willing, Addressed to J.S. Mill*. Boston: Lee and Shepard, 1869

867 [Headicar, B.M.] 'A John Stuart Mill Collection,' *Bulletin of the British Library of Political and Economic Science*, 36 (1926), 29-30. (Signed B.M.H. Describes collection of letters, MSS, etc. acquired by the library.)

868 Hearnshaw, F.J.C. *Democracy at the Crossways*. London: Macmillan, 1918. (Passing references to JSM, *passim*)

869 Hedge, F.H. 'The Best Government,' *Christian Examiner*, 72, 5th ser, 10 (1862), 313-36. (Long review of *Considerations on Representative Government*)

870 Heertje, Arnold, and Evert Schoorl. 'Jean-Baptiste Say and the Education of John Stuart Mill,' *Mill News Letter*, VIII, 1 (1972), 10-15

871 Heinemann, Fritz. 'Theodor Gomperz und John Stuart Mill, mit unveröffentlichen Briefen,' *Philosophia*, 3 (1938), 516-23

872 Henley, Kenneth. 'Children and the Individualism of Mill and Nozick,' *Personalist*, 59 (1978), 415-19

873 Henrici, Julius. 'Einführung in die induktive Logik ans Bacons Beispiel (der Warme) nach Stuart Mills Regeln.' In *Festschrift zur Grosshertzogliche Gymnasium in Heidelburg*. Leipzig: Teubner, 1894, 15-27

874 Henshaw, S.E. 'John Stuart Mill and Mrs Taylor,' *Overland Monthly*, 13 (1874), 516-23

875 Hertel, Rudolf. *Die Erklärung der Krisen bei John Stuart Mill und Marx*. Cologne, 1928

876 Herzen, Aleksandr Ivanovich. 'Dzhon-Styuart Mill' i yevo kniga "On Liberty"' ['John Stuart Mill and His Book "On Liberty"'], *Kolokol* [*The Bell*], 15 Apr. 1859. Reprinted in *Polyarnaya zvezda* [*The North Star*], Bk V, 1859; and in Herzen's memoirs, translated into English by Constance Garnett as *My Past and Thoughts*. 6 vols. London: Chatto and Windus, 1924-27

877 Hessler, C.A. 'John Stuart Mill och Religions-Friheten.' In his *Civibus et rei publicae*. Uppsala: Amgrist and Wiksell, 1960, 176-85

878 Hibben, John Grier. 'The Heart and the Will in Belief - Romanes and Mill,' *North American Review*, 166 (1898), 121-3

879 [Hickson, W.E.] 'Life and Immortality,' *Westminster Review*, ns 56 (1871), 168-228. (Quotes *Logic*)

880 [——] 'Malthus,' *Westminster Review*, 52 (1849), 133-201. (Treats, *inter alia*, Malthus's *Essay* and JSM's *Principles of Political Economy*; 1st section, 'Ratios of Population and Capital,' 135-54, concerns JSM)

881 [——] '*Principles of Political Economy*,' *Westminster Review*, 49 (1848), 289-314. (Review)

882 Hill, Charles J. 'Theme and Image in *The Egoist*,' *University of Kansas City Review*, 20 (1954), 281-5. (Claims that Meredith, in *The Egoist*, dramatizes ideas from *Subjection of Women*)

883 Hill, Rev George. 'Theism and Christianity,' *Universalist Quarterly and General Review*, 34, ns 14 (1877), 299-308

884 Hill, Rev Thomas. 'Fundamental Laws of Reasoning,' *Christian Examiner*, 40, 4th ser, 5 (1846), 363-84. (Discussion of the *Logic*)

885 Himes, Norman E. 'John Stuart Mill's Attitude to Neo-Malthusianism,' *Economic History*, Suppl. to the *Economic Journal*, 4 (1929), 457-84

886 —— 'The Place of John Stuart Mill and of Robert Owen in the History of English Neo-Malthusianism,' *Quarterly Journal of Economics*, 42 (1928), 627-40

887 Himmelfarb, Gertrude. *On Liberty and Liberalism: The Case of John Stuart Mill*. New York: Knopf, 1974

888 —— 'The Other John Stuart Mill.' In her *Victorian Minds*. New York: Knopf, 1968, 113-54

889 —— 'The Politics of Democracy: The English Reform Act of 1867,' *Journal of British Studies*, 6 (1966), 97-138

890 —— 'Reply to Louis B. Zimmer on Mill's "Negative Argument,"' *Journal of British Studies*, 17 (1977), 138-40. (See also Zimmer)

891 ——, introd. *Essays on Politics and Culture. By John Stuart Mill*. New York: Doubleday, 1962. (Presents her view of the 'conservative' JSM)

892 ——, introd. *On Liberty. By John Stuart Mill*. Harmondsworth: Penguin, 1974

893 Hinsdale, Burke Aaron. *The History of a Great Mind: A Survey of the Education and Opinions of John Stuart Mill*. Cincinnati: Bosworth Chase and Hall, nd. Reprinted from *Christian Quarterly*, 6 (1874), 145-74. (Review of *Autobiography*)

894 Hippler, Fritz. *Staat und Gesellschaft bei Mill, Marx, Lagarde: Ein Beitrag zum soziologischen Denken der Gegenwart*. Berlin: Junker and Dünnhaupt, 1934

895 Hirsch, Gordon D. 'Organic Imagery and the Psychology of Mill's *On Liberty*,' *Mill News Letter*, X, 2 (1975), 3-13

896 Hirst, W.A. 'The Manuscript of Carlyle's "French Revolution,"'

Nineteenth Century, 123 (1938), 93-8. (Argues that Mrs Taylor
deliberately destroyed the manuscript)

897   Hobhouse, Leonard Trelawney. 'Gladstone and Mill.' In his
      Liberalism. New York: Holt, 1911. Frequently reprinted

898   —— 'John Stuart Mill,' *Nation*, 7 (1910), 246-7

899   —— 'Liberalism and Socialism.' In his *Democracy and Reaction*.
      London: T. Fisher Unwin, 1904. (223-5 quotes *Autobiography* on the
      socialistic ideal)

900   —— 'Mill and Mazzini: A Contrast,' *Marlburian*, 18 (1883), 81-4

901   Hodgson, Shadworth H. 'De Quincey as Political Economist; or, De
      Quincey and Mill on Supply and Demand.' In his *Outcast Essays and
      Verse Translations*. London: Longmans, 1881, 67-98

902   Høffding, Harald. 'John Stuart Mill.' In his *Geschichte der neuern
      Philosophie*. 2 vols. Leipzig: Reisland, 1896, II, 439-86. Trans.
      B.E. Myer as *A History of Modern Philosophy*. 2 vols. London:
      Macmillan, 1900, II, 394-433

903   Hoffman, Robert. 'A Note on Mill's Method of Residues,' *Journal of
      Philosophy*, 59 (1962), 495-7

904   Holbeach, Henry. See William Brighty Rands

905   Holland, Norman N. 'Prose and Minds: A Psychoanalytic Approach to
      Non-Fiction.' In *The Art of Victorian Prose*. Ed. George Levine and
      William Madden. New York: Oxford University Press, 1968, 314-37

906   Hollander, Jacob Harry. 'Letters of John Stuart Mill,' *Political
      Science Quarterly*, 26 (1911), 697-706. (Review of Elliot's edition of
      the letters)

907   ——, ed. *Two Letters on the Measure of Value. By John Stuart
      Mill*. A Reprint of Economic Tracts. Baltimore: Johns Hopkins, 1936.
      (Reprints of JSM's letters to the *Traveller*, 6 and 13 Dec. 1822,
      along with editorials from the *Traveller* and a short introduction by
      Hollander. These are JSM's first published writings [see
      Autobiography, Chap. 4].)

908   Hollander, Samuel. 'Attack the Best Defense,' *History of Political
      Economy*, 7 (1975), 115-22. (An appendix to Pedro Schwartz, 'Teaching
      the History of Economic Thought: Report of a Symposium at Bristol 1973,'
      ibid., 112-15. Hollander's outline discusses JSM's place in the
      curriculum.)

909 —— 'Ricardianism, J.S. Mill, and the Neo-classical Challenge.' In *James and John Stuart Mill: Papers of the Centenary Conference.* Ed. John M. Robson and Michael Laine. Toronto: University of Toronto Press, 1976, 67-85

910 —— 'The Role of Fixed Technical Coefficients in the Evolution of the Wages-Fund Controversy,' *Oxford Economic Papers*, 20 (1968), 320-41

911 —— 'The Role of the State in Vocational Training: The Classical Economists' View,' *Southern Economic Journal*, 34 (1968), 513-25. (Discusses, *inter alia*, JSM's views on education)

912 —— 'Technology and Aggregate Demand in J.S. Mill's Economic System,' *Canadian Journal of Economics and Political Science*, 30 (1964), 175-84

913 Hollis, Martin. 'J.S. Mill's Political Philosophy of Mind,' *Philosophy*, 47 (1972), 334-47

914 Holloway, Harry A. 'Mill and Green on the Modern Welfare State,' *Western Political Quarterly*, 13 (1960), 389-405

915 —— 'Mill's *Liberty*, 1859-1959,' *Ethics*, 71 (1961), 130-2. (A reply to A.W. Levi, 'The Value of Freedom,' which see)

916 Holman, Harriet R. 'J.S. Mill's Library: A Further Note,' *Mill News Letter*, VII, 1 (1971), 18

917 —— 'J.S. Mill's Library, Provence, 1906,' *Mill News Letter*, VI, 1 (1970), 20-1

918 —— 'What Did Mill Mean to Poe?' *Mill News Letter*, VI, 2 (1971), 20-1

919 Holmes, George F. 'Slavery and Freedom,' *Southern Quarterly Review*, 1 (1856), 62-95. (Reviews *Principles of Political Economy* along with G. Fitzhugh's *Sociology for the South* and several others)

920 Holt, Winifred. *A Beacon for the Blind, Being a Life of Henry Fawcett.* London: Constable, 1915

921 Holthoon, F.L. van. See van Holthoon

922 Holyoake, George Jacob. *Bygones Worth Remembering.* 2 vols. London: Unwin, 1905. (Two chapters on JSM, I, 259-80)

923 —— *John Stuart Mill as Some of the Working Classes Knew Him. 'An Answer to a Letter Circulated by "The Author of the Articles in the Times" on Mr Mill's Death.'* London: Trübner, 1873. (Refers to Abraham Hayward)

924 —— *A New Defence of the Ballot: In Consequence of Mr Mill's Objection to It*. London: Book Store, 282 Strand, 1868. (Pamphlet)

925 —— *Sixty Years of an Agitator's Life*. 2 vols. London: Unwin, 1892. (Several references to JSM)

926 Honderich, Ted. 'Mill on Liberty,' *Inquiry*, 10 (1967), 292-7

927 —— 'The Worth of Mill's *On Liberty*,' *Political Studies*, 22 (1974), 463-70

928 Hooker, Isabella Beecher. 'Correspondence with John Stuart Mill.' In her *Womanhood: Its Sanctities and Fidelities*. Boston: Lee and Shepard; New York: Lee, Shepard, and Dillingham, 1874, 28-37. (Her 9 Aug. 1869 letter to JSM, his reply 13 Sept. and short commentary)

929 Horne, Kathryn A. 'John Stuart Mill: Culture and the Man of Reason,' *Quest*, 24 (1973), 15-17

930 Horny, Friedrich. 'John Stuart Mills Voschläge sur Hebung der arbeitenden Klasse,' *Vierteljahrsschrift für Volkswirtschaft, Politik und Kulturgeschichte*, 88 (1885)

931 [Horton, Samuel Dana.] *The Parity of Moneys as Regarded by Adam Smith, Ricardo and Mill*. London: Macmillan, 1888. (Signed 'Amicus Curiae')

932 Hough, Graham. 'Books in General: Mill on Liberty,' *New Statesman*, ns 32 (1946), 361. (Deals with JSM's education)

933 Houghton, Walter Edward. *The Victorian Frame of Mind: 1830-1870*. New Haven: Published for Wellesley College by Yale University Press, 1957

934 Hourani, George F. *Ethical Value*. Ann Arbor: University of Michigan Press, 1956

935 Housman, Laurence. 'Fire-Lighters: A Dialogue on a Burning Topic,' *London Mercury*, 19 (1929), 263-77. (On the burning of Carlyle's manuscript of the *French Revolution*. Later dramatized.)

936 Howe, Mark De Wolfe. *Justice Oliver Wendell Holmes: The Shaping Years*. Cambridge: Belknap Press of Harvard University Press, 1957. (Discussion of the influence of JSM's works on Holmes with brief description of meetings with JSM in 1866)

937 ——, ed. *The Holmes-Laski Letters*. 2 vols. Boston: Harvard University Press, 1953

938 Hubbard, Elbert. *John Stuart Mill and Harriet Taylor*. Little

Journeys to Homes of Great Lovers, 18. East Aurora, NY: The
Roycrofters, 1906

939   Hübner, Walter. 'Wandepunkte des Freiheitsbegriffs: Eine kritische
Interpretation von J.S. Mills Abhandlung "On Liberty,"'
Neuphilologische Monatsschrift, 10 (1939), 1-24

940   Huffer, E.J.E. 'Bij het eeuwfeest van een logica-boek,' *Algemeen
Nederlands Tijdschrift voor Wijsbegeerte en Psychologie*, 37 (1943-44),
2-11

941   Hughes, William H. 'More on Mill's Socialism,' *Mill News Letter*,
VII, 2 (1972), 9-13

942   Hull, Alban. *The Political Ideas of John Stuart Mill*. Halifax:
Ashworth, 1935

943   Hunter, Laurence C. 'Mill and Cairnes on the Rate of Interest,' *Oxford
Economic Papers*, ns 11 (1959), 63-87

944   —— 'Mill and the Law of Markets: Comment,' *Quarterly Journal of
Economics*, 74 (1960), 158-62. (Comment on Balassa's paper, which see)

945   Hunter, W.A. 'John Stuart Mill: His Position as a Philosopher,'
Examiner, 17 May 1873, 517-18. Reprinted in *Popular Science
Monthly*, 3 (1973), 386-8; and in *John Stuart Mill: Notices of His
Life and Works*. Ed. H.R. Fox Bourne. London: Dallow, 1873, 91-6

946   —— 'John Stuart Mill: His Studies in Morals and Jurisprudence,'
Examiner, 17 May 1873, 512. Reprinted in *John Stuart Mill: Notices of
His Life and Works*. Ed. H.R. Fox Bourne. London: Dallow, 1873, 62-4

947   Hutchison, Terrence W. 'J.S. Mill and the Doctrine of "The Impossibility
of General Overproduction."' In his *A Review of Economic Doctrines,
1870-1929*. Oxford: Clarendon Press, 1953, 346-56

948   [Hutton, R.H.] 'Carlyle and Mill,' *Spectator*, 61 (1888), 1131-2.
(Review of Edward Jenks's *Thomas Carlyle and John Stuart Mill*,
which see)

949   [——] 'Considerations on Representative Government by John Stuart
Mill,' *Economist*, 19 (1861), 511-12, 540-1. (Review)

950   [——] 'Dissertations and Discussions ... by John Stuart Mill,'
Economist, 18 (1860), 227-8. (Review)

951   [——] 'The "Dublin Review" on Free Will,' *Spectator*, 47 (1874),
600-1. (Regrets that JSM did not live to see and reply to W.G.
Ward's criticisms, which see)

952 [——] 'John Stuart Mill on the Civil War,' *Spectator*, 35 (1862), 126-7

953 [——] 'John Stuart Mill on Free Will and Necessity,' *Spectator*, 38 (1865), 642-4. (3rd part of review of *Sir William Hamilton's Philosophy*)

954 [——] 'John Stuart Mill on Sir William Hamilton,' *Spectator*, 38 (1865), 584-5, 614-15. (Review. See also Hutton's 'John Stuart Mill on Free Will and Necessity,' above.)

955 [——] 'The Latest Phase of the Utilitarian Controversy,' *British Quarterly Review*, 50 (1869), 68-91

956 [——] 'Mill and Whewell on the Logic of Induction,' *Prospective Review*, 6 (1850), 77-111

957 [——] 'Mill on Liberty,' *National Review*, 8 (1859), 393-425

958 [——] 'Mr Courtney on Mill,' *Spectator*, 52 (1879), 309-10. (Review of W.L. Courtney, *The Metaphysics of John Stuart Mill*, which see)

959 [——] 'Mr John Stuart Mill as a Politician,' *Spectator*, 38 (1865), 325-6. (Favourable comment on JSM's nomination)

960 [——] 'Mr John Stuart Mill's Autobiography,' *Spectator*, 46 (1873), 1337-9. Reprinted in *Every Saturday*, 3rd ser, 4 (1873), 583-5; and in his *Criticisms on Contemporary Thought and Thinkers*. 2 vols. London: Macmillan, 1894, I, 171-82. (Review. See also Hutton's 'Mr J.S. Mill's Philosophy as Tested in His Life,' below.)

961 [——] 'Mr J.S. Mill,' *Spectator*, 41 (1868), 1529-30. (Comment on JSM's parliamentary career and his defeat in the 1868 election)

962 [——] 'Mr J.S. Mill on Utilitarianism,' *Spectator*, 36 (1863), 1868-9. (Review)

963 [——] 'Mr J.S. Mill's Philosophy as Tested in His Life,' *Spectator*, 46 (1873), 1370-2. Reprinted in his *Criticisms on Contemporary Thought and Thinkers*. 2 vols. London: Macmillan, 1894, I, 183-92. (Continues review of *Autobiography*)

964 [——] 'Mr J.S. Mill's Religious Confession,' *Spectator*, 47 (1874), 1325-7. Reprinted in *Eclectic Magazine*, 84 (1874), 108; *Littell's Living Age*, 123 (1874), 508; and in his *Aspects of Religious and Scientific Thought*. Ed. Elizabeth M. Roscoe. London: Macmillan, 1899, 302-12. (Refers to *Three Essays on Religion*)

965 [——] 'Mr Mansell's Reply to Mill,' *Spectator*, 39 (1866), 1255-7. (Review of *The Philosophy of the Conditioned*, which see)

966 [——] 'Mr Mill's Case for Women,' *Spectator*, 40 (1867), 574-5. (Comment on JSM's amendment to the Reform Bill proposing to enfranchise women)

967 [——] 'Mr Mill's Essays on Religion,' *Spectator*, 47 (1874), 1366-7. Reprinted in his *Criticisms on Contemporary Thought and Thinkers*. 2 vols. London: Macmillan, 1894, I, 193-203. (Review)

968 Hyde, Francis E. 'Utility and Radicalism, 1825-1837: A Note on the Mill-Roebuck Friendship,' *Economic History Review*, 16 (1946), 38-44

969 Hyde, William J. 'Theoretic and Practical Unconventionality in *Jude the Obscure*,' *Nineteenth-Century Fiction*, 20 (1965), 155-64. (Hardy's use of JSM, especially *On Liberty*, in *Jude the Obscure*)

970 Ierson, Henry. 'The Religious Views of John Stuart Mill,' *Unitarian Review*, 1 (1874), 101-12

971 Iggers, Georg G. 'Further Remarks about Early Uses of the Term "Social Science,"' *Journal of the History of Ideas*, 20 (1959), 433-6

972 'Index.' See George Vasey

973 Irons, William Josiah. *An Examination of Mr Mill's Three Essays on Religion*. London: Hardwicke, 1875

974 Irvine, William. 'Shaw, the Fabians, and the Utilitarians,' *Journal of the History of Ideas*, 8 (1947), 218-31

975 Jackson, Reginald. *An Examination of the Deductive Logic of J.S. Mill*. Oxford: Oxford University Press, 1941. (Originally, and at greater length, dissertation, St Andrews)

976 —— 'Mill's Joint Method,' *Mind*, ns 46 (1937), 417-36; ns 47 (1938), 1-17

977 —— 'Mill's Treatment of Geometry - A Reply to Jevons,' *Mind*, 50 (1941), 22-42. Reprinted in *Mill: A Collection of Critical Essays*. Ed. J.B. Schneewind. Garden City, NY: Doubleday, 1968, 84-110. (Refers to W.S. Jevons, 'John Stuart Mill's Philosophy Tested,' which see)

978 Jacobs, Herbert. *Rechtsphilosophie und politische Philosophie bei John Stuart Mill*. Bonn: Bouvier, 1965

979 Jacobs, L. 'The Talmudic Hermeneutical Rule of "binyan 'abh" and J.S. Mill's "Method of Agreement,"' *Journal of Jewish Studies*, 4 (1953), 59-64

980 Jacobs, Willis D. 'Carlyle and Mill,' *CEA Critic*, 21 (1959), 5

981 James, Henry, Sr. 'Some Personal Recollections of Carlyle,' *Atlantic Monthly*, 47 (1881), 593-609. (Brief reference to JSM)

982 James, William. 'Bushnell's Women's Suffrage and Mill's Subjection of Women,' *North American Review*, 109 (1869), 556-65

983 —— *Principles of Psychology*. 2 vols. New York: Holt, 1890

984 Janes, George M. 'J.S. Mill's Education,' *Quarterly Journal of the University of North Dakota*, 21 (1931), 107-18

985 —— 'Mill's Unwritten Work,' *Quarterly Journal of the University of North Dakota*, 22 (1931), 46-50. (Refers to the 'Ethology or a science of character' mentioned in *Logic*)

986 Janet, Paul. 'De la valeur du syllogisme,' *Revue Philosophique*, 12 (1881), 105-18

987 —— 'Mill et Hamilton: le problème de l'existence des corps,' *Revue des Deux Mondes*, 83 (1869), 944-72

988 Jenks, Edward. 'A Reply to J.S. Mill,' *Economica*, 5 (1925), 7-9. (On JSM's debating speech on lawyers, published *ibid.*, 1-6)

989 —— *Thomas Carlyle and John Stuart Mill*. Orpington: George Allen, 1888

990 Jennings, Richard. *Natural Elements of Political Economy*. London: Longman, Brown, Green, and Longmans, 1855. (Brief quotations from *Principles of Political Economy* and reference to problems of classification found in *Logic*)

991 [Jennings, William.] 'Tendencies of Modern Logic,' *Dublin Review*, 36 (1854), 436-45. (This review article of *Logic* quarrels with JSM's philosophy because his system does not require a 'First, Great, Efficient Cause, or God ...' [438])

992 Jevons, William Stanley. *Elementary Lessons in Logic*. London: Macmillan, 1870. New ed., London and New York, 1876. ('An easy introduction to some of the most important points of Mr Mill's treatise on Logic')

993 —— 'John Stuart Mill's Philosophy Tested,' *Contemporary Review*,

31 (1877), 166-82; (1878), 256-75; 32 (1878), 88-99. Reprinted in *Popular Science Monthly*, 2 (1878), 279-88, 317-28; 3 (1878), 85-92, and (abridged) as Pt II of his *Pure Logic*. London and New York: Macmillan, 1890. (See also Strachey, Jackson, and Robertson)

994 —— 'J.S. Mill's Philosophy Tested by Professor Jevons,' *Mind*, 3 (1878), 284-7. (Reply to G.C. Robertson, which see)

995 —— *Principles of Economics*. London: Macmillan, 1905

996 —— *Principles of Science*. London: Macmillan, 1874

997 —— *The Theory of Political Economy*. London and New York: Macmillan, 1871. (Treats Economy as 'a Calculus of Pleasure and Pain.' Critical of JSM especially of Wage Fund Theory.)

998 Joad, C.E.M. *Liberty Today*. London: Watts, 1934

999 —— 'Objective Utilitarianism: John Stuart Mill.' In his *Guide to the Philosophy of Morals and Politics*. London: Gollancz, 1938

1000 Johnson, Alvin S. 'Protection and Capital,' *Political Science Quarterly*, 23 (1908), 220-41

1001 [Johnson, Andrew.] 'Mr Mill, *On Representative Government*,' *Westminster Review*, ns 20, (1861), 91-114. (Review)

1002 Jones, Ernest. *Sigmund Freud: Life and Works*. 2 vols. London: Hogarth Press, 1953. (Refers to Freud's translation of some of JSM's essays and of the 'Enfranchisement of Women' [I, 61-2]. Quotes Freud on the woman question, on JSM's style and on *Autobiography*, which he saw as 'so prudish or so ethereal that one could never gather from it that human beings consist of men and women' [I, 191-2].)

1003 Jones, Hardy. 'Mill's Argument for the Principle of Utility,' *Philosophy and Phenomenological Research*, 38 (1978), 338-54

1004 Jones, Harry W. 'Freedom and Opportunity as Competing Social Values: Mill's Liberty and Ours.' In *Liberty*. Ed. Carl J. Friedrich. *Nomos* (Yearbook of the American Society for Political and Legal Philosophy), IV. New York: Atherton; London: Prentice-Hall, 1962, 227-42

1005 Jones, Iva G. 'Trollope, Carlyle, and Mill on the Negro: An Episode in the History of Ideas,' *Journal of Negro History*, 52 (1967), 185-99

1006 [Jordan, Wilhelm.] 'Nachrichten über das Schuljahr, 1869-70.' In *Programm des Königlichen. Gymnasiums in Stuttgart*. Stuttgart: Kleeblat, 1870

1007 —— 'Die Zweideutigkeit der Copula bei Stuart Mill.' In *Programm des Königlichen. Gymnasiums in Stuttgart*. Stuttgart: Kleeblatt, 1870

1008 Joy, Glenn C. *'On Liberty*: A Note on Mill's Use of Logic,' *Mill News Letter*, VIII, 2 (1973), 7-10

1009 Juleus, Nels. 'The Rhetoric of Opposites: Mill and Carlyle,' *Pennsylvania Speech Annual*, 1966

1010 Kamm, Josephine. *John Stuart Mill in Love*. London: Gordon and Cremonesi, 1977

1011 Kannwischer, Arthur. 'Psychology and Ethics in John Stuart Mill's Logic,' *University of Pittsburgh Abstracts of Dissertations*, 49 (1953), 25-30

1012 Kantzer, E. Marcel. *La Religion de J. Stuart Mill*. Caen: Valin, 1906

1013 Karinsky, Mikhail Ivanovich. *Klassifikatsiya vyvodov [A Classification of Inferences]*. St Petersburg, 1880

1014 —— *Raznoglasiye v shkole novovo empirizma po voprosu ob istinakh samoochevidnakh [The Discord in the Modern Empiricist School on the Question of Self-Evident Truths]*. Moscow, 1914. Originally published serially from 1901 to 1914 in *Zhurnal ministerstva narodnovo prosveshcheniya [Journal of the Ministry of Public Education]*

1015 Karns, C. Franklin. 'Causal Analysis and Rhetoric: A Survey of the Major Philosophical Conceptions of Cause Prior to John Stuart Mill,' *Speech Monographs*, 32 (1965), 36-48

1016 Kaspary, J. *Natural Laws; or, The Infallible Criterion*. London: Brook, 1876

1017 Kaufmann, Felix. *Methodology of the Social Sciences*. New York: Humanities Press, 1958

1018 Kaufmann, Walter. 'The Origin of Justice,' *Review of Metaphysics*, 23 (1969), 209-39. (Contains a full discussion of Chap. 5 of *Utilitarianism*. See also Rohatyn.)

1019 Kaulla, Rudolf. 'John Stuart Mill.' In his *Die geschichtliche Entwicklung der modernen Werttheorien*. Tübingen: Laupp, 1906, 184-9

1020 Kell, S.C. *The Ballot. Shall the Vote Be Free or Watched? The Voter's Own or Some One's Else?* Bradford: Hanson, 186?. (Pamphlet)

1021 Keller, Paul. *Dogmengeschichte des wohlstandspolitischen Interventionismus*. Winterthur: Keller, 1955

1022 Kemp, Murray C. 'The Mill-Bastable Infant Industry Dogma,' *Journal of Political Economy*, 68 (1960), 65-7. (Discusses JSM's and Bastable's ideas concerning the protection of new industries)

1023 Kendall, Willmoore. 'The "Open Society" and Its Fallacies,' *American Political Science Review*, 54 (1960), 972-9. Reprinted in *Limits of Liberty: Studies of Mill's 'On Liberty.'* Ed. Peter Radcliffe. Belmont: Wadsworth, 1966, 27-42; and in *On Liberty*. Ed. David Spitz. New York: Norton, 1975, 154-67. (Suggests that an 'open society' as proposed by JSM rests on a misconception of human behaviour in society and might promote intolerance and fail to serve the interests of truth)

1024 ——, and George W. Carey. 'The "Roster Device": J.S. Mill and Contemporary Elitism,' *Western Political Quarterly*, 21 (1968), 20-39. (Examines *Representative Government*, discussing principles in it by which politicians may be ranked)

1025 Kennedy, William F. *Humanist versus Economist: The Economic Thought of Samuel Taylor Coleridge*. University of California Publications in Economics, Vol. 17. Berkeley: University of California Press, 1958. (Especially 48-54)

1026 Kent, C.B. Roylance. *The English Radicals: An Historical Sketch*. London: Longmans, Green, 1899

1027 Kent, Christopher. 'Helen Taylor's "Experimental Life" on the Stage, 1856-58,' *Nineteenth-Century Theatre Research*, 5 (1977), 45-54

1028 Kern, Paul B. 'Universal Suffrage with Democracy: Thomas Hare and John Stuart Mill,' *Review of Politics*, 34 (1972), 306-22

1029 Ketchan, Carl H. 'Dorothy Wordsworth's Unpublished Journals and the Dates of Mill's Visits with Wordsworth, 1831,' *Mill News Letter*, XI, 1 (1976), 7-10. (See also Anna J. Mill, 'John Stuart Mill's Visit to Wordsworth')

1030 Keynes, John Maynard. *The End of Laissez-faire*. London: Hogarth Press, 1926. (Only passing reference to JSM)

1031 —— *A Treatise on Probability*. London: Macmillan, 1921, 265-77. Reprinted New York: Harper and Row, 1962

1032 Keynes, John Neville. *The Scope and Method of Political Economy*. London and New York: Macmillan, 1891

1033 —— *Studies and Exercises in Logic*. London: Macmillan, 1870. 4th ed. rev. and enlarged with index provided, 1906. Reprinted 1928

1034 Killick, A.H. *The Student's Handbook Synoptical and Explanatory of Mr J.S. Mill's System of Logic*. London: Longmans, Green, Reader, and Dyer, 1870

1035 Kinlock, Tom Fleming. *Six English Economists*. London: Gee, 1928, 38-52. (Smith, Malthus, Ricardo, JSM, Jevons, Marshall)

1036 Kinzer, Bruce L. 'J.S. Mill and the Secret Ballot,' *Historical Reflections*, 5 (1978), 19-39

1037 —— 'A Note on William Longman, J.S. Mill, and the 1865 Westminster Election,' *Mill News Letter*, XIII, 2 (1978), 12-13

1038 —— 'Tocqueville and His English Interpreters, J.S. Mill and Henry Reeve,' *Mill News Letter*, XIII, 1 (1978), 2-10

1039 Kirkman, Thomas Pennington. *On a So-called Theory of Causation, vide 'System of Logic,' by J.S. Mill, Book III, Chapter v*. Liverpool, 1862. (Read before the Liverpool Literary and Philosophical Society, 24 Feb. 1862)

1040 Kirkus, William. See Emma Sara Williamson

1041 Kitchel, Anna Theresa. *George Lewes and George Eliot*. New York: Day, 1933. (Discusses Lewes' friendship with JSM, 27-40)

1042 Knickerbocker, Frances Wentworth. *Free Minds - John Morley and His Friends*. Cambridge: Harvard University Press, 1943

1043 Knight, Frank H. 'Some Notes on Political Freedom and on a Famous Essay.' In *Liberty*. Ed. Carl J. Friedrich. *Nomos* (Yearbook of the American Society for Political and Legal Philosophy), IV. New York: Atherton; London: Prentice-Hall, 1962, 110-18

1044 Knight, William. 'Unpublished Letters of J.S. Mill to Professor John Nichol,' *Fortnightly Review*, 61 (1897), 660-78

1045 Knights, Ben. 'The Reconstruction of Opinion: John Stuart Mill.' In his *The Idea of the Clerisy in the Nineteenth Century*. Cambridge and New York: Cambridge University Press, 1978, 140-77

1046 Knox, B.A. 'The British Government and Governor Eyre,' *Historical Journal*, 19 (1976), 877-900. (Discusses, in passing, JSM's role in the House)

1047 Kohn, Benno. *Untersuchungen über das Causalproblem auf dem Boden einer Kritik der einschlägigen Lehren J.S. Mills*. Vienna: Gerold, 1881

1048   Kohn, Hans. 'England: J.S. Mill.' In his *Prophets and Peoples: Studies in Nineteenth Century Nationalism*. New York: Macmillan, 1946, 12-42

1049   Koizumi, Takashi. 'Analysis of Nishi Amane's Conceptions of Legislation, "Tenpo (natural laws)" and "Ten (the Heaven)" - in Comparison with Ogyu Sorai and J.S. Mill,' *East and West: Studies of History of Ideas*, 1 (1969), 1-12

1050   Kornberg, Jacques. 'Feminism and the Liberal Dialectic: John Stuart Mill on Women's Rights,' *Historical Papers 1974* (Canadian Historical Association), 37-63. (Paper presented at the 1974 Annual Meeting at Toronto)

1051   —— 'John Stuart Mill: A View from the Bismarckian Reich,' *Mill News Letter*, XII, 1 (1977), 3-18

1052   Kort, Fred. 'Issue of a Science of Politics in Utilitarian Thought,' *American Political Science Review*, 46 (1952), 1140-52

1053   Kotarbiński, Tadeusz. 'L'Utilitarisme dans la morale de Mill et de Spencer.' In *Mysliodziataniu*, Vol. I of *Wybór pism*. Warsaw, 1957. Published separately in Polish, Cracow, 1915

1054   Krenis, Lee. 'Authority and Rebellion in Victorian Autobiography,' *Journal of British Studies*, 18 (1978), 107-30

1055   Kretzmann, Norman. 'Desire as Proof to Desirability,' *Philosophical Quarterly*, 8 (1958), 246-58. Reprinted in *Mill: Utilitarianism*. Ed. S. Gorovitz. Indianapolis and New York, 1971, 231-41; and in *Mill's 'Utilitarianism.'* Ed. J.M. Smith and E. Sosa. Belmont: Wadsworth, 1969, 110-1

1056   Kriegel, Friedrich. *J. St. Mills Lehre vom Wert, Preis und der Bodenvente*. Berlin: Puttkammer and Mühlbrecht, 1897

1057   Krieger, Leonard. 'Stages in the History of Political Freedom.' In *Liberty*. Ed. Carl J. Friedrich. *Nomos* (Yearbook of the American Society for Political and Legal Philosophy), IV. New York: Atherton: London: Prentice-Hall, 1962, 1-28

1058   Krook, Dorothea. 'Rationalist Humanism: J.S. Mill's *Three Essays on Religion*.' In her *Three Traditions of Moral Thought*. London: Cambridge University Press, 1959, 181-201

1059   Krumme, E. *Du libéralisme classique à l'individualisme social; la place de John Stuart Mill dans l'histoire des doctrines économiques*. Paris: Giard and Brière, 1913. Reprinted from *Revue Internationale de Sociologie*, 21 (1913), 492-535, 601-28

1060   Kubitz, Oskar Alfred. *Development of John Stuart Mill's 'System of Logic.'* Illinois Studies in the Social Sciences, 18:1-2. Urbana: University of Illinois, 1932. (Published dissertation)

1061   Lachs, John. 'Two Views of Happiness in Mill,' *Mill News Letter*, IX, 1 (1973), 16-20

1062   Ladenson, Robert F. 'Mill's Conception of Individuality,' *Social Theory and Practice*, 4 (1977), 167-82

1063   Laine, Michael. 'On the Character of Catiline' by J.S. Mill,' *Mill News Letter*, VII, 2 (1972), 2-9. (Previously unpublished debating speech [1826]; edited with introduction)

1064   ——, and John M. Robson, eds. *James and John Stuart Mill: Papers of the Centenary Conference.* See Robson

1065   Lakeman, Enid. 'Centennial - Mill: Representative Government,' *Contemporary Review*, 199 (1961), 204-7

1066   La Nauze, J.A. 'A Letter of J.S. Mill to Charles Kingsley,' *Australian Quarterly*, 18 (1946), 30-4

1067   Lancaster, Lane W. 'John Stuart Mill.' In his *Masters of Political Thought*, Vol. III. Ed. W.T. Jones. Boston: Houghton Mifflin, 1959, 101-59

1068   Land, Berel, and Gary Stahl. 'Mill's "Howlers" and the Logic of Naturalism,' *Philosophy and Phenomenological Research*, 29 (1969), 562-74

1069   Langbaum Robert. *The Poetry of Experience.* London: Chatto and Windus; New York: Random House, 1957. Reprinted New York: Norton, 1963. (Short comment on *Autobiography* and quotes, briefly, JSM's remarks on Browning's *Pauline*)

1070   Lange, Friedrich A. *J.S. Mills Ansichten über die sociale Frage und die angebliche Umwälzung der Socialwissenschaft durch Carey.* Dinsburg: Bleuler, Hausheer, 1866

1071   Larkin, Henry. 'Carlyle and Mrs Carlyle: A Ten Years' Reminiscence,' *British Quarterly Review*, 74 (1881), 28-84. (Describes, 73, Carlyle's reaction to *On Liberty*. No other reference to JSM.)

1072   Laski, Harold J., introd. *Autobiography. By John Stuart Mill.* London: Oxford University Press, 1924. (Also contains six debating speeches. General introduction by Laski mentions the 1922 Sotheby sale of JSM's papers. See Britton and Robson, 'Mill's Debating Speeches.')

1073   Laugel, Auguste. 'Les Confessions de John Stuart Mill,' *Revue des Deux Mondes*, 108 (1873), 906-37. Reprinted in his *Grandes Figures historiques*. Bibliothèque contemporaine. Paris: Lévy, 1875, 175-255. (Review)

1074   —— *Etude sur Stuart Mill*. Paris, 1885

1075   Laughlin, J. Laurence, ed. *Principles of Political Economy, Abridged, with Notes and a Sketch of the History of Political Economy*. New York: Appleton, 1884

1076   ——, ed. *A Synopsis of the First Three Books of J.S. Mill's Principles of Political Economy, as Revised by J.L. Laughlin. With an Appendix Containing Recent Examination Papers on Political Economy*. Cambridge, Mass.: Wheeler, 1888

1077   Lauret, Henri. *Philosophie de Stuart Mill*. Neufchateau: Kienne; Paris: Alcan, 1885. (Published dissertation)

1078   Laurie, H. 'Methods of Inductive Inquiry,' *Mind*, 18 (1893), 319-38

1079   Laurie, Simon Somerville. 'New Utilitarianism - Mr Mill.' In his *Notes Expository and Critical on Certain British Theories of Morals*. Edinburgh: Edmonston and Douglas, 1868, 98-127

1080   Laveleye, Emile L.V. de. *Lettres inédites de Stuart Mill*. Paris: Germer-Baillière, 1885. Reprinted from *Revue de Belgique*, 15 Jan. 1885, 5-25; republished in his *Essais et études*, 3e sér, 1897

1081   —— 'Les Tendances nouvelles de l'économie politique en Angleterre,' *Revue des Deux Mondes*, 44 (1881), 623-46

1082   Lavine, George. 'Determinism and Responsibility in the Works of George Eliot,' *PMLA*, 77 (1962), 268-79. (Draws on Bk VI of JSM's *Logic*)

1083   Lavrov, Pyotr Lavrovich. 'Ocherk teorii lichnosti' ['An Outline of the Theory of Individualty'], *Otechestvennyye zapiski* [*Annals of the Fatherland*], no 11 (1859), 207-42; no 12, 555-610

1084   —— 'Zadachi Pozitivizma i ikh resheniye' ['The Problems of Positivism and Their Solution'], *Sovremennoye obozreniye* [*Contemporary Review*], no 5 (1868), 117-54. (Review of *Auguste Comte and Positivism*)

1085   Leader, R.E., ed. *Autobiography and Letters of John Arthur Roebuck*. London: Arnold, 1897

1086   Leavis, F.R. 'Mill, Beatrice Webb, and the "English School,"'

Scrutiny, 16 (1949), 104-26. Reprinted as the Introduction to his edition, *Mill on Bentham and Coleridge*. London: Chatto and Windus, 1950

1087　Lecky, William Edward Hartpole. *History of European Morals from Augustus to Charlemagne*. 2 vols. London: Longmans, Green, 1869; 3rd ed. rev., 1877. Reprinted 1920. 1st chap. reprinted as *Survey of English Ethics*. Ed. W.A. Hurst. London: Longmans, 1903

1088　Lees, Frederic Richard. *Law and Liberty: With Especial Relation to the Temperance Question, the Prohibition of the Liquor Traffic, and the Objections of J.S. Mill*. Leeds: Lees, 1860

1089　—— *Relations of Liberty to the Temperance Question*. London: Clowes, 1860

1090　Legros, G.V. *La Vie de J.H. Fabre, naturaliste*. Paris: Delagrove, 1913, 59-64, 70-1. Reprinted 1924. Trans. Bernard Miall as *Fabre, Poet of Science*. London and Leipsic: T. Fisher Unwin, 1913, 84-90, 97-9

1091　Lennard, Reginald V. 'Mill - and Others - on Liberty,' *Hibbert Journal*, 57 (1959), 342-8. (Berlin, Bosanquet, Hobhouse, Hegel, McTaggart, Toynbee, Goethe)

1092　Le Rossignol, James Edward. 'Mill on Machinery,' *American Economic Review*, 30 (1940), 115-16

1093　Leroux, Emmanuel, and André Leroy. *La Philosophie anglaise classique*. Paris: Conlin, 1951

1094　Leroux, R. 'Guillaume de Humboldt et J. Stuart Mill,' *Etudes Germaniques*, 6 (1951), 262-74; 7 (1952), 81-7

1095　Lesevich, Vladimir Viktorovich. 'Dzhon Styuart Mill'' ['John Stuart Mill'] . In *Sobraniye sochineni V.V. Lesevicha* [*Collected Works of V.V. Lesevich*]. Moscow, 1915, II, 41-80

1096　Leslie, Thomas Edward Cliffe. 'John Stuart Mill.' In his *Essays in Political and Moral Philosophy*. London: Longmans, 1879, 243-7. Reprinted from *Academy*, 8 (1875)

1097　—— 'On the Philosophical Method of Political Economy.' In his *Essays in Political and Moral Philosophy*. London: Longmans, 1879, 216-42

1098　—— 'Utilitarianism and the Common Good,' *Macmillan's Magazine*, 8 (1863), 152-60

1099   Letwin, Shirley Robin. 'Morality & Law,' *Encounter*, 43 (1974),
       35-43. (Includes, *inter alia*, a critique of the 'suppressed
       assumptions' in JSM's individualism)

1100   —— *The Pursuit of Certainty: David Hume, Jeremy Bentham, John
       Stuart Mill, Beatrice Webb*. London: Cambridge University Press, 1965

1101   Levi, Albert William. 'The Idea of Socrates: The Philosophic Hero in the
       Nineteenth Century,' *Journal of the History of Ideas*, 17 (1956), 89-108

1102   —— 'The "Mental Crisis" of John Stuart Mill,' *Psychoanalytic Review*,
       32 (1945), 86-101

1103   —— *A Study in the Social Philosophy of John Stuart Mill*. Chicago:
       University of Chicago, 1940. (Published typescript reproduction
       of 1938 dissertation)

1104   —— 'The Value of Freedom: Mill's *Liberty*, 1859-1959,' *Ethics*,
       70 (1959), 37-46. Reprinted in *Limits of Liberty: Studies of Mill's
       'On Liberty.'* Ed. Peter Radcliffe. Belmont: Wadsworth, 1966, 6-18;
       and in *On Liberty*. Ed. David Spitz. New York: Norton, 1975, 191-203.
       (See also Holloway)

1105   —— 'The Writing of Mill's *Autobiography*,' *Ethics*, 61 (1951),
       284-96

1106   Levin, Harvey J. 'Standards of Welfare in Economic Thought,' *Quarterly
       Journal of Economics*, 70 (1956), 117-38. (Discussion of social values
       by economists. Several references to JSM)

1107   Levin, Thomas Woodhouse. *Notes on Inductive Logic, Book I, Being an
       Introduction to Mill's System of Logic*. Cambridge: Deighton, Bell,
       1885

1108   Levine, George. 'Determinism and Responsibility in the Works of George
       Eliot,' *PMLA*, 77 (1962), 268-79. (Presents Eliot's determinism as
       being very close to JSM's)

1109   Levy, J.H. 'John Stuart Mill: His Work in Philosophy,' *Examiner*, 17
       May 1873, 511-12. Reprinted in *Popular Science Monthly*, 3 (1873),
       379-81; and in *John Stuart Mill: Notices of His Life and Works*. Ed.
       H.R. Fox Bourne. London: Dallow, 1873, 55-61

1110   —— 'Mill's Propositions and Inferences of Mere Existence,' *Mind*,
       10 (1885), 417-20

1111   —— *The Outcome of Individualism*. London: Personal Rights
       Association, P.S. King and Son [1890]. 3rd ed. revised and enlarged
       [1892]. (See also Roland K. Wilson *et al.*)

1112 Lévy-Bruhl, L. 'A. Comte et Stuart Mill, d'après leur correspondance,' *Revue Philosophique*, 23 (1898), 627-44

1113 ——, ed. *Lettres inédites de J.S. Mill à Auguste Comte*. Paris: Alcan, 1899

1114 Lewels, Maximillian. *John Stuart Mill: Die Stellung eines Empiristen zur Religion*. Münster: Theissing'schen Buchhandlung, 1903. (Inaugural dissertation, Münster)

1115 Lewes, George Henry. 'Auguste Comte,' *Fortnightly Review*, 3 (1866), 385-410. (Review of JSM on Comte and of Littré's *Auguste Comte et Stuart Mill*, which see)

1116 —— *The Biographical History of Philosophy, from Its Origin in Greece down to the Present Day*. Library Edition, enlarged and revised. New York: Appleton, 1875. 1st ed., 1845-46. (*Logic*, n. xxi, 587)

1117 —— 'Comte and Mill,' *Fortnightly Review*, 6 (1866), 385-406

1118 [——] 'Public Affairs,' *Fortnightly Review*, 1 (1865), 623-30. (On JSM's election to Parliament, 624)

1119 Lewis, C.I. 'A Pragmatic Conception of the *a priori*,' *Journal of Philosophy*, 20 (1923), 169-77. Reprinted in *Readings in Philosophical Analysis*. Ed. Herbert Feigl and Wilfrid Sellars. New York: Appleton-Century-Crofts, 1949, 286-94. (Refers to JSM's challenging the *a priori* character of arithmetic; says JSM was mistaken)

1120 Lewis, Gilbert F., ed. *Letters of Rt Hon. Sir G.C. Lewis*. London: Longmans, Green, 1870. (JSM's letter to Duff-Gordon, 153-4)

1121 Lewisohn, David H. 'Mill and Comte on the Methods of Social Science,' *Journal of the History of Ideas*, 33 (1972), 315-24

1122 Lewisohn, Ludwig. 'The Democrat's Handbook,' *Nation*, 117 (1923), 19. (*On Liberty*)

1123 Liard, Louis. *Les Logiciens anglais contemporains*. Paris: Baillière, 1878

1124 'A Liberal.' *A Review of J.S. Mill's Essay 'On Liberty,' and an Investigation of His Claim to Be Considered the Leading Philosopher and Thinker of the Age. Also a Refutation of His Two Statements: 1. That Christian morality teaches us to be selfish. 2. That the working classes of this country are mostly habitual liars*. London: Watson and Gardner, 1867

1125 Lichtman, Richard. 'Surface and Substance of Mill's Defence of Freedom,' *Social Research*, 30 (1963), 469-94

1126 Lilla, V. *Critica della dottrina etica-giuridica di J.S. Mill*. Naples: Gargiulo, 1889

1127 Lincoln, Heman. 'Autobiography of J.S. Mill,' *Baptist Quarterly*, 8 (1874), 233-50

1128 Lindley, Dwight N. 'John Stuart Mill: The Second Greatest Influence,' *Victorian Newsletter*, 11 (1957), 25-6. (Review of I.W. Mueller's *John Stuart Mill and French Thought*, which see)

1129 Lindquist, Emory. *John Stuart Mill's Essay On Liberty: A Centennial Review*. University of Wichita Bulletin, University Studies, 42. Wichita, Kan.: University of Wichita, 1959

1130 Lindsay, Alexander Dunlop. 'T.H. Green and the Idealists.' In *The Social and Political Ideas of Some Representative Thinkers of the Victorian Age*. Ed. F.J.C. Hearnshaw. London: Harrap, 1922, 150-64

1131 ——, introd. *Utilitarianism, Liberty and Representative Government. By John Stuart Mill*. Everyman's Library. London: Dent; New York: Dutton, 1910. Frequently reprinted

1132 Link, Robert G. *English Theories of Economic Fluctuations, 1815-48*. New York: Columbia University Press, 1959

1133 Linnenberg, Clem Charles, Jr. 'The Laissez-faire State in Relation to National Economy,' *Southwestern Social Science Quarterly*, 24 (1943), 101-17, 230-48

1134 Lippincott, Benjamin Evans. *The Victorian Critics of Democracy*. Minneapolis: University of Minnesota Press, 1938

1135 Littré, Maximilien Paul Emile. *Auguste Comte et Stuart Mill*. Printed with G. Wyrouboff's *Stuart Mill et la philosophie positive*. Paris: Germer-Baillière, 1866. (Littré's book reprinted from *Revue des Deux Mondes*, 64 [1866], 829-66)

1136 Lively, Jack. *The Social and Political Thought of Alexis de Tocqueville*. Oxford: Clarendon Press, 1962

1137 Lloyd, Walter. 'J.S. Mill's Letters to Auguste Comte,' *Westminster Review*, 153 (1900), 421-6

1138 Löchen, Arne. *Om. J. Stuart Mill's Logik: En kritisk Studie*. Christiana and Copenhagen: Huseby, 1885

1139 Lockwood, Michael. 'On Predicating Proper Names,' *Philosophical Review*, 84 (1975), 471-98

1140 Long, W. 'The Legend of Mill's "Proofs,"' *Southern Journal of Philosophy*, 5 (1967), 36-47

1141 Longe, Francis Davey. *A Critical Examination of George's 'Progress and Poverty' and Mill's Theory of Wages*. London: Simpkin and Marshall, 1883

1142 —— *A Refutation of the Wage-fund Theory of Modern Political Economy as Enunciated by Mr Mill, MP and Mr Fawcett, MP*. London: Longmans, Green, 1866. Ed. with Introduction and Notes by Jacob H. Hollander. Baltimore: Johns Hopkins, 1904, 1934

1143 Lorimer, James. *The Institutes of Law*. Edinburgh: Clark, 1872; 2nd ed. rev. Edinburgh: Blackwood, 1880. (1st ed. contains few references to JSM)

1144 [——] 'Mr Mill on Representative Government,' *North British Review*, 35 (1861), 534-63

1145 Loring, L. 'Moore's Criticism of Mill,' *Ratio*, 9 (1967), 84-90

1146 Louch, A.R. 'Sins and Crimes,' *Philosophy*, 43 (1968), 38-50. (Uses JSM to discuss the legal and moral aspects of sexual problems)

1147 Lubac, Jean. *J.S. Mill et le socialisme*. Paris: Giardet and Brière, 1902

1148 [Lucas, Edward.] 'Mill on Liberty,' *Dublin Review*, ns 13 (1869), 62-75. ('In this paper we are only engaged in showing Mr Mill's inconsistencies')

1149 —— 'Mr Mill on Liberty of the Press.' In *Essays on Religion and Literature*. Ed. Henry Edward Manning. 3rd ser. London: King, 1874, 142-73

1150 Ludwig, Mario. *Die Sozialethik des John Stuart Mill*. Zurich: Polygraphischer Verlag A.G., 1963

1151 Lyall, Alfred. 'Mill's "System of Logic."' In his *Agonistes; or, Philosophical Strictures, Suggested by Opinions, Chiefly, of Contemporary Writers*. London: Rivington, 1856, 307-85

1152 Lynd, Helen Merrell. *England in the Eighteen-Eighties: Toward a Social Basis for Freedom*. Oxford: Oxford University Press, 1945. (References to JSM, particularly to *On Liberty*)

1153 Lyons, David. 'Mill's Theory of Morality,' *Nous*, 10 (1976), 101-20

1154 Lytton, Victor Alexander George. *The Life of Edward Bulwer, First Lord Lytton*. 2 vols. London: Macmillan, 1913. (A few references to JSM and letters from him to Bulwer-Lytton)

1155 Mabbott, J.D. 'Interpretations of Mill's Utilitarianism,' *Philosophical Quarterly*, 6 (1956), 115-20. Reprinted in *Mill: A Collection of Critical Essays*. Ed. J.B. Schneewind. Garden City, NY: Doubleday, 1968, 190-8; and in *Mill's 'Utilitarianism.'* Ed. James M. Smith and E. Sosa. Belmont: Wadsworth, 1969, 126-32. (See also Mandelbaum, Smart, Urmson)

1156 —— 'Punishment,' *Mind*, 48 (1939), 152-67. Reprinted in *Mill: Utilitarianism*. Ed. S. Gorovitz. Indianapolis and New York: Bobbs-Merrill, 1971, 88-98

1157 McCabe, Joseph. *Life and Letters of George Jacob Holyoake*. 2 vols. London: Watts, 1908. (Several references to JSM)

1158 MacCaig, Donald. *A Reply to John Stuart Mill, on the Subjection of Women*. Philadelphia: Lippincott, 1870

1159 Maccall, William. 'Mill's Refutation of Hamilton,' *National Reformer*, 6 (1865), 477-8, 493-4, 509-10, 525-6, 541-2. Reprinted in his *The Newest Materialism: Sundry Papers on the Books of Mill, Comte, Bain, Spencer, Atkinson, and Feuerbach*. London: Farrah, 1873

1160 McCallum, R.B. 'The Individual in the Mass: Mill on Liberty and the Franchise.' In *1859: Entering an Age of Crisis*. Ed. Philip Appleman, *et al*. Bloomington: Indiana University Press, 1959, 147-61

1161 —— 'John Stuart Mill, 1806-1873.' In *Great Democrats*. Ed. A. Barratt Brown. London: Nicholson and Watson, 1934

1162 McCarthy, Justin. 'The English Positivists,' *Galaxy*, 7 (1869), 373-82. (Brief reference to JSM as the greatest Positivist, but one who rejects Comte's 'fantastic religion.' Deals with the influence of those who 'go much farther, and accept Comte's religious teaching as a law of life,' on the political scene; especially, Richard Congreve, Harrison, Beasley, and Morley.)

1163 —— 'The Liberal Triumvirate,' *Galaxy*, 7 (1869), 33-44. (Some comments about JSM's term in Parliament)

1164 McCloskey, H.J. 'A Critique of the Ideals of Liberty,' *Mind*, 74 (1965), 483-508

1165 —— 'An Examination of Restricted Utilitarianism,' *Philosophical Review*, 66 (1957), 466-85. Reprinted in *Mill: Utilitarianism*. Ed. S. Gorovitz. Indianapolis and New York: Bobbs-Merrill, 1971, 204-16

1166 —— *John Stuart Mill: A Critical Study*. London: Macmillan, 1971

1167 —— 'Liberalism,' *Philosophy*, 49 (1974), 13-32. (Distinguishes between a liberalism based upon respect for persons as ends in themselves [Kant] and one based on utilitarian ethical theories concerned with pleasure and reduction of pain. Also distinguishes positive and negative liberty - a distinction which he claims JSM does not make.)

1168 —— 'Liberty of Expression: Its Grounds and Limits,' *Inquiry*, 13 (1970), 219-37. (See also D.H. Monro)

1169 —— 'Mill's Liberalism,' *Philosophical Quarterly*, 13 (1963), 143-56. (Reply by A. Ryan, 'Mr McCloskey on Mill's Liberalism,' which see; reply by McCloskey, 'Mill's Liberalism: A Rejoinder to Mr Ryan,' *ibid.*, 16 [1966], 64-8. 'Mill's Liberalism' reprinted in *Essays in the History of Political Thought*. Ed. Isaac Kramnick. Englewood Cliffs, NJ: Prentice-Hall, 1969, 371-84. Reconsiders JSM as the theorist of a limited liberal state, contending that he envisioned a more active, intervening one)

1170 —— 'The Problem of Liberalism,' *Review of Metaphysics*, 19 (1965), 248-75

1171 Maccoby, Simon. *English Radicalism*. 6 vols. London: Allen and Unwin, 1935-36, Vols III, IV, *passim*

1172 Maccoll, Norman. 'Mr Mill's Autobiography,' *Athenaeum*, 25 Oct. 1873, 521-2

1173 McCosh, James. *An Examination of Mr J.S. Mill's Philosophy, Being a Defence of Fundamental Truth*. London: Macmillan, 1866. 2nd ed., 1877, includes as an appendix the second paper from McCosh's *Philosophical Papers*. (See also Guy)

1174 —— 'Mill's Reply to His Critics,' *British and Foreign Evangelical Review*, 17 (1868), 332-62. Reprinted in *American Presbyterian and Theological Review*, ns 6 (1868), 350-91

1175 —— *Philosophical Papers. I: Examination of Sir William Hamilton's Logic. II: Reply to Mr Mill's Third Edition* [of *Sir William Hamilton's Philosophy*]. *III: Present State of Moral Philosophy in Britain*. London: Macmillan, 1868. (See McCosh, *An Examination*)

1176   —— Supplement and Questions to *Outlines of Moral Philosophy by Dugald Stewart, with a Supplement by James McCosh*. London, 1865

1177   McCready, H.W. 'The Defence of Individualism,' *Queen's Quarterly*, 52 (1945), 71-6

1178   Maccunn, John. 'The Utilitarian Optimism of J.S. Mill.' In his *Six Radical Thinkers: Bentham, J.S. Mill, Cobden, Carlyle, Mazzini, T.H. Green*. New York: Russell and Russell, 1964, 39-87

1179   McDonnell, James. '"A Season of Awakening": An Analysis of Chapter Five of Mill's "Autobiography,"' *Modern Language Review*, 72 (1977), 773-83

1180   —— 'Success and Failure: A Rhetorical Study of the First Two Chapters of Mill's *Autobiography*,' *University of Toronto Quarterly*, 45 (1976), 109-22

1181   MacFie, R.A. *Speech Delivered at a Meeting of the Liverpool Reform League, Including Extracts from Archibishop Whately and Mr J.S. Mill on Plurality of Votes*. London: Longmans, Green, 1867

1182   McGee, John Edwin. *A Crusade for Humanity: The History of Organized Positivism in England*. London: Watts, 1931

1183   Machann, Clinton. 'J.S. Mill's Mental Crisis: An Adlerian Interpretation,' *Journal of Individual Psychology*, 29 (1973), 76-87

1184   MacIver, Robert M., Bertrand Russell, and Lyman Bryson. 'John Stuart Mill: *On Liberty*,' *Invitation to Learning: Discussion of Great Books and Significant Ideas*, 1 (1951-52), 356-63. (Edited transcript of a radio discussion heard over CBS, 28 Oct. 1951)

1185   McJarrow, John S. 'John Stuart Mill's "On Liberty,"' *Holborn Review*, 73 (1931), 510-15

1186   Mack, Mary Peter. 'The Fabians and Utilitarianism,' *Journal of the History of Ideas*, 16 (1955), 76-88

1187   McKechnie, W.S. *The State and the Individual*. Glasgow: MacLehose, 1896

1188   McKeon, Richard P. 'The Ethics of International Influence,' *Ethics*, 70 (1960), 187-203. (JSM provides a 'monument' marking the transition from 'accountability' to 'responsibility.' Cites *On Liberty*, *Utilitarianism*)

1189   —— *Freedom and History: The Semantics of Philosophical Controversies and Ideological Conflicts*. New York: Noonday, 1962.

(Short discussion of JSM's attitude to democracy. Cites *Autobiography, On Liberty*.)

1190 Mackie, J.L. 'Mill's Method of Induction.' In *The Encyclopaedia of Philosophy*. Ed. Paul Edwards. 8 vols. New York: Macmillan and Free Press; London: Collier-Macmillan, 1967, V, 324-32

1191 McKingsley, Erskine. 'The Problem of "Underdevelopment" in the English Classical School,' *Quarterly Journal of Economics*, 69 (1955), 235-52

1192 McLaren, Charles B.B. 'Hamilton's Natural Dualism, Mill's Psychological Theory and Berkeley's Spiritual Realism.' In *University Essays in Metaphysics, Moral Philosophy, and English Composition*. Edinburgh: privately printed, 1870

1193 MacLeod, Henry Dunning. *The History of Economics*. New York: Putnam's; London: Bliss, Sands, 1896, 10-19, 120-35, and *passim*. (Critical of JSM's methods and theory of value)

1194 McMahan, Anna Benneson. 'An Interesting Memorial of Two Great Authors,' *Dial*, 31 (1901), 229-30. (Description of JSM's annotated copy of Browning's *Pauline*)

1195 McMahon, Patrick. 'Tillage - Waste Lands - Fixity of Tenure,' *Dublin Review*, 25 (1848), 332-4. (JSM and the Irish question)

1196 MacMinn, Ney, J.R. Hainds, and James MacNab McCrimmon. *Bibliography of the Published Writings of John Stuart Mill*. Northwestern University Studies in the Humanities, no 12. Evanston, Ill.: Northwestern University Press, 1945. Reprinted Lincoln: University of Nebraska Press; New York: AMS Press, 1970

1197 McNaughton, Robert. 'A Metrical Conception of Happiness,' *Philosophy and Phenomenological Research*, 14 (1953), 171-83

1198 McNeilly, F.C. 'Pre-Moral Appraisals,' *Philosophical Quarterly*, 8 (1958), 97-111. (Bearing on the naturalistic fallacy - JSM and Nowell-Smith)

1199 McNiece, Gerald. 'Shelley, John Stuart Mill, and the Secret Ballot,' *Mill News Letter*, VIII, 2 (1973), 2-7

1200 Macpherson, C.B. 'The Economic Penetration of Political Theory: Some Hypotheses,' *Journal of the History of Ideas*, 39 (1978), 101-18. (JSM figures prominently in the discussion)

1201 —— *The Life and Times of Liberal Democracy*. Oxford: Oxford University Press, 1977. (JSM figures prominently in Chap. 3)

1202 McPherson, Thomas. *Social Philosophy*. London: Van Nostrand Reinhold, 1970, 41-5, 103-6, 125-9. (Introduction and summary of JSM's ideas on the subject as found in *Utilitarianism*, *Liberty*, and *Representative Government*. Some criticism.)

1203 MacRae, Donald Gunn. *Ideology and Society*. London: Heinemann, 1961

1204 McRae, Robert F. 'Phenomenalism and J.S. Mill's Theory of Causation,' *Philosophy and Phenomenological Research*, 9 (1948), 237-50

1205 Magid, Henry M. 'Mill and the Problem of Freedom of Thought,' *Social Research*, 21 (1954), 43-61

1206 ——, ed. *On the Logic of the Moral Sciences*. Indianapolis: Bobbs-Merrill, 1967. (Bk VI of the *Logic* with introduction by Magid)

1207 Magnino, Bianca. *Storia del positivismo*. Rome: Mazara, 1956

1208 Mahaffy, J.P. 'Anticipation of Mill's Theory of Syllogism by Locke,' *Mind*, 1 (1876), 287-8

1209 Makato, Tehtearo. *Japanese Notions of English Political Economy*. Glasgow: Scottish Single Tax League, 1899. (Two brief sketches of JSM)

1210 Mallock, W.H. *Socialism*. New York: National Civic Federation, 1907. (Cites *Principles of Political Economy* in a discussion of labour theory of value, 49-52)

1211 Man, Glenn K.S. 'The Imaginative Dimension in the Writings of John Stuart Mill,' *Mill News Letter*, VI, 1 (1970), 21-3

1212 —— 'John Stuart Mill and Harriet Taylor,' *Antigonish Review*, 14 (1973), 43-50

1213 Mandelbaum, Maurice. 'On Interpreting Mill's Utilitarianism,' *Journal of the History of Philosophy*, 6 (1968), 35-46. Reprinted in *Mill: Utilitarianism*. Ed. S. Gorovitz. Indianapolis and New York: Bobbs-Merrill, 1971, 380-90

1214 —— 'Two Moot Issues in Mill's Utilitarianism.' In *Mill: A Collection of Critical Essays*. Ed. J.B. Schneewind. Garden City, NY: Doubleday, 1968, 206-33. (See also Mabbot, Smart, Urmson)

1215 Mansel, Henry Longueville. 'Appendix D,' *Prolegomena Logica*. Oxford: Graham, 1851. (Deals with JSM's logic of the moral sciences)

1216 —— 'The Limits of Demonstrative Science Considered: A Letter to the

Rev. Wm. Whewell. 12 April 1853.' In his *Letters, Lectures and Reviews*. Ed. H.W. Chandler. London: Murray, 1873, 79-106

1217 —— 'On Utility as a Ground for Moral Obligation.' In his *Letters, Lectures and Reviews*. Ed. H.W. Chandler. London: Murray, 1873, 363-78

1218 —— *The Philosophy of the Conditioned: Comprising Some Remarks on Sir W. Hamilton's Philosophy, and on Mr J.S. Mill's Examination of That Philosophy*. London and New York: Alexander Strahan, 1866. Reprinted, with additions, from the *Contemporary Review*, 1 (1866), 31-49, 185-219

1219 —— 'Supplementary Remarks on Mr Mill's Criticism of Sir William Hamilton,' *Contemporary Review*, 6 (1867), 18-31

1220 Marchand, Leslie. 'The Symington Collection,' *Journal of Rutgers University Library*, 12 (1948), 1-15. (The Symington Collection includes some JSM materials, particularly correspondence of Mrs Gaskell concerning her reference to and quotation of HTM in her biography of Charlotte Brontë)

1221 Marcuse, Herbert. See Robert Paul Wolff

1222 Margolis, Joseph. 'Mill's Utilitarianism Again,' *Australasian Journal of Philosophy*, 45 (1967), 179-84. Reprinted in *Mill: Utilitarianism*. Ed. S. Gorovitz. Indianapolis and New York: Bobbs-Merrill, 1971, 376-9. (Concise argument that, whatever the status of JSM's 'proof' of the principle of utility, he in fact held that desirability is neither a necessary nor a sufficient condition of goodness)

1223 Maritain, Jacques. *Eléments de philosophie*. 2 vols. Paris: Téqui, 1923-25. Vol. II: *Petite Logique*. Trans. Imelda Choquette as *Introduction to Logic*. London: Sheed and Ward, 1937

1224 Marshall, Alfred. 'On Mr Mill's Theory of Value.' In *Memorials of Alfred Marshall*. Ed. A.C. Pigou. London: Macmillan, 1925, 119-33. Republished from *Fortnightly Review*, 112 (1876), 591-602

1225 —— *Principles of Economics*. 2 vols. London: Macmillan, 1890. Reprinted, ed. E.W. Guillebaud. 2 vols. London: Macmillan for The Royal Economic Society, 1961

1226 Marshall, J. 'The Proof of Utility and Equity in Mill's Utilitarianism,' *Canadian Journal of Philosophy*, 3 (1973), 13-26

1227 Marston, Mansfield. *The Life of John Stuart Mill, Politician and Philosopher, Critic and Metaphysician, with a Record of His Claims upon the Regards of the People as a Philanthropist and Friend.* London: Farrah, 1873

1228 Martin, David E. 'Land Reform.' In *Pressure from Without in Early Victorian England.* Ed. Patricia Hollis. London: Arnold, 1974, 131-58

1229 —— 'The Rehabilitation of the Peasant Proprietor in Nineteenth-Century Economic Thought: A Comment,' *History of Political Economy,* 8 (1976), 297-302

1230 Martin, Ged. 'A Letter from John Stuart Mill to John Plummer,' *Mill News Letter,* IX, 2 (1974), 7-9

1231 Martin, Peter E. 'Carlyle and Mill: The "Anti-Self Consciousness" Theory,' *Thoth,* 6 (1965), 20-34

1232 Martin, Rex. 'A Defence of Mill's Qualitative Hedonism,' *Philosophy,* 47 (1972), 140-51. (See also West)

1233 Martinazzoli, A. *La teorica dell'individualismo secondo Stuart Mill.* Milan: Hoepli, 1905

1234 Martineau, James. 'John Stuart Mill,' *National Review,* 9 (1859), 474-508. Reprinted in his *Essays Philosophical and Theological.* 2 vols. New York: Holt, 1879, I, 63-120

1235 —— 'John Stuart Mill's Philosophy.' In his *Essays, Reviews, and Addresses.* 4 vols. London: Longmans, 1890-91, III, 489-536

1236 Marwick, James D. 'John Stuart Mill and Liberty,' *Scottish Bankers' Magazine,* 40 (1948), 41-3

1237 Marx, Karl. 'Auflösung der Ricardoschen Schule: s. 7, John Stuart Mill.' In *Theorien über den Mehrwert.* Ed. K. Kautsly. 3 vols. Stuttgart: Dietz, 1905. Reprinted Berlin: Dietz, 1956-62, III, 191-234; also I, 5, 145; II, 40, 112, 498. Trans. R. Simpson in *Theory of Surplus Value.* London: Lawrence and Wishart, 1969

1238 Mason, Michael York. '*Middlemarch* and Science: Problems of Life and Mind,' *Review of English Studies,* 22 (1972), 151-69. (Suggests the relations of the scientific ideas of the characters to views of scientific method held by JSM and Whewell)

1239 Mason, Will E. 'The Stereotypes of Classical Transfer Theory,' *Journal of Political Economy,* 64 (1956), 492-506. (Some references to JSM's monetary theories)

1240 Masson, David. *Recent British Philosophy: A Review with Criticism;*

Including Some Comments on Mr Mill's Answer to Sir William Hamilton.
London and Cambridge: Macmillan, 1865. 3rd ed. enlarged, 1877

1241 Matthews, Charles. 'Argument through Metaphor in John Stuart Mill's
On Liberty,' Language and Style, 4 (1971), 221-89

1242 Mattison, J.T. 'Was Mill a Democrat?' *History Today,* 8 (1958), 431

1243 Mattu, Antonio, ed. *The Prose of J.S. Mill: 'Utilitarianism' and
'Principles of Political Economy.'* Caliari: Sarda Fossarto, 1968.
(Selections with introduction and bibliography)

1244 Maurice, F.D. 'Mr Maurice on the Satanic School,' *Spectator,* 38
(1865), 668. (Supports JSM in controversy over religious views
expressed in *Sir William Hamilton's Philosophy*)

1245 Maurice, Frederick, ed. *The Life of Frederick Denison Maurice.*
2 vols. London: Macmillan, 1884. (Several references to JSM)

1246 Mavrinac, Albert A. 'Freedom, Authority, Conscience, and Development:
Mill, Acton, and Some Contemporary Catholic Thinkers.' In *Liberty.*
Ed. Carl J. Friedrich. *Nomos* (Yearbook of the American Society for
Political and Legal Philosophy), IV. New York: Atherton: London:
Prentice-Hall, 1962, 57-88

1247 Maxey, Chester Collins. *Political Philosophies.* 1938; rev. New York:
Macmillan, 1948, 474-89. (Conventional treatment)

1248 Mayer, David Y. 'John Stuart Mill and Classical Democracy,'
Politics, 3 (1968), 55-64

1249 Mayer, J.P. *Alexis de Tocqueville: A Biographical Study in Political
Science.* New York: Harper, 1960. Rev. ed. of his *Prophet of the Mass
Age,* below. (Several references to JSM)

1250 —— 'Alexis de Tocqueville and John Stuart Mill,' *Listener,* 43
(1950), 471-2

1251 —— 'Letters from Mill to Tocqueville,' *Times Literary Supplement,*
1 Sept. 1950, 556; 8 Sept. 1950, 572; 15 Sept. 1950, 588. Reprinted
in Tocqueville's *Oeuvres.* Ed. J.P. Mayer. Vol. VI. Paris:
Gallimard, 1954, 289-352

1252 —— *Prophet of the Mass Age: A Study of Alexis de Tocqueville.*
London: Dent, 1939. Revised as *Alexis de Tocqueville,* above

1253 Mayo, A.D. 'John Stuart Mill on Women,' *Monthly Review and Religious
Magazine,* 43 (1870), 226-33

1254   Mazlish, Bruce. *James and John Stuart Mill*. New York: Basic Books, 1975

1255   —— 'James Mill and the Utilitarians,' *Daedalus*, 97 (1968), 1036-61

1256   Mead, G.H. *Movements of Thought in the Nineteenth Century*. Ed. Merritt H. Moore. Chicago: University of Chicago Press, 1936

1257   Mears, John W. 'Theistic Reactions in Modern Speculation,' *Presbyterian Quarterly and Princeton Review*, ns 4 (1875), 329-47. (Review of *Three Essays on Religion* and works by other authors)

1258   Medawer, P.B. 'Is the Scientific Paper Fraudulent?' *Saturday Review of Literature*, 1 Aug. 1964, 42-3. (Discusses JSM's inductive logic vis-à-vis method in scientific papers)

1259   Meek, Ronald L. 'The Decline of Ricardian Economics in England,' *Economica*, ns 17 (1950), 43-62

1260   Megill, Allan D. 'J.S. Mill's Religion of Humanity and the Second Justification for the Writing of *On Liberty*,' *Journal of Politics*, 34 (1972), 612-29

1261   Melden, A.I. 'Two Comments on Utilitarianism,' *Philosophical Review*, 60 (1951), 508-24. Reprinted in *Mill: Utilitarianism*. Ed. S. Gorovitz. Indianapolis and New York: Bobbs-Merrill, 1971, 117-28

1262   Mellor, Enoch. *An Examination of Some of the Points in Mr Mill's Critique of the Philosophy of Sir William Hamilton*. Liverpool: Marples [printer], [1866]

1263   Melvin, James R. 'Mill's Law of International Value,' *Southern Economic Journal*, 36 (1969), 107-16

1264   Menger, Carl. 'John Stuart Mill.' In *Kleinere Schriften zur Methode und Geschichte der Volkswirtschaftlehre*. Vol. III of *The Collected Works of Carl Menger*. London: London School of Economics, 1935, 283-91. Reprinted from *National-Zeitung*, 22 May 1906

1265   Mercer, Thomas W. *John Stuart Mill and Co-operation*. Manchester: National Co-operative Publishing Society, 1923. Reprinted from *Co-operative News*, 5 May 1923

1266   Metz, Rudolph. *A Hundred Years of British Philosophy*. London: Allen and Unwin, 1938

1267   Mévil, André. 'Un Ami de John Stuart Mill,' *Journal des Débats* (Edition Hébdomadaire, 13 Apr. 1934), 41 (1934), 597. (Obit. of Pasteur Rey)

1268 Michaëlis, Carl Theodor. *Stuart Mills Zahlbegriff*. Berlin: Gaertner, 1888

1269 Michel, Henry. *De Stuart Milli individualissmo*. Paris: Hachette, 1895. (Published dissertation in Latin)

1270 Mikhailov, Mikhail Larionovich. 'Dzh. St. Mill' o emansipatsii zhenshchin' ['J.S. Mill on the Emancipation of Women'], *Sovremennik* [*The Contemporary*], no 11 (1860)

1271 Mikhailovsky, Nikolay Konstantinovich. *Sochineniya N.K. Mikhailovskovo* [*Works of N.K. Mikhailovsky*]. St Petersburg: Vol'f, 1896, II, 551-66. (A review of JSM's *Principles of Political Economy* and *Autobiography* originally published in *Otechestvennyye zapiski* [*Annals of the Fatherland*], Jan. 1874)

1272 Mill, Anna J. 'Another of J.S. Mill's Reticences,' *Mill News Letter*, IV, 1 (1968), 15-16

1273 —— *Carlyle and Mill: Two Scottish University Rectors*. Occasional Papers of the Carlyle Society, Edinburgh, no 1. Edinburgh: Carlyle Society, 1966

1274 —— 'The Education of John - Some Further Evidence,' *Mill News Letter*, XI, 1 (1976), 10-14

1275 —— 'The First Ornamental Rector at St Andrews University,' *Scottish Historical Review*, 43 (1964), 131-44

1276 —— 'John Stuart Mill and the Picturesque,' *Victorian Studies*, 14 (1970), 151-63. (JSM's Lake District journal)

1277 —— 'John Stuart Mill's Visit to Wordsworth,' *Modern Language Review*, 44 (1949), 341-50

1278 —— 'J.S.M., Conservationist,' *Mill News Letter*, X, 1 (1975), 2-3

1279 —— 'Some Notes on Mill's Early Friendship with Henry Cole,' *Mill News Letter*, IV, 2 (1969), 2-8. (See also Mineka, 'A Note on "Some Notes"')

1280 ——, ed. *John Mill's Boyhood Visit to France: A Journal and Notebook*. Toronto: University of Toronto Press, 1960. (Valuable Introduction and Notes on editorial practice and MSS)

1281 Miller, Kenneth E. 'John Stuart Mill's Theory of International Relations,' *Journal of the History of Ideas*, 22 (1961), 493-514

1282 Millet, J. *An Millius veram mathematicorum axiomatum originem invenirit*. Paris: Didier, 1867. (Published dissertation)

1283 Millet, René. 'Le Parti radical en Angleterre: un manifeste de M. Stuart Mill,' *Revue des Deux Mondes*, 97 (1872), 932-59

1284 Millett, Kate. 'The Debate over Women: Ruskin versus Mill,' *Victorian Studies*, 14 (1970), 63-82. Adapted from her *Sexual Politics*. New York: Doubleday, 1970

1285 Millhauser, Milton. 'The Two Boyhoods,' *Hartford Studies in Literature*, 4 (1972), 36-51. (Ruskin and Mill)

1286 Mindle, Grant. 'Man's Insatiable Appetites: The Political Philosophy of Adam Smith,' *Claremont Journal of Public Affairs*, 1 (1972), 27-40. (Discusses JSM's rejection of a social contract and his 'collision of truths' theory in referring to *On Liberty*)

1287 Mineka, Francis E. 'The *Autobiography* and the Lady,' *University of Toronto Quarterly*, 32 (1963), 301-6

1288 —— *The Dissidence of Dissent: The Monthly Repository, 1806-38.* Chapel Hill: University of North Carolina Press, 1944. (JSM's contributions to the *Monthly Repository*, and his friendship with William Johnson Fox, its editor)

1289 —— 'John Stuart Mill and Neo-Malthusianism, 1873,' *Mill News Letter*, VIII, 1 (1972), 3-10

1290 —— 'John Stuart Mill: Letters on the French Revolution of 1830,' *Victorian Studies*, 1 (1957), 137-54

1291 —— 'A Note on "Some Notes,"' *Mill News Letter*, V, 1 (1969), 10-11. (See Anna J. Mill, 'Some Notes on Mill's Early Friendship with Henry Cole')

1292 ——, and William E.S. Thomas, eds. 'New Letters of J.S. Mill to Sir William Molesworth,' *Mill News Letter*, VI, 1 (1970), 1-13

1293 Minto, William. 'John Stuart Mill: His Place as a Critic,' *Examiner*, 17 May 1873, 510-11. Reprinted in *Popular Science Monthly*, 3 (1873), 377-9; and in *John Stuart Mill: Notices of His Life and Works*. Ed. H.R. Fox Bourne. London: Dallow, 1873, 49-54

1294 —— 'J.S. Mill,' *Encyclopaedia Britannica*, 9th ed., 1883, XVI, 307-14. With John Malcolm Mitchell, *ibid.*, 11th ed., 1911, XVIII, 454-9

1295 Mitchell, Basil. *Law, Morality and Religion in a Secular Society.* London: Oxford University Press, 1967

1296   Mitchell, Dorothy. 'Mill's Theory of Value,' *Theoria*, 36 (1970), 100-15

1297   Mitchell, Ellen M. 'John Stuart Mill. (Extracts from Hildebrand's "Aus und über England"),' *Western*, ns 3 (1877), 555-61

1298   Miyoshi, Masao. 'Mill and *Pauline*: The Myth and Some Facts,' *Victorian Studies*, 9 (1965), 154-63. (The argument, based on the fullest account yet given of JSM's marginal comments in the Victoria and Albert copy of *Pauline*, is that Browning did not change the course of his poetic career as a result of JSM's criticism, and that the criticism was not wholly unpleasant to Browning)

1299   Moffat, Robert Scott. *The Economy of Consumption*. London: Kegan Paul, 1878. Includes *The Principles of a Time Policy*, below. (Strongly critical of JSM's views on capital and on property. See especially, I, ii and III, iii.)

1300   —— *The Principles of a Time Policy: Being an Exposition of a Method of Settling Disputes between Employers and Labourers: With a Preface and Appendix Containing a Re-criticism of the Theories of Ricardo and J.S. Mill on Rent, Value and Cost of Production*. London: Kegan Paul, 1878. Reprints II, iv of *The Economy of Consumption*, above, plus Preface and Appendix

1301   Monahan, John. 'J.S. Mill on the Liberty of the Mentally Ill: A Historical Note,' *American Journal of Psychiatry*, 134 (1977), 1428-9

1302   Monck, W.H.S. 'Mill's Doctrine of Natural Kinds,' *Mind*, 12 (1887), 637-9. (Comment on Towry's article, which see. See also F. and C.L. Franklin.)

1303   Monro, D.H. 'Liberty of Expression: Its Grounds and Limits,' *Inquiry*, 13 (1970), 238-53. (See also H.J. McCloskey)

1304   Montague, Francis C. *The Limits of Individual Liberty*. London: Rivington, 1885

1305   Montague, William Pepperal. *The Missing Link in the Case for Utilitarianism*. Studies in the History of Ideas, Department of Philosophy, Columbia University, Vol. 2. New York: Columbia University Press, 1925

1306   Moore, Barrington, Jr. See Robert Paul Wolff

1307   Moore, David Cresap. *The Politics of Deference: A Study of the Mid-Nineteenth Century English Political System*. Hassocks and New York: Harvester, 1976

1308 Moore, George Edward. *Principia Ethica*. Cambridge: Cambridge University Press, 1903. (Chap. 3, 'Hedonism.' See also Smith and Sosa.)

1309 Morgan, Peter F. 'Francis Place's Copy of the Westminster Review,' *Notes and Queries*, 211 (1966), 330-2. (Some attributions to JSM, and Place's observations on his articles)

1310 —— 'The Poetic in the Early Life of John Stuart Mill,' *Wordsworth Circle*, 9 (1978), 121-8

1311 Morlan, George. *America's Heritage from John Stuart Mill*. New York: Columbia University Press, 1936. (Primarily concerned with what America should learn rather than what America has learned from JSM)

1312 Morley, John. 'Contemporary Opinions,' *Fortnightly Review*, 7 (1867), 388. Reprinted *ibid.*, ns 173 (1953), 256-7. (On the *Inaugural Address*)

1313 —— 'The Death of Mr Mill,' *Fortnightly Review*, ns 13 (1873), 669-76. Reprinted in *Littell's Living Age*, 118 (1873), 159-62; and in his *Critical Miscellanies*. 2nd ser. London: Chapman and Hall, 1877

1314 —— 'John Stuart Mill: An Anniversary,' *Times Literary Supplement*, 18 May 1906, 173-5. Reprinted in his *Critical Miscellanies*. 4th ser. London and New York: Macmillan, 1908

1315 —— 'Mr Lecky's First Chapter,' *Fortnightly Review*, ns 5 (1869), 519-38. (Refers to W.E.H. Lecky, *History of European Morals*, which see)

1316 —— 'Mr Mill's Autobiography,' *Fortnightly Review*, ns 15 (1874), 1-20. Reprinted in his *Critical Miscellanies*. 2nd ser. London: Chapman and Hall, 1877

1317 —— 'Mr Mill's Doctrine of Liberty,' *Fortnightly Review*, ns 14 (1873), 234-56. Republished in revised and abbreviated form in *On Compromise*. Vol. III of *The Works of Lord Morley*. London: Macmillan, 1921, 151-66

1318 —— 'Mr Mill's Three Essays on Religion,' *Fortnightly Review*, ns 16 (1874), 634-51; ns 17 (1875), 103-31. Reprinted in his *Critical Miscellanies*. 2nd ser. London: Chapman and Hall, 1877

1319 —— 'A Political Prelude,' *Fortnightly Review*, ns 14 (1868), 103-14. (Deals with JSM's writing on Ireland)

1320 —— *Recollections*. 2 vols. London: Macmillan, 1917, I, especially 52-67. (Account of his friendship with JSM)

1321　—— 'Valedictory,' *Fortnightly Review*, ns 32 (1882), 512-21. (Contains tribute to JSM)

1322　——, and Mary Augusta Ward. 'Anthony Trollope,' *Macmillan's Magazine*, 49 (1883), 47-56. (Review of Trollope's *Autobiography*; recounts briefly a visit by Trollope to JSM)

1323　Morris, Clarence. 'On Liberation and Liberty: Marcuse's and Mill's Essays Compared,' *University of Pennsylvania Law Review*, 118 (1970), 735-45. Reprinted in his *The Justification of the Law*. Philadelphia: University of Pennsylvania Press, [1971], 65-76

1324　Morris, George Sylvester. 'John Stuart Mill.' In his *British Thought and Thinkers: Introductory Studies, Critical, Biographical, and Philosophical*. Chicago: Griggs, 1880, 302-36

1325　Morris, John N. *Versions of the Self: Studies in English Autobiography from Milton to John Stuart Mill*. New York: Basic Books, 1966

1326　Moser, S. 'A Comment on Mill's Argument for Utilitarianism,' *Inquiry*, 6 (1963), 308-18

1327　[Mozley, Anne.] 'Mr Mill *On the Subjection of Women*,' *Blackwood's Magazine*, 106 (1869), 309-21

1328　[Mozley, John Rickards.] 'Mr John Stuart Mill and His School,' *Quarterly Review*, 133 (1872), 77-118

1329　Mueller, Iris. *John Stuart Mill and French Thought*. Urbana: University of Illinois Press, 1956. (See also Lindley)

1330　Mukherjee, Sobhanlal. *The Political Philosophy of John Stuart Mill*. Calcutta: Gupta, 1965

1331　Munro, C.J. 'Locke's Alleged Anticipation of Mill's Theory of the Syllogism,' *Mind*, 1 (1876), 560-6

1332　Murphy, Gardner. *Historical Introduction to Modern Psychology*. New York: Harcourt Brace, 1949

1333　Murray, Henry. 'John Stuart Mill,' *Bookman*, 38 (1910), 165. (Review of Elliot's ed. of JSM's letters)

1334　Murray, James G. 'Mill on De Quincey: *Esprit Critique* Revoked,' *Victorian Newsletter*, 37 (1970), 7-12

1335　Murray, Robert Henry. 'J.S. Mill: Optimistic Democrat.' In his *Studies in the English Social and Political Thinkers of the Nineteenth Century*. 2 vols. Cambridge: Heffer, 1929, I, 376-431

1336 Musaccio, Enrico. 'Utilitarismo, econismo e calcolo della felicità,'
De homine, 42-43 (1971), 197-228

1337 Musgrave, Anthony. 'Capital: Mr Mill's Fundamental Propositions,'
Contemporary Review, 24 (1874), 728-49

1338 —— *Studies in Political Economy*. London: Henry S. King, 1875.
(Reprints above, 55-102; contains chap. 'Some Thoughts on Value'
dealing primarily with JSM, 103-56. References to JSM *passim*.)

1339 Myers, Garry Cleveland. 'How Wordsworth Saved John Stuart Mill from
Insanity,' *High School Teacher*, 8 (1932), 230

1340 Myers, Minor, Jr. 'Intended Speech at the Cooperative Society by John
Stuart Mill,' *Connecticut College Library Bulletin*, no 2 (1975),
15-28. (MS, gift of Laski, in possession of the College)

1341 Myint, H. 'The 'Classical Theory' of International Trade and the
Underdeveloped Countries,' *Economic Journal*, 68 (1958), 317-37

1342 N., I. 'Vozrazheniya na ekonomicheskoye ucheniye Dzhona Styuarta
Millya' ['Objections to the Economic Doctrine of John Stuart Mill'],
Slovo [*Word*], no 7 (1879), 139-78; no 8, 75-120

1343 'N., N.' *Thirteen Pages on Intellectual Property Written with
Reference to a Doubtful Doctrine of the Late John Mill, by One of His
Pupils*. Manchester: Heywood, [1876]

1344 Nagel, Ernest, ed. *John Stuart Mill's Philosophy of Scientific
Method*. New York: Hafner, 1950

1345 Nakhnikian, George. 'Value and Obligation in Mill,' *Ethics*, 62
(1951), 33-40

1346 Napier, Joseph. *The Miracles: Butler's Argument on Miracles, Explained
and Defended, with Observations on Hume, Baden Powell, and J.S. Mill.
To Which Is Added a Critical Dissertation by H.L. Mansel*. Dublin:
Hodges, Smith, 1863

1347 Napier, Macvey [the younger], ed. *Selections from the Correspondence
of the Late Macvey Napier*. London: Macmillan, 1879. (Includes JSM
letters)

1348 Narveson, Jan. *Morality and Utility*. Baltimore: Johns Hopkins Press,
1967

1349 Neale, R.S. 'John Stuart Mill on Australia: A Note,' *Historical
Studies: Australia and New Zealand*, 13 (1968), 239-45. (Chiefly

JSM's letters to H.S. Chapman, 1858-63. See also Neale, 'H.S. Chapman and the "Victorian" Ballot,' *ibid.*, 12 (1967), 506-21.)

1350 Neatby, W.B. 'The Existential Import of Propositions,' *Mind*, ns 6 (1897), 542-3

1351 Neff, Emery Edward. *Carlyle and Mill: Mystic and Utilitarian*. New York: Columbia University Press, 1924. Republished as *Carlyle and Mill: An Introduction to Victorian Thought*. New York: Columbia University Press, 1926

1352 ——, introd. *On Liberty and Other Essays, by John Stuart Mill*. Modern Reader Series. New York: Macmillan, 1926

1353 Negro Pavon, Dalmacio. *Liberalismo y socialismo: la encrucijada intelectual de Stuart Mill*. Madrid: Instituto de Estudios Politicos, 1975

1354 —— 'Tocqueville y Stuart Mill,' *Revista de occidente*, 19 (1967), 103-14

1355 Nesbitt, George L. *Benthamite Reviewing: The First Twelve Years of the Westminster Review, 1824-36*. New York: Columbia University Press, 1934

1356 Newman, Francis W. 'Epicureanism, Ancient and Modern,' *Fraser's Magazine*, 84 (1871), 606-17. Reprinted in his *Miscellanies*, V. London: Kegan Paul, 1891, 99-114. (Sees Utilitarianism as the new Epicureanism)

1357 Nielsen, Kai. 'Mill's Proof of Utility.' In *New Dimensions in the Humanities and Social Sciences*. Ed. Harry R. Garvin. Lewisburg, Pa.: Bucknell University Press; London: Associated University Presses, 1977, 110-23

1358 Noble, F.A. 'Obedience and Liberty,' *Presbyterian Quarterly and Princeton Review*, ns 3 (1874), 65-86. (Answer to *On Liberty*)

1359 Nogaro, Bertrand. 'John Stuart Mill et le classicisme au milieu de XIXe siècle.' In his *Le Développement de la pensée économique*. Paris: Librarie Générale de Droit et de Jurisprudence, 1944, 142-203

1360 Nordquest, David. 'A Note on Mill's Discussion of Liberty,' *Mill News Letter*, X, 1 (1975), 16

1361 Norman, Richard. *Reasons for Actions: A Critique of Utilitarian Morality*. New York: Barnes and Noble, 1971. (Published dissertation)

1362 Norris, Stephen E. 'Being Free to Speak and Speaking Freely.' In

Social Ends and Political Means. Ed. Ted Honderich. Boston and
London: Routledge and Kegan Paul, 1976, 13-28

1363 Northrop, F.S.C. *The Logic of the Sciences and the Humanities.* New
York: Macmillan, 1948

1364 Norton, Sarah, and M.A. DeWolfe Howe, eds. *The Letters of Charles
Eliot Norton.* 2 vols. Boston: Houghton Mifflin, 1913. (Many references
to JSM)

1365 Nyman, Alf T. *Leviathan och Folkviljan. Betraktelser
över förstatligande byrakratl och skattetryck. Tillika en commentar till
Stuart Mill's skrift 'Om Friheten.'* Stockholm: Natur og Kulture, 1948

1366 O'Brien, D.P. 'The Longevity of Adam Smith's Vision: Paradigms,
Research Programmes and Falsifiability in the History of Economic
Thought,' *Scottish Journal of Political Economy*, 23 (1976), 133-51

1367 O'Brien, George. 'J.S. Mill and J.E. Cairnes,' *Economica*, ns 10
(1943), 273-85

1368 O'Hanlon, Hugh Francis. *A Criticism of J.S. Mill's Pure Idealism; and
an Attempt to Shew That, if Logically Carried Out, It Is Pure
Nihilism.* Oxford and London: Parker, 1866

1369 Okey, Thomas. *The Story of Avignon.* London: Dent; New York: Dutton,
1911. (Brief description of JSM's house and grave with a short
commentary)

1370 Okin, Susan M. 'John Stuart Mill's Feminism: The Subjection of Women
and the Improvement of Mankind,' *New Zealand Journal of History*,
7 (1973), 105-27

1371 Oldershaw, Lucian R.F. *Analysis of Mill's Principles of Political
Economy.* Oxford: Blackwell, 1915

1372 [Oliphant, Margaret.] 'The Great Unrepresented,' *Blackwood's Magazine*,
100 (1866), 367-79. (JSM and the enfranchisement of women)

1373 [——] 'Mill's *The Subjection of Women*,' *Edinburgh Review*, 130
(1869), 572-602. (Also reviews briefly Josephine Butler's *Woman's
Work and Woman's Culture*)

1374 Olivier, Sydney H. 'John Stuart Mill on Socialism,' *To-day: The
Monthly Magazine of Scientific Socialiam*, ns 2 (1884), 490-504

1375 Ong, Walter J. 'J.S. Mill's Pariah Poet,' *Philological Quarterly*, 29
(1950), 333-44. Reprinted in his *Rhetoric, Romance and Technology:*

Studies in the Interaction of Expression and Culture. Ithaca and London: Cornell University Press, 1971, 237-54. (Discusses the associationist origins of JSM's ideas of poetry and maintains that JSM saw the poet as an 'anomaly')

1376 Orr, J. 'J.S. Mill and Christianity,' *Theological Monthly*, 6 (1891), 108-21

1377 Oswald, Eugene. *Reminiscences of a Busy Life*. London: De la Mare Press, 1911. (Oswald translated, with Joseph Coulthard, von Humbolt's *The Sphere and Duties of Government*. Here claims great influence of von Humbolt on *On Liberty*.)

1378 Ouvry, Henry Aimé. *Stein and His Reforms in Prussia, with Reference to the Land Question in England: and an Appendix Containing the Views of Richard Cobden, and J.S. Mill's Advice to Land Reformers*. London: Kerby and Endean, 1873

1379 Packe, Michael St John. *The Life of John Stuart Mill*. London: Secker and Warburg, 1954

1380 Paden, William D. 'Tennyson and the Reviewers (1829-1835).' In *Studies in English in Honor of Raphael Norman O'Leary and Selden Lincoln Whitcomb*. University of Kansas Publications, Humanities Studies 4:4. Lawrence: University of Kansas, 1940, 14-39. (Mentions in passing JSM's review of *Poems of 1832*. Makes much of the Benthamite bias of other reviewers, especially W.J. Fox.)

1381 Paepe, César de. 'John Stuart Mill, socialiste,' *Société Nouvelle*, 2 (1885), 250-63

1382 [Palgrave, Francis Turner.] 'John Stuart Mill's *Autobiography*,' *Quarterly Review*, 136 (1874), 150-79. (Review)

1383 Palladini, F. 'Interpretazioni della "prova" milliana de "principio di utilita,"' *La cultura*, 4 (1971)

1384 Pankhurst, Richard Keir Pethick. *The Saint Simonians, Mill and Carlyle*. [London:] Sidgwick and Jackson, [1957]

1385 Paoli, Alesssandreo. *Dei concetti divettivi di J.S. Mill nella logica e nella psicologia*. Rome, 1877

1386 Pap, Arthur. *An Introduction to the Philosophy of Science*. Glencoe: The Free Press, 1962. (Discusses JSM's theory of induction, *passim*)

1387 Pappé, H.O. *John Stuart Mill and the Harriet Taylor Myth*. Melbourne: Melbourne University Press, 1960. (See also Rees)

1388 —— 'Mill and Tocqueville,' *Journal of the History of Ideas*, 25 (1964), 217-34

1389 —— 'The Mills and Harriet Taylor,' *Political Science*, 8 (1956), 19-30

1390 —— 'On Liberty and Liberalism,' *Times Literary Supplement*, 15 Oct. 1976, 1307. (A letter relating to Himmelfarb's book, which see)

1391 Park, Roy. 'Hazlitt and Bentham,' *Journal of the History of Ideas*, 30 (1969), 369-84

1392 Parker, Joseph. *Job's Comforters; or, Scientific Sympathy*. 2nd ed. New York: Funk and Wagnalls, 1862. (Anti-positivist tract casting JSM in the role of an inadequate comforter)

1393 —— *John Stuart Mill on Liberty: A Critique*. London: Pitman, 1865

1394 Passmore, John. 'John Stuart Mill and British Empiricism.' In his *A Hundred Years of Philosophy*. London: Duckworth, 1957, 1-32. Reprinted 1966; and Harmondsworth: Penguin, 1968. (References to JSM *passim*)

1395 Patinkin, Don. 'Keynes's Misquotation of Mill: Comment,' *Economic Journal*, 88 (1978), 341-2

1396 Patten, Simon Nelson. 'Interpretation of John Stuart Mill,' *Annals of the American Academy on Political and Social Science*, 44 (1912), 31-5

1397 Patterson, Jerry E. 'A Letter of John Stuart Mill,' *Yale University Library Gazette*, 30 (1956), 163-6. (Letter to W.M. Dickson, 1 Sept. 1865, acquired by Yale)

1398 Pattison, Mark. 'J.S. Mill on Hamilton,' *Reader*, 5 (1865), 562-3

1399 Payot, Jules. *Quia apud Millium Spencerumque de externis rebus disserentes sit reprehendum*. Orléans: Michau, 1895

1400 Peabody, Andrew P. 'Mill on Representative Government,' *North American Review*, 95 (1862), 228-55

1401 Pearlman, Mari Ann. 'The Other Argument in *On Liberty*,' *Style*, 11 (1977), 39-55. (Rhetorical analysis)

1402 Perkins, Moreland, and Irving Singer. 'The Definition of "More Valuable,"' *Analysis*, 13 (1952-53), 140-3

1403 Perry, T.S. 'Autobiography,' *North American Review*, 118 (1874), 185-8

1404 Peterfreund, Shelden P. 'On Mill's Higher and Lower Pleasures,' *Personalist*, 57 (1976), 411-12

1405 Peters, Richard Stanley. *Ethics and Education*. London: Allen and Unwin, 1966. Reprinted 1970

1406 Peterson, William S., and Fred. L. Standley. 'The J.S. Mill Marginalia in Robert Browning's *Pauline*: A History and Transcription,' *Papers of the Bibliographical Society of America*, 66 (1972), 135-70

1407 Phelps, William Lyon. 'Freedom and Literature.' In *Freedom: Its Meaning*. Ed. Ruth Nada Anshen. New York: Harcourt Brace, 1940, 428-36. (Not included in English ed.)

1408 —— 'Notes on Browning's *Pauline*,' *Modern Language Notes*, 47 (1932), 292-9. (JSM's marginal notes)

1409 Phelps Brown, E.H. 'Prospects of Labour,' *Economica*, ns 16 (1949), 1-10

1410 Phillipps, Lucy F. March. *The Battle of Two Philosophers, by An Inquirer*. London: Longmans, Green, 1866. (Deals with *Sir William Hamilton's Philosophy*)

1411 Phillips, M.A. 'John Stuart Mill and Browning's "Pauline,"' *Cornhill Magazine*, ns 32 (1912), 671-7

1412 Pick, G. Vesian. *Digest of Political Economy: The Principles of John Stuart Mill*. London: Sonnenschein, 1892

1413 Pierce, Christine. 'Hart on Paternalism,' *Analysis*, 35 (1975), 205-7. (Refers to H.L.A. Hart's *Law, Liberty and Morality*, which see)

1414 Pigou, Arthur Cecil. 'Mill and the Wages Fund,' *Economic Journal*, 59 (1949), 171-80

1415 Pike, Edgar Royston. 'Hearts and Intellects: The "most animating" and Invigorating Thought of John Stuart Mill.' In his *Pioneers of Social Change*. [London:] Barrie and Rockcliff, 1963, 188-211

1416 Pikler, Julius. 'The Genesis of the Cognition of Physical Reality,' *Mind*, 15 (1890), 394-400. (Defence of JSM against Stout, which see. See also Baldwin.)

1417 —— 'J.S. Mill's Theory of the Belief in an External World.' In his *The Psychology of the Belief in Objective Existence. Part I: Objectiva Capable of Presentation*. London: Williams and Norgate, 1890, 62-7. (Subsequent parts never published)

1418 Pillon, F. 'John Stuart Mill au point de vue religieux,' *La Critique Philosophique*, 2:1 (1873), 283-8. (Includes letter by Rey and concerns JSM and French Positivists)

1419 —— 'John Stuart Mill socialiste,' *La Critique Philosophique*, 2:1 (1873), 350-5, 363-72

1420 —— 'L'Origine de la justice selon Bentham et M. Stuart Mill,' *La Critique Philosophique*, 2:1 (1873), 129-36

1421 —— 'Polémique de Mahaffy contre l'école associationniste,' *La Critique Philosophique*, 2:2 (1873), 43-8

1422 —— 'Polémique de M. Mahaffy contre Stuart Mill au sujet des jugements mathématiques,' *La Critique Philosophique*, 2:2 (1873), 58-64

1423 —— 'La Raison profonde de la crise mentale de Stuart Mill; contradiction entre l'éducation intellectuelle et l'éducation morale dans la doctrine associationniste,' *La Critique Philosophique*, 4:1 (1875), 339-45

1424 —— 'La Science de la morale selon Bentham et Stuart Mill,' *La Critique Philosophique*, 3:1 (1874), 137-42

1425 [Pipping, Hugo E.] 'John Stuart Mill och Harriet Taylor,' *Nya Argus*, 44 (1951), 192-5. (Review of F.A. Hayek. Signed H.E.P.)

1426 Pira, Carl. *Framställning och Kritik af J. St. Mills. Lotzes och Sigwarts Läror om begreppsbildningen i logiken*. Stockholm: Palmquist, 1897

1427 Pizer, Donal. 'The Ethical Unity of *The Rise of Silas Lapham*,' *American Literature*, 32 (1960-61), 322-7. (Suggests that the 'ethical core' of Howells' novel rests on the Principle of Utility as interpreted by JSM)

1428 Plamenatz, John. *Mill's 'Utilitarianism.' Reprinted with A Study of the English Utilitarians*. Oxford: Blackwell, 1949

1429 —— *The English Utilitarians*. 2nd ed. rev. Oxford: Blackwell, 1958

1430 [Plummer, John.] 'Philosophical Politicians,' *Working Man*, 2 (1866), 73-4. (JSM in Parliament)

1431 [——] 'Remarkable Men: Members of the New Parliament, No 1: John Stuart Mill,' *Cassell's Illustrated Family Paper*, 3rd ser., 16 Sept. 1865, 87-8

1432   Political Economy Club. *Names of Members 1821-1860: - Rules of the Club: - and List of Questions Discussed, 1833-60*. London: printed for the Club, 1860. Vol. II: *List of Members 1821-72: - List of Questions Discussed, 1860-72*. London: printed for the Club, 1872. Vol. IV: *Minutes of Proceedings, 1821-82. Role of Members and Questions Discussed*. London: printed for the Club, 1882. Vol. VI [Centenary Volume]: *Minutes of Proceedings, 1899-1920: Role of Members and Questions Discussed, 1821-1920; with Documents Bearing on the History of the Club*. London: Macmillan, 1921

1433   Popkin, Richard H. 'A Note on the "Proof" of Utility in J.S. Mill,' *Ethics*, 61 (1950), 66-8

1434   Popper, Karl. *The Open Society and Its Enemies*. 2 vols. London: Routledge and Kegan Paul, 1945. Frequently reprinted. Vol. II, Chap. 14, 'The Autonomy of Sociology,' reprinted in *Mill: A Collection of Critical Essays*. Ed. J.B. Schneewind. Garden City, NY: Doubleday, 1968, 426-42

1435   Porter, Noah. 'John Stuart Mill,' *International Review*, 1 (1874), 385-406. (See also Daniel G. Thompson)

1436   Power, M. Susan. 'Democracy, Representation, and John Stuart Mill,' *Susquehanna University Studies*, 7 (1965), 231-45

1437   Powers, Richard H. 'John Stuart Mill: Morality and Inequality,' *South Atlantic Quarterly*, 58 (1959), 206-12

1438   Pradhan, S.V. 'Mill on India: A Reappraisal,' *Dalhousie Review*, 56 (1976), 5-22

1439   Preyer, Robert. 'The Utilitarian Poetics: John Stuart Mill,' *University of Kansas City Review*, 19 (1953), 131-6

1440   [Price, Bonamy.] 'Mr Mill on Land,' *Blackwood's Magazine*, 110 (1871), 30-45

1441   Price, H.H. 'Mill's View of the External World,' *Proceedings of the Aristotelian Society*, ns 27 (1926-27), 109-40

1442   Price, L.L. 'John Stuart Mill, 1806-1873: The Theory of Value.' In his *A Short History of Political Economy in England*. London: Methuen, 1891, 87-114

1443   Prichard, Harold Arthur. 'Does Moral Philosophy Rest on a Mistake?' *Mind*, 21 (1912), 21-37. Reprinted in *Mill: Utilitarianism*. Ed. S. Gorovitz. Indianapolis and New York: Bobbs-Merrill, 1971, 61-72

1444   Pringle, G.O.S. 'Mill's Humanity,' *Westminster Review*, 150 (1898), 159-62

1445   Pringle-Pattison, A.S. See Andrew Seth

1446   Pugh, Evelyn L. 'John Stuart Mill, Harriet Taylor, and Women's Rights in America, 1850-1873,' *Canadian Journal of History*, 13 (1978), 423-42

1447   —— 'Politics and Light Verse: Another Look at J.S. Mill,' *Mill News Letter*, XII, 2 (1977), 7-22

1448   Purnell, Thomas. 'Literary Men in Parliament.' In his *Literature and Its Professors.* London: Bell and Daldy, 1867, 47-62

1449   Qualter, T.H. 'John Stuart Mill, Disciple of de Tocqueville,' *Western Political Quarterly*, 13 (1960), 880-9

1450   Quesnel, Leo. 'Les Deux Mill,' *Bibliothèque Universelle et Revue Suisse* [Partie Littéraire, Lausanne], 3e période, 13 (1882), 463-96. (Review article of Bain's *James Mill* and *John Stuart Mill*)

1451   Quinton, Anthony. 'The Neglect of Victorian Philosophy,' *Victorian Studies*, 1 (1958), 245-54. (Discussion of current misinterpretation and neglect of JSM and other Victorian philosophers)

1452   —— *Utilitarian Ethics*. London: Macmillan, 1973. (Especially 'John Stuart Mill,' 38-81)

1453   R., G. 'Mr Mill on Wages,' *National Reformer*, 5 (1864), 337-8; 'The True Cause of Low Wages,' *ibid.*, 356-7; 'Popular Remedies for Low Wages,' *ibid.*, 372-3; 'True Remedies for Low Wages I,' *ibid.*, 389-90; 'True Remedies for Low Wages II,' *ibid.*, 406-7. (Five articles, chiefly summary)

1454   R., J. 'Mr Mill's New Book,' *National Reformer*, 14 (1869), 6-7. (Short notice for *Subjection of Women*)

1455   —— 'A Visit to the Tomb of Mill,' *National Reformer*, 24 (1874), 33-4

1456   Radcliffe, Peter, ed. *Limits of Liberty: Studies of Mill's 'On Liberty.'* Belmont: Wadsworth, 1966. (Contains papers by S.I. Benn, Isaiah Berlin, H.L.A. Hart, W. Kendall, A.W. Levi, J.C. Rees, M.G. Singer, and Fitzjames Stephen, which see)

1457   Ralph, P.L. 'Mo Ti and the English Utilitarians,' *Far Eastern Quarterly*, 9 (1949), 42-62

1458   Randall, John Herman, Jr. *The Career of Philosophy*. 2 vols. New

York: Columbia University Press, 1962-66. (A study of nineteenth-century British philosophy with particular reference to JSM, II, 485-637)

1459 —— 'John Stuart Mill and the Working-Out of Empiricism,' *Journal of the History of Ideas*, 26 (1965), 59-88

1460 —— 'T.H. Green and Liberal Idealism.' In his *Philosophy after Darwin: Chapters for the Career of Philosophy Volume III and Other Essays*. New York: Columbia University Press, 1977, 65-96. (JSM mentioned 90-5)

1461 —— 'T.H. Green: The Development of English Thought from J.S. Mill to F.H. Bradley,' *Journal of the History of Ideas*, 27 (1966), 217-44

1462 [Rands, William Brighty.] Henry Holbeach (pseud). *Henry Holbeach: Student in Life and Philosophy: A Narrative and Discussion*. 2 vols. London: Strahan, 1865. ('The Sphere of Law' a 'Controversial Letter' to JSM, II, 3-33)

1463 [——] Henry Holbeach (pseud). 'Mr Mill's Autobiography and Mr Fitzjames Stephen on "Liberty,"' *Saint Paul's Magazine*, 13 (1873), 686-701

1464 [——] Matthew Browne (pseud). 'The Subjection of Women,' *Contemporary Review*, 14 (1870), 273-86

1465 Raphael, D. Daiches. 'Fallacies in and about Mill's Utilitarianism,' *Philosophy*, 30 (1955), 344-57

1466 Ratcliffe, Barrie M., and W.H. Chaloner, eds. *A French Sociologist Looks at Britain: Gustave D'Eichthal and British Society in 1828*. Manchester: Manchester University Press, 1977. (A translation of D'Eichthal's notes and an intellectual portrait by Ratcliffe)

1467 Rawls, John. 'Justice as Reciprocity.' In *Mill: Utilitarianism*. Ed. S. Gorovitz. Indianapolis and New York: Bobbs-Merrill, 1971, 242-68

1468 —— *A Theory of Justice*. Cambridge: Belknap Press of Harvard University Press, 1971

1469 —— 'Two Concepts of Rules,' *Philosophical Review*, 64 (1955), 3-32. Reprinted in *Mill: Utilitarianism*. Ed. S. Gorovitz. Indianapolis and New York: Bobbs-Merrill, 1971, 175-94

1470 Ray, Jean. *La Méthode de l'économie politique d'après J.S. Mill*. Paris: Sirey, 1914

1471 Read, Carveth. 'A Posthumous Chapter by J.S. Mill,' *Mind*, ns 17

(1908), 74-8. (Concerns *On Social Freedom*. Read doubts, but finally accepts, HT's judgement.)

1472   Rees, John Collwyn. *Equality*. London: Pall Mall Press; New York: Praeger, 1971. Reprinted London: Macmillan, 1972

1473   —— 'H.O. Pappé's "John Stuart Mill and the Harriet Taylor Myth,"' *Political Studies*, 10 (1962), 198-202

1474   —— *Mill and His Early Critics*. Leicester: University College, 1956. (See also Cranston)

1475   —— 'A Note on Macaulay and the Utilitarians,' *Political Studies*, 4 (1956), 315-17

1476   —— 'A Phase in the Development of Mill's Ideas on Liberty,' *Political Studies*, 6 (1958), 33-44

1477   —— 'The Reaction to Cowling on Mill,' *Mill News Letter*, I, 2 (1966), 2-11

1478   —— 'A Re-reading of Mill on Liberty,' *Political Studies*, 8 (1960), 113-29. Reprinted, slightly abridged and with new conclusion, in *Limits of Liberty: Studies of Mill's 'On Liberty.'* Ed. Peter Radcliffe. Belmont: Wadsworth, 1966, 87-107; and in *Essays in the History of Political Thought*. Ed. Isaac Kramnick. Englewood Cliffs, NJ: Prentice-Hall, 1969, 357-71

1479   —— 'The Thesis of the Two Mills,' *Political Studies*, 25 (1977), 369-82. (Critique of Himmelfarb, 'The Other John Stuart Mill,' which see)

1480   —— 'Was Mill for Liberty?' *Political Studies*, 14 (1966), 72-7. (Review of Cowling's *Mill and Liberalism*)

1481   Reeve, Henry. 'Autobiography of John Stuart Mill,' *Edinburgh Review*, 139 (1874), 91-129

1482   [——] 'J.S. Mill's *Essays on Theism*,' *Edinburgh Review*, 141 (1875), 1-31. (Review)

1483   Reichel, H. 'Darstellung und Kritik von J. St. Mills Theorie der induktiven Methode,' *Zeitschrift für Philosophie und philosophische Kritik*, 122 (1903), 176-97; 123 (1904), 33-46, 121-51

1484   Remnant, Peter. 'The Relevance of Mill,' *Queen's Quarterly*, 77 (1970), 513-29

1485   Rémusat, Charles de. 'De la liberté civile et politique, à propos des ouvrages de MM. Jules Simon et Stuart Mill,' *Revue des Deux Mondes*, 22 (1859), 322-52

1486   Renner, H. 'John Stuart Mill,' *Philosophische Wochenschrift und Literatur-Zeitung*, 2 (1906), 270-1

1487   Renouvier, Charles-Bernard. 'De l'esprit de la philosophie anglaise. L'Utilitarianisme: Robert Owen et Stuart Mill,' *La Critique Philosophique*, 2:1 (1873), 17-25

1488   [——] 'La Mort de J. Stuart Mill,' *La Critique Philosophique*, 2:1 (1873), 235-7

1489   —— 'L'Opinion de Stuart Mill sur la liberté et la nécessité des actes,' *La Critique Philosophique*, 3:1 (1874), 225-31

1490   —— 'Le Principe du socialisme d'après "L'Autobiographie" de Stuart Mill,' *La Critique Philosophique*, 2:2 (1873), 258-65

1491   —— 'Les Rapports du criticisme avec philosophie de Stuart Mill,' *La Critique Philosophique*, 2:1 (1873), 273-82. (Kant, Hume and JSM)

1492   Ressler, Anny. *Die beiden Mills*. Ichenhausen: Wagner, 1929

1493   Restaino, Franco. *J.S. Mill e la cultura filosofica britannica*. Florence: La Nuova Italia Editrice, 1968

1494   —— 'J.S. Mill: gli anni del distacco dal benthamismo (1831-1836),' *Giornale critico della filosofia italiana*, 4 (1970), 512-58

1495   —— 'J.S. Mill *radical philosopher*: gli anni della milizia politica benthamiana (1822-1829),' *Studi storici*, 8 (1967), 282-324

1496   ——, ed. and trans. *John Stuart Mill: scritti scelti*. Milan: Principato, 1969. Includes extracts from *Logic*, *Principles of Political Economy*, *On Liberty*, *Utilitarianism*, *Sir William Hamilton's Philosophy*

1497   Rey, Louis. 'John Stuart Mill in Avignon' introduced by a 'Discourse de M. Edward Vicars, Consul Général britannique, Doyen du Corps Consulaire à Marseille,' *Annales de l'Ecole Palatine d'Avignon*, 1921, 2e sem., 148-60. Reprinted without introduction as *John Stuart Mill en Avignon, conférence donnée dans la grande salle des fêtes de l'Hôtel de Ville d'Avignon sous les auspices de l'Ecole Palatine, sous la présidence de M. Vicars consul général britannique à Marseilles, par M. le pasteur Rey, le 23 avril 1921*. Vaison: Macabet, 1922

1498   —— 'The Romance of John Stuart Mill,' *Nineteenth Century*, 74 (1913), 502-26. Also published as *Le Roman de John Stuart Mill*. Paris, 1913

1499 Reybaud, Louis [Marie-Roch]. *Economistes modernes: R. Cobden, Fr. Bastiat, M. Chevalier, John Stuart Mill, L. Faucher, Pellegrino Rossi*. Paris: Lévy, 1862

1500 —— 'John Stuart Mill et l'économie politique en Angleterre,' *Revue des Deux Mondes*, 10 (1855), 117-48

1501 [Rhind, Neil.] 'Mill's House at Blackheath,' *Mill News Letter*, X, 2 (1975), 15-16

1502 [Ribot, Théodule Armand.] 'Auguste Comte, lettres à John Stuart Mill (1841-1846),' *Revue Philosophique*, 3 (1877), 542-3. (Review of Littré's edition of these letters, signed Th.R.)

1503 —— 'La Philosophie contemporaine en Angleterre: M. John Stuart Mill et son influence philosophique,' *Revue Politique et Littéraire*, 11 (1873), 1154-9

1504 —— *La Psychologie anglaise contemporaine (école experimentale)*. Paris, 1870. Trans. as *English Psychology*. London: Kegan Paul, Trench, Trübner, 1873

1505 Richter, Melvin. *The Politics of Conscience: T.H. Green and His Age*. London: Weidenfeld and Nicolson, 1964

1506 Rickaby, Joseph. *Free Will and Four English Philosophers*. London: Burns and Oates, 1906. Reprinted Freeport, NY: Books for Libraries Press, 1969. (An attack by a Catholic theologian on JSM's determinism)

1507 —— 'Mr Mill on the Utility of Religion,' *Month*, ns 4 (1875), 393-408; ns 5 (1875), 169-80

1508 —— 'Mr Mill's Essay on Nature,' *Month*, ns 4 (1875), 50-65

1509 Rinehart, Keith. 'John Stuart Mill's *Autobiography*: Its Art and Appeal,' *University of Kansas City Review*, 19 (1953), 265-73

1510 Ritchie, David G. *The Principles of State Interference: Four Essays on the Political Philosophy of Mr Herbert Spencer, J.S. Mill, T.H. Green*. London: Sonnenschein, 1891. (Essay on JSM referring to *On Liberty* reprinted from *Time*, ns 13 (1886), 29-44; short note on Utilitarianism)

1511 Ritchie, J. Ewing. 'John Stuart Mill.' In his *British Senators; or, Political Sketches, Past and Present*. London: Tinsley Brothers, 1869, 295-301

1512   Roach, John. 'Liberalism and the Victorian Intelligentsia,' *Cambridge Historical Journal*, 13 (1957), 58-81. (Chiefly discussion of Fitzjames Stephen and the 'old Liberal' view)

1513   Robbins, Larry M. 'Mill and *Middlemarch*: The Progress of Public Opinion,' *Victorian Newsletter*, 31 (1967), 37-9. (An examination of the role of public opinion in *Middlemarch* with reference to the ideas of *On Liberty)*

1514   Robbins, Lionel. 'The Classical Economists and Socialism: John Stuart Mill.' In his *The Theory of Economic Policy in English Classical Political Economy*. London: Macmillan, 1952, 142-68

1515   —— *Political Economy Past and Present*. London: Macmillan, 1976

1516   —— *Robert Torrens and the Evolution of Classical Economics*. London: Macmillan, 1958

1517   —— *The Theory of Economic Development in the History of Economic Thought*. London and New York: Macmillan, 1968. (Lord Robbins' Chichele Lectures revised and extended. Frequent references to JSM.)

1518   Robbins, William. *The Newman Brothers*. London: Heinemann; Toronto: Bellhaven House, 1966. (Passing references to JSM)

1519   Robertson, George Croom. 'Courtney's Metaphysics of John Stuart Mill,' *Mind*, 4 (1879), 421-6. (See also Courtney, *The Metaphysics of John Stuart Mill)*

1520   [——] 'J.S. Mill's Philosophy Tested by Professor Jevons,' *Mind*, 3 (1878), 141-4. (Signed 'Editor.' See also Jevons, Strachey)

1521   Robertson, John M. 'John Stuart Mill.' In his *Modern Humanists*. London: Sonnenschein, 1895, 62-111

1522   —— 'John Stuart Mill.' In his *Modern Humanists Reconsidered*. London: Watts, 1927, 132-65

1523   Robinson, Henry Crabb. *On Books and Their Writers*. Ed. Edith Morley. 3 vols. London: Dent, 1938. (Brief references to JSM)

1524   Robson, Ann P. 'Bertrand Russell and His Godless Parents,' *Russell*, 7 (1972), 3-9. (JSM and Helen Taylor were Russell's godparents)

1525   —— 'Legal Proof of Dissertations and Discussions,' *Mill News Letter*, XI, 2 (1976), 22-5

1526   ——, and John M. 'John Stuart Mill's Annotated "Examiner" Articles,' *Victorian Periodicals Newsletter*, 7 (1974), 3-6

1527 Robson, John M. 'Editing J.S. Mill's *Principles of Political Economy,*'
University of Toronto Press Notes, 3 (1961), np

1528 —— '"Feminine" and "Masculine": Mill vs Grote,' *Mill News
Letter,* XII, 1 (1977), 18-22

1529 —— 'Harriet Taylor and John Stuart Mill: Artist and Scientist,'
Queen's Quarterly, 73 (1966), 167-86

1530 —— *The Improvement of Mankind: The Social and Political Thought of
John Stuart Mill.* Toronto: University of Toronto Press; London:
Routledge and Kegan Paul, 1968

1531 —— 'John Stuart Mill.' In *The New Cambridge Bibliography of
English Literature.* Ed. George Watson. Vol. III: *1800-1900.*
Cambridge: Cambridge University Press, 1969, 1551-76. (This new edition,
revised and up-dated throughout, of the standard reference work on the
period, contains, as well as the strictly literary sections, listings of
works in History, Philosophy, Religion, etc.)

1532 —— 'John Stuart Mill.' In *Victorian Prose: A Guide to Research.*
Ed. David J. DeLaura. New York: Modern Language Association of
America, 1973, 185-218. (Critical and bibliographical survey of research)

1533 —— 'John Stuart Mill and Jeremy Bentham, with Some Observations on
James Mill.' In *Essays in English Literature from the Renaissance to
the Victorian Age Presented to A.S.P. Woodhouse.* Ed. M. MacLure and
F.W. Watt. Toronto: University of Toronto Press, 1964, 245-68

1534 —— '"Joint Authorship" Again: The Evidence in the Third Edition of
Mill's Logic,' *Mill News Letter,* VI, 2 (1971), 15-20

1535 —— 'J.S. Mill's Theory of Poetry,' *University of Toronto Quarterly,*
29 (1960), 420-38. Reprinted in *Mill: A Collection of Critical Essays.*
Ed. J.B. Schneewind. Garden City, NY: Doubleday, 1968, 251-79

1536 —— 'Mill and Arnold: Liberty and Culture - Friends or Enemies,'
Humanities Association Bulletin, 12 (1961), 20-32. Reprinted in *Of
Several Branches: Studies from the Humanities Association Bulletin,
1954-65.* Ed. G.S. McCaughey and M. Legris. Toronto: University of
Toronto Press, 1968, 125-42

1537 —— 'Mill's *Autobiography*: The Public and the Private Voice,'
College Composition and Communication, 16 (1965), 97-101

1538 —— 'A Note on Mill Bibliography,' *University of Toronto Quarterly,*
34 (1964), 93-7

1539 —— 'Principles and Methods in the Collected Edition of John Stuart Mill.' In *Editing Nineteenth Century Texts*. Ed. John M. Robson. Toronto: University of Toronto Press, 1967, 96-122

1540 —— 'Rational Animals and Others.' In *James and John Stuart Mill: Papers of the Centenary Conference*. Ed. John M. Robson and Michael Laine. Toronto: University of Toronto Press, 1976, 143-60

1541 —— 'The Rhetoric of J.S. Mill's Periodical Articles,' *Victorian Periodicals Newsletter*, 10 (1977), 122-9

1542 —— 'Victorian Liberals,' *University of Toronto Quarterly*, 31 (1962), 242-5

1543 ——, introd. *John Stuart Mill: A Selection of His Works*. Toronto: Macmillan, 1966

1544 ——, and Karl Britton. 'Mill's Debating Speeches,' *Mill News Letter*, I, 1 (1965), 2-6

1545 ——, and Michael Laine, eds. *James and John Stuart Mill: Papers of the Centenary Conference*. Toronto: University of Toronto Press, 1976. (Articles by Edward Alexander, Karl W. Britton, J.H. Burns, L.S. Feuer, Joseph Hamburger, Samuel Hollander, John M. Robson, J.B. Schneewind, George J. Stigler, which see)

1546 Rockmore, Tom. 'The Moral Philosophy of J.S. Mill Revisited,' *Personalist*, 55 (1974), 380-7

1547 Rodgers, Brian. 'John Stuart Mill - The Avignon Years,' *Memoirs & Proceedings of the Manchester Literary and Philosophical Society*, 117 (1974-75), 52-74

1548 [Roebuck, J.A.] 'Bentham's *Rational of Judicial Evidence*,' *Westminster Review*, 9 (1828), 198-250. (One paragraph [216] on JSM's editing of Bentham's MSS. Does not mention him by name.)

1549 Roellinger, Francis X., Jr. 'Mill on Education,' *Journal of General Education*, 6 (1952), 246-59

1550 Roerig, Franziska. *Die Wandlungen in der geistigen Grundhaltung John Stuart Mills zu volkswirtschaftlichen Problemen*. Cologne: Bergisch-Gladbach, 1930

1551 Rogers, Arthur K. *English and American Philosophy since 1800*. London: Macmillan, 1922, 64-86

1552 Rogers, Frederic [Lord Blachford]. 'The Reality of Duty: As Illustrated by the *Autobiography* of Mr John Stuart Mill,' *Contemporary Review*, 28 (1876), 508-36

1553 Rogin, Leo. *The Meaning and Validity of Economic Theory: A Historical Approach*. New York: Harper, 1956

1554 Rohatyn, Dennis Anthony. 'Hall and Mill's Proof,' *Southwestern Journal of Philosophy*, 2 (1972), 113-18. (See Hall)

1555 —— 'Mill, Kant, and Negative Utility,' *Philosophia*, 5 (1975), 515-21

1556 —— 'A Note on Kaufmann and Justice,' *Mill News Letter*, VI, 2 (1971), 23-5. (See Kaufmann)

1557 —— 'On Behalf of Ebel and Berlin,' *Mill News Letter*, V, 1 (1969), 6-9. (See Berlin and Ebel)

1558 Romilly, Henry. *Public Responsibility and Vote by Ballot by an Elector. Second Edition. To Which Are Appended a Letter from J.S. Mill, MP to the Editor of 'The Reader,' 29th April 1865 and Observations Thereon*. London, 1867. 1st ed., London: Ridgway, 1865. Reprinted appended to his *Punishment by Death*. London: Murray, 1866

1559 Rosenberg, A. 'Mill and Some Contemporary Critics on "Cause,"' *Personalist*, 54 (1973), 123-9

1560 Ross, Janet. *Three Generations of English Women: Memoirs and Correspondence of Mrs John Taylor, Mrs Sarah Austin, and Lady Duff-Gordon*. London: Murray, 1888. (Author is the daughter of Lady Duff-Gordon and granddaughter of Sarah Austin)

1561 Ross, Sydney. 'Sir John Herschel's Marginal Notes on Mill's *On Liberty*, 1859,' *Journal of the History of Ideas*, 29 (1968), 123-30

1562 Rossel', Yuri Andreyevich. 'Dzhon Styuart Mill' i yevo shkola' ['John Stuart Mill and His School'], *Vestnik Yevropy* [*Herald of Europe*] (1874), 221:5-33, 473-511; 222:132-68, 667-706; 223:654-84; 224:672-719

1563 Rossi, Alice S., ed. *John Stuart Mill and Harriet Taylor Mill. Essays on Sex Equality*. Chicago: University of Chicago Press, 1970. (Contains the 'Early Essays on Marriage and Divorce,' reprinted from F.A. Von Hayek's *John Stuart Mill and Harriet Taylor*; Harriet Taylor Mill's 'Enfranchisement of Women'; JSM's *The Subjection of Women*; and an introductory essay by Rossi, 'Sentiment and Intellect,' which appeared in abridged form in *Midway* [1970])

1564 Rover, Constance. *Love, Morals and the Feminists*. London: Routledge and Kegan Paul, 1970

1565 —— *The Punch Book of Women's Rights*. London: Hutchinson, 1967.
Reprinted New York: Barnes, 1970. (Reproduces, with short comment,
cartoons: 'Mill's Logic' and 'The Lady's Advocate')

1566 —— *Women's Suffrage and Party Politics in Britain, 1866-1914*.
London: Routledge and Kegan Paul: Toronto: University of Toronto Press,
1967

1567 Rozhdestvensky, M.N. *O znachenii Dzhona Styuarta Millya v ryadu
sovremennykh ekonomistov* [*On the Significance of John Stuart Mill in
the Ranks of Contemporary Economists*]. St Petersburg: Prats, 1867

1568 Rudman, Harry. 'Mill on Perpetual Endowments,' *History of Ideas
Newsletter*, 3 (1957), 70-2

1569 Russell, Bertrand. See also Robert M. MacIver

1570 —— 'John Stuart Mill,' *Proceedings of the British Academy*, 41 (1955),
43-59. Reprinted London: Oxford University Press, 1955. Also in his
Portraits from Memory and Other Essays. London: Allen and Unwin,
1956, 114-34; and in *Mill: A Collection of Critical Essays*. Ed.
J.B. Schneewind. Garden City, NY: Doubleday, 1968, 1-21

1571 —— 'Toleration.' In his *Ideas and Beliefs of the Victorians*.
London: Sylvan Press, 1949, 268-76. Reprinted New York: Dutton, 1966.
(A transcript of a BBC Third Programme broadcast. Claims JSM went
to prison over birth control episode. See also Ayer.)

1572 ——, and Patricia Russell. *The Amberley Papers*. 2 vols. London:
Hogarth Press, 1937. (References to the Amberleys' friendship with
JSM from 1865 onwards)

1573 Russell, Edward Richard. *On the Autobiography of John Stuart Mill,
etc.* Liverpool: Marples, 1874

1574 Rutkovsky, Leonid Vasil'yevich. 'Kritika metodov induktivnovo
dokazatel'stva' ['A Critique of Methods of Inductive Proof'], *Zhurnal
ministerstva narodnovo prosveshcheniya* [*Journal of the Ministry of
Public Education*], nos 6, 7 (1899)

1575 Ryan, Alan. 'John Stuart Mill and the Open Society,' *Listener*, 89
(1973), 633-5

1576 —— 'John Stuart Mill's Art of Living,' *Listener*, 74 (1965), 620-2.
(See also Wharton)

1577 —— *J.S. Mill*. London and Boston: Routledge and Kegan Paul, 1974

1578 —— 'Mill and the Naturalistic Fallacy,' *Mind*, ns 75 (1966), 422-5

1579 —— 'Mr McCloskey on Mill's Liberalism,' *Philosophical Quarterly*, 14 (1964), 253-60. (See McCloskey)

1580 —— 'The Open Society and Utility,' *Government and Opposition*, 6 (1971), 235-42

1581 —— *The Philosophy of John Stuart Mill*. London: Macmillan, 1970. As *John Stuart Mill*. New York: Pantheon, 1970

1582 —— 'Two Concepts of Politics and Democracy: James and John Stuart Mill.' In *Machiavelli and the Nature of Political Thought*. Ed. Martin Fleisher. New York: Atheneum, 1972; London: Croom Helm, 1973, 76-113

1583 —— 'Utilitarianism and Bureaucracy: The Views of J.S. Mill.' In *Studies in the Growth of Nineteenth-Century Government*. Ed. Gillian Sutherland. London: Routledge and Kegan Paul, 1972, 33-62

1584 Ryle, Gilbert. 'The Theory of Meaning.' In *British Philosophy in the Mid-Century*. Ed. C.A. Mace. London: Allen and Unwin, 1957, 239-64. (Refers to *Logic*)

1585 Sabine, George Holland. 'Liberalism Modernized.' In his *A History of Political Theory*. London: Harrap, 1937 ; 3rd ed. rev. New York: Holt, Rinehart and Winston, 1961, 701-54

1586 Sampson, R.V. 'J.S. Mill: An Interpretation,' *Cambridge Journal*, 3 (1950), 232-9

1587 Sanderson, David R. 'Metaphor and Method in Mill's *On Liberty*,' *Victorian Newsletter*, 34 (1968), 22-5

1588 Sangar, James Mortimer. *Episcopal Vows: What Do They Mean? A Letter to the Lord Bishop of St David's on His Recent Endorsement of the Alleged Infidelity of J.S. Mill, Esq, MP*. London: William Hunt, [1866]. (See Thirlwall)

1589 Sänger, Samuel. 'John Stuart Mill als Philosoph,' *Archiv für Geschichte der Philosophie*, 9 (1896), 344-60

1590 —— *John Stuart Mill: Sein Leben und Lebenswerk*. Stuttgart: Frommann, 1901

1591 —— 'Mills Theodizee,' *Archiv für Geschichte der Philosophie*, 13 (1900), 402-29

1592 Scanlan, James P. 'John Stuart Mill in Russia: A Bibliography,' *Mill News Letter*, IV, 1 (1968), 2-6

1593 —— 'J.S. Mill and the Definition of Freedom,' *Ethics*, 68 (1958), 194-206

1594 Schapiro, Jacob S. 'Comment,' *Journal of the History of Ideas*, 10 (1949), 303-4. (On Feuer on Mill and Marxian socialism; see also Feuer)

1595 —— 'John Stuart Mill, Pioneer of Democratic Liberalism in England,' *Journal of the History of Ideas*, 4 (1943), 127-60. Reprinted in his *Liberalism and the Challenge of Fascism*. New York: McGraw-Hill, 1949, 256-89

1596 —— 'Utilitarianism and the Foundations of English Liberalism,' *Journal of Social Philosophy*, 4 (1939), 121-37

1597 Schatz, Albert. *L'Individualisme économique et social*. Paris: Colin, 1907. (Especially 216-57)

1598 Schauchet, Pauline. *Individualistische und sozialistische Gedanken in den Lehren John Stuart Mills*. Geissen, 1926. (Published dissertation)

1599 Scheffler, Israel. *Anatomy of Inquiry*. New York: Knopf, 1963. (Refers to *Logic, passim*)

1600 Schérer, Edmond Henri Adolphe. *Etudes critiques sur la littérature contemporaine*. 10 vols. Paris: Lévy, 1863, I, 290-320. Trans. G. Saintsbury as *Essays on English Literature*. New York: Scribner's, 1891, 13-35

1601 Schiel, J. *Die Methode der inductiven Forschung als die Methode der Naturforschung in gedrängter Darstellung. Hauptsächlich nach J.S. Mill*. Braunschweig: Friedrich Vieweg und Sohn, 1865

1602 Schmid, J. von. 'John Stuart Mill's Logica der Geesteswetenschappen,' *Algemeen Nederlands Tijdschrift voor Wijsbegeerte en Psychologie*, 37 (1943-44), 11-20

1603 Schneewind, Jerome B. 'Concerning Some Criticisms of Mill's *Utilitarianism*, 1861-76.' In *James and John Stuart Mill: Papers of the Centenary Conference*. Ed. John M. Robson and Michael Laine. Toronto: University of Toronto Press, 1976, 35-54

1604 —— 'John Stuart Mill.' In *The Encyclopaedia of Philosophy*. Ed. Paul Edwards. 8 vols. New York: Macmillan and Free Press: London: Collier-Macmillan, 1967, V, 314-23

1605 —— *Sidgwick's Ethics and Victorian Moral Philosophy*. Oxford: Clarendon Press, 1977

1606 —— 'Two Unpublished Letters of John Stuart Mill to Henry Sidgwick,' *Mill News Letter*, IX, 2 (1974), 9-11

1607 ——, ed. *Mill: A Collection of Critical Essays*. Garden City, NY: Doubleday, 1968. (Includes articles by Noel Annan, R.P. Anschutz, Jean Austin, J.H. Burns, Maurice Cowling, J.P. Day (2), Richard B. Friedman, Everett W. Hall, R.J. Halliday, Reginald Jackson, J.D. Mabbott, Maurice Mandelbaum, Karl Popper, John M. Robson, Bertrand Russell, J.D. Urmson, G.N.A. Veney, Mary Warnock, which see)

1608 ——, ed. 'Moral Problems and Moral Philosophy in the Victorian Period,' Supplement to *Victorian Studies*, 9 (1965), 29-46. (Discussion of the controversy between Utilitarians and Intuitionists as illustrated in the novels of Charlotte M. Yonge, Mrs Gaskell, William Hale White, and George Eliot)

1609 ——, introd. *Mill's Essays on Literature & Society*. New York: Collier, 1965

1610 ——, introd. *Mill's Ethical Writings*. New York: Collier, 1965

1611 Schneider, Herbert W. 'Mill's Methods and Formal Logic.' In *Studies in the History of Ideas*, III. Ed. Columbia University Department of Philosophy. New York: Columbia University Press, 1935, 407-26. Reprinted 1970

1612 Schneidermeyer, Wilma. 'John Stuart Mill's Principle of Liberty and Legislative Reality,' *Journal of Human Relations*, 20 (1972), 147-55

1613 Schoelcher, Victor. 'Mr Mill and His Clergymen Supporters,' *National Reformer*, 6 (1865), 478-9. (Controversy over remarks in *Sir William Hamilton's Philosophy*)

1614 Schumpeter, J.A. *History of Economic Analysis*. New York: Oxford University Press, 1954. (Many references, particularly to *Principles of Political Economy* and the *Logic*; Chaps. 5, 6)

1615 Schwartz, Pedro. 'Distribucion e instituciones en J.S. Mill,' *Anales de economia*, ns 8 (1964), 709-40

1616 —— 'John Stuart Mill and Laissez Faire: London Water,' *Economica*, ns 33 (1966), 71-83. (Title refers to Metropolitan Sanitary Association and problem with London Water supply bills 1840-51. Cites JSM's correspondence with Chadwick.)

1617 —— 'John Stuart Mill and Socialism,' *Mill News Letter*, IV, 1 (1968), 11-15

1618 —— 'John Stuart Mill y el "laissez-faire,"' *Moneda y credito*, 91 (1964), 59-130

1619 —— *La nueva economia politica de J.S. Mill*. Madrid: Tecnos, SA, 1968. Trans. as *The New Political Economy of J.S. Mill*. London: London School of Economics and Political Science, Weidenfeld and Nicolson; Durham: Duke University Press, 1972

1620 Schweik, Robert C. 'Rhetorical Art and Literary Form in Mill's *The Subjection of Women*,' *Quarterly Journal of Speech*, 61 (1975), 23-30

1621 [Scrope, George Poulett.] 'Irish Clearances, and Improvement of Waste Lands,' *Westminster Review*), 50 (1848), 163-87. (Article quotes JSM on the Irish problem, 173-4)

1622 Seal, Horace. 'The Individual Always the Unit,' *Westminster Review*, 147 (1897), 5-10. (In response to Frederic Harrison [*Nineteenth Century*, 1896], a defence of JSM's comprehension that individuals rather than family units are used in calculations involving the social sciences and politics)

1623 Seccombe, John T. *Science, Theism, and Revelation, Considered in Relation to Mr Mill's Essays on Nature, Religion and Theism*. London: Simpkin, Marshall, 1875

1624 Sée, Henri. 'Stuart Mill et la propriété foncière,' *Revue Internationale de Sociologie*, 32 (1924), 606-19

1625 Selem, Alessandro. 'La teoria dell'induzione di J.S. Mill,' *Studia patavina*, 6 (1959), 524-39

1626 Semmel, Bernard. *The Governor Eyre Controversy*. London: MacGibbon and Kee, 1962

1627 —— *The Rise of Free Trade Imperialism: Classical Political Economy, the Empire of Free Trade and Imperialism, 1750-1850*. Cambridge: Cambridge University Press, 1970

1628 Senior, Nassau William. *Four Introductory Lectures on Political Economy*. London: Longman, Brown, Green, and Longmans, 1852. (Lecture IV denies *contra* JSM that Political Economy is a hypothetical science. Quotes from and analyses *Some Unsettled Questions of Political Economy*.)

1629 —— Letter of 18 Dec. 1844. In *Selections from the Correspondence of the Late Macvey Napier*. Ed. Macvey Napier [the younger]. London:

Macmillan, 1879, 480. (Discusses future articles for the *Edinburgh Review*: 'Factory Labour must be left to Mill. He will be ingenious and original, though I own I do not quite trust his good sense.')

1630 —— 'Mill, The Principles of Political Economy,' *Edinburgh Review*, 88 (1848), 293-339

1631 —— 'Relief of Irish Distress in 1847 and 1848,' *Edinburgh Review*, 89 (1849), 221-68. Reprinted in his *Journals, Conversations and Essays Relating to Ireland*. 2 vols. London: Longmans, Green, 1868, I, 195-264. (Considers Thornton's and JSM's proposals for colonizing Ireland's waste lands, 253-4)

1632 Senn, Peter R. 'The Earliest Use of the Term "Social Science,"' *Journal of the History of Ideas*, 19 (1958), 569-70. (JSM used this term in 1836)

1633 Seth, Andrew [A. Seth Pringle-Pattison]. *The Philosophical Radicals and Other Essays*. Edinburgh and London: Blackwood, 1907

1634 Seth, James. 'The Alleged Fallacies in Mill's "Utilitarianism,"' *Philosophical Review*, 17 (1908), 469-88). Reprinted in his *Essays in Ethics and Religion*. Ed. A. Seth Pringle-Pattison. Edinburgh and London: Blackwood, 1926

1635 —— 'The English Development of Hume's Empiricism.' In his *English Philosophers and Schools of Philosophy*. Channels of English Literature Series. London: Dent; New York: Dutton, 1912, 240-97

1636 —— *A Study of Ethical Principles*. Edinburgh and London: Blackwood, 1894

1637 Shairp, J.C. 'Moral Theories and Christian Ethics,' *North British Review*, ns 8 (1867), 1-46

1638 Shannon, Edgar Finley. *Tennyson and the Reviewers*. Cambridge: Harvard University Press, 1952. 2nd ed. rev. Hamden, Conn.: Archon Books, 1967. (Several references to JSM's 1835 article)

1639 Sharpless, F. Parvir. *The Literary Criticism of John Stuart Mill*. The Hague: Mouton, 1967

1640 —— 'William Johnson Fox and Mill's Essays on Poetry,' *Victorian Newsletter*, 27 (1965), 18-21

1641 ——, introd. *Essays on Poetry by John Stuart Mill*. Columbia: University of South Carolina Press, 1976

1642 Shaw, George Bernard. *The Intelligent Woman's Guide to Socialism and Capitalism*. London: Constable, 1928. (Few references to JSM. Appendix claims JSM 'began as a Ricardian and ended as an avowed socialist.')

1643 Sheddon, Thomas. 'On Sir William Hamilton and Mr Mill.' In his *Three Essays on Philosophical Subjects*. London: Longmans, 1866

1644 Shee, William Archer. *My Contemporaries*. London: Hurst and Blackett, 1893. (Especially 171, 293-5, 306. 'I shall be much surprised if the British House of Commons does not vote him a bore.')

1645 Shine, Hill. 'J.S. Mill and an Open Letter to the Saint-Simonian Society in 1832,' *Journal of the History of Ideas*, 6 (1945), 102-8. (See also Hainds)

1646 Shorey, Paul. 'Mill Revealed in His Letters,' *Dial*, 48 (1910), 417-19. (Review of Elliot's edition of JSM's letters)

1647 Shoul, Bernice. 'Similarities in the Work of John Stuart Mill and Karl Marx,' *Science and Society*, 29 (1965), 18-21

1648 Shumaker, Wayne. *English Autobiography: Its Emergence, Materials, and Form*. Berkeley: University of California Press, 1954, 142-6

1649 Sidgwick, Arthur, and Eleanor Mildred Sidgwick. *Henry Sidgwick: A Memoir*. London: Macmillan, 1906. (Frequent references to JSM especially regarding *Considerations on Representative Government* and *Sir William Hamilton's Philosophy*)

1650 Sidgwick, Henry. 'Bentham and Benthamism in Politics and Ethics,' *Fortnightly Review*, ns 21 (1877), 627-52. Reprinted in his *Miscellaneous Essays and Addresses*. London: Macmillan, 1904, 135-69

1651 —— 'The Economic Lessons of Socialism,' *Economic Journal*, 5 (1895), 336-46. Reprinted in his *Miscellaneous Essays and Addresses*. London: Macmillan, 1904, 235-48

1652 —— 'John Stuart Mill,' *Academy*, 15 May 1873, 193

1653 —— *The Methods of Ethics*. London: Macmillan, 1874. (Revised through 6 eds [6th ed. rev. London: Macmillan, 1901]. Preface to 6th ed. contains an account prepared posthumously from MS material in which Sidgwick discusses the progress of his ethical thought and his debt to and divergence from that of JSM.)

1654 —— 'Philosophy at Cambridge,' *Mind*, 1 (1876), 235-45. (Mentions JSM's strong influence, 244)

1655 —— 'Pleasure & Desire,' *Contemporary Review*, 19 (1872), 664-72.
(In revised form became Bk I, Chap. 4 of *Methods of Ethics*)

1656 Sidgwick, Rose. 'The Library of John Stuart Mill,' *Cornhill
Magazine*, ns 21 (1906), 674-82

1657 Simcox, Edith. 'Influence of J.S. Mill's Writings,' *Contemporary
Review*, 22 (1873), 297-317

1658 Simon, David. *John Stuart Mill und Pestalozzi*. Vienna: Manz, 1904

1659 Simon, Thomas Collins. *Hamilton versus Mill: A Thorough Discussion of
Each Chapter in Mill's Examination of Hamilton*. 2 pts. Edinburgh,
1866, 1868

1660 Simon, W.M. *European Positivism in the Nineteenth Century: An Essay in
Intellectual History*. Ithaca: Cornell University Press, 1963, 172-301.
(Discusses JSM's role in introducing Positivist ideas to England
and his relations with Comte)

1661 Singer, Marcus George. 'Actual Consequence Utilitarianism,' *Mind*, 86
(1977), 67-77

1662 —— *Generalizations on Ethics*. New York: Knopf, 1961. 311-18
reprinted as 'Duties to Oneself.' In *Limits of Liberty: Studies of
Mill's 'On Liberty.'* Ed. Peter Radcliffe. Belmont: Wadsworth, 1966,
108-14

1663 —— 'On Rawls On Mill On Liberty and So On,' *Journal of Value
Inquiry*, 11 (1977), 141-8. (See Rawls)

1664 Sirkin, Gerald, and Natalie Robinson Sirkin. 'John Stuart Mill and
Disutilitarianism in Indian Education,' *Journal of General Education*,
24 (1973), 231-85

1665 —— 'Mill in India House: A Little Bureaucratic Tale in Two Letters,'
Mill News Letter, IX, 2 (1974), 3-7

1666 Smart, J.J.C. 'Extreme and Restricted Utilitarianism,' *Philosophical
Quarterly*, 6 (1956), 344-54. Reprinted in *Mill: Utilitarianism*.
Ed. S. Gorovitz. Indianapolis and New York: Bobbs-Merrill, 1971,
195-203. (See also Mabbott, Mandelbaum, Urmson)

1667 —— *An Outline of a System of Utilitarian Ethics*. Parkerville:
Melbourne University Press, 1961. Reprinted in his and Barnard Williams'
Utilitarianism For and Against. Cambridge: Cambridge University Press,
1973, 3-74

1668 Smith, Colin. *John Stuart Mill, ou la réalité des sensations*. Paris: Seshers, 1973. (General discussion and selection of texts translated into French)

1669 Smith, Henry Boynton. 'Mill's Examination of Hamilton's Philosophy,' *American Presbyterian and Theological Review*, 4 (1866), 126-62

1670 Smith, James M., and Ernest Sosa, eds. *Mill's 'Utilitarianism': Text and Criticism*. Belmont: Wadsworth, 1969. (Includes articles by: Jean Austin, F.H. Bradley [from *Ethical Studies*], N. Kretzmann, J.D. Mabbott, G.E. Moore [from *Principia Ethica*], Ernest Sosa, J.O. Urmson, which see)

1671 [Smith, William Henry.] 'J.S. Mill on Our Belief in the External World,' *Blackwood's Magazine*, 99 (1866), 20-45

1672 [——] 'Mill's *Logic*,' *Blackwood's Magazine*, 54 (1843), 415-30. (Review)

1673 [——] '*Political Economy*, by J.S. Mill,' *Blackwood's Magazine*, 64 (1848), 407-28. (Review)

1674 Solly, Henry. *These Eighty Years*. 2 vols. London: Simpkin and Marshall, 1893. (Reminiscences of JSM as a young man)

1675 Somervell, D.C. *English Thought in the Nineteenth Century*. London: Methuen, 1926. (JSM discussed 93-8 and mentioned *passim*. 'That so dry a writer should have been widely read is in itself a testimonial to the seriousness of his age.')

1676 Sosa, Ernest. 'Mill's *Utilitarianism*.' In *Mill's 'Utilitarianism'*. Ed. J.M. Smith and Ernest Sosa. Belmont: Wadsworth, 1969, 155-72

1677 Souday, P. 'La Correspondance de Stuart Mill et d'Auguste Comte,' *Le Temps*, 31 Jan. 1899

1678 Spahr, Margaret. 'Mill on Paternalism in Its Place.' In *Liberty*. Ed. Carl J. Friedrich. *Nomos* (Yearbook of the American Society for Political and Legal Philosophy), IV. New York: Atherton; London: Prentice-Hall, 1962, 162-75

1679 Spalding, J.L. 'Review of Autobiography of John Stuart Mill,' *Catholic World*, 18 (1874), 721-33. ('Dr Newman's Apologia ... will be read with delight when Mill and his book have been forgotten')

1680 Spence, G.W. 'John Stuart Mill, an Imperialist with a Philosophy of History,' *Cambridge Review*, 89A (1968), 380-2

1681 —— 'The Psychology behind J.S. Mill's "Proof,"' *Philosophy*, 43
(1968), 18-28. (Uses, *inter alia*, JSM's notes to his father's
Analysis)

1682 Spencer, Herbert. 'John Stuart Mill: His Moral Character,' *Examiner*,
17 May 1873, 508-9. Reprinted in *Popular Science Monthly*, 3 (1873),
373-5; in *John Stuart Mill: Notices of His Life and Works*. Ed. H.R.
Fox Bourne. London: Dallow, 1873, 38-42; and as 'John Stuart Mill's
Moral Character,' *Appleton's Journal*, 9 (1873), 791-2

1683 —— 'Mill *versus* Hamilton - The Test of Truth,' *Fortnightly Review*,
1 (1865), 531-50

1684 Spengler, Joseph J. 'J.S. Mill on Economic Development.' In *Theories
of Economic Growth*. Ed. B.F. Hoselitz, *et al*. Glencoe, Ill.: Free
Press, 1960, 113-54

1685 Spiegelberg, Herbert. '"Accident of Birth": A Non-utilitarian Motif in
Mill's Philosophy,' *Journal of the History of Ideas*, 22 (1961),
475-92. (An examination JSM's use of 'accident of birth' and related
phrases and of its importance in supplementing his definition of
justice)

1686 Spitz, David. 'Freedom and Individuality: Mill's *Liberty* in Retrospect.'
In *Liberty*. Ed. Carl J. Friedrich. *Nomos* (Yearbook of the
American Society for Political and Legal Philosophy), IV. New York:
Atherton; London: Prentice-Hall, 1962, 176-226. Reprinted in *On Liberty*.
Ed. David Spitz. New York: Norton, 1975, 203-38

1687 —— 'The Pleasures of Misunderstanding Freedom,' *Dissent*, 13
(1966), 729-39. (A reply to Michael Walzer's 'On the Nature of Freedom,'
ibid., 725-8, which discusses Spitz's article, 'Pure Tolerance,'
which see)

1688 —— 'Politics and the Realms of Being,' *Dissent*, 6 (1959), 56-65.
(Mainly criticism of Hannah Arendt's attitude to segregation;
compares her argument to JSM's in *On Liberty*)

1689 —— 'Pure Tolerance: A Critique of Criticisms,' *Dissent*, 13
(1966), 510-25. (See also *ibid*., 729-39. Review article of Robert
Wolff, Barrington Moore, and Herbert Marcuse, *A Critique of Pure
Reason*, which see. Highly critical of what he sees as distortions of
JSM's ideas. See also Green, Wolff.)

1690 ——, ed. *On Liberty*. Norton Critical Edition. New York: Norton,
1975. (Includes Anon., 'Mill on Liberty,' *National Review* [1859];

and articles by Maurice Cowling [from *Mill and Liberalism*], Patrick Devlin, H.L.A. Hart, Willmoore Kendall, A.W. Levi, David Spitz, Fitzjames Stephen [from *Liberty, Equality, Fraternity*], C.L. Ten, which see)

1691 Spivey, Edward. 'Carlyle and the Logic Choppers: J.S. Mill and Diderot.' In *Carlyle and His Contemporaries: Essays in Honor of Charles Richard Sanders*. Ed. John Clubbe. Durham, NC: Duke University Press, 1976, 60-73

1692 —— '"Here Is a New Mystic,"' *Mill News Letter*, V, 2 (1970), 5-6. (On Carlyle and *The Spirit of the Age*)

1693 Sprague, A.P. ['Mill and Agassiz,'] *National Quarterly Review*, 28 (1873), 234

1694 Stammhammer, Josef. 'John Stuart Mill.' In his *Handwörterbuch der Staatswissenschaft*. 5 vols., 2 supplements. Jena: Gustav Fischer, 1890-97, IV, 1182-4. Revised by C. Meitzel, 1925, IV, 583-4

1695 Stamp, Josiah Charles. 'New Letters of John Stuart Mill,' *The Times*, 29 Dec. 1938, 9-10

1696 Stebbing, L. Susan. *Modern Introduction to Logic*. London: Methuen, 1930. Revised 1933

1697 Stebbing, William. *Analysis of Mr Mill's System of Logic*. London: Longman, Green, Longman, Roberts, and Green, 1864

1698 Steele, E.D. *Irish Land and British Politics*. [London:] Cambridge University Press, 1974

1699 —— 'J.S. Mill and the Irish Question: The Principles of Political Economy, 1848-1865,' *Historical Journal*, 13 (1970), 216-36

1700 —— 'J.S. Mill and the Irish Question: Reform and the Integrity of the Empire, 1865-1870,' *Historical Journal*, 13 (1970), 419-50

1701 Stegenga, James A. 'John Stuart Mill's Concept of Liberty and the Principle of Utility,' *Journal of Value Inquiry*, 7 (1973), 281-9

1702 Steintrager, James. *Bentham*. London: Allen and Unwin, 1977

1703 —— 'Morality and Belief: The Origin and Purpose of Bentham's Writings on Religion,' *Mill News Letter*, VI, 2 (1971), 3-15

1704 Stephen, James Fitzjames. *Liberty, Equality, Fraternity*. London: Smith Elder, 1873. Reprinted with introduction by R.J. White. Cambridge: Cambridge University Press, 1967. Selections reprinted in *Limits of*

Liberty: Studies of Mill's 'On Liberty.' Ed. Peter Radcliffe. Belmont: Wadsworth, 1966, 43-57; and in *On Liberty.* Ed. David Spitz. New York: Norton, 1975, 142-53. Trans. M. Muromtsev as *Svoboda, ravenstuo, i bratstvo.* St Petersburg: Benke, 1907. (Anti-positivist, anti-democratic critique of JSM's views in *On Liberty*)

1705 —— 'Mr Spencer on Mr Mill,' *Saturday Review*, 12 Aug. 1865, 199-201

1706 —— 'A Note on Utilitarianism.' In his *Liberty, Equality, Fraternity.* London: Smith Elder, 1873, 335-50. (A shortened reprint of his 'Utilitarianism,' *Pall Mall Gazette*, 1869. 'Suggested by some criticisms on a work of Mr Lecky's, which have lost their interest. I have accordingly omitted all reference to Mr. Lecky and his critics....')

1707 [Stephen, Leslie.] 'The Comtist Utopia,' *Fraser's Magazine*, 80 (1869), 1-21. (A survey of Comtist doctrine and a discussion of JSM's points of disagreement with the Comtists)

1708 —— *The English Utilitarians.* 3 vols. London: Duckworth, 1900. (Vol. III devoted to JSM)

1709 —— 'John Stuart Mill,' *Dictionary of National Biography* (1837-38), XIII, 390-9

1710 —— 'The Late Stuart Mill,' *Nation*, 16 (1873), 382-3

1711 —— *Life of Henry Fawcett.* London: Smith Elder, 1885. (Shows Fawcett's debt to JSM)

1712 —— [?]. 'Mr Lecky's *History of European Morals*,' *Fraser's Magazine*, 80 (1869), 273-84. (Houghton attribution uncertain)

1713 —— 'Mr Mill and the Land Laws,' *Nation*, 16 (1873), 71-2

1714 —— 'Mr Mill on the Land Question,' *Nation*, 12 (1871), 414-15

1715 —— 'Some Early Impressions,' *National Review*, 42 (1903), 208-24. (A brief sketch of JSM's influence on the young Stephen and impressions of JSM's performance in the House of Commons)

1716 Stevenson, Lionel. '1859: Year of Fulfillment,' *Centennial Review*, 3 (1959), 337-56. (The most notable books published in 1859, including *On Liberty*)

1717 Stewart, H.L. 'J.S. Mill's *Logic*: A Post-centenary Appraisal,' *University of Toronto Quarterly*, 17 (1947), 361-71

1718   Stigler, George L. 'The Nature and Role of Originality in Scientific Progress,' *Economica*, ns 22 (1955), 293-302. Reprinted in his *Essays in the History of Economics*. Chicago: University of Chicago Press, 1965, 1-15. (Discussion of six important contributions by JSM to economic thought, usually overlooked as original because JSM did not trumpet forth his originality)

1719   —— 'The Scientific Uses of Scientific Biography, with Special Reference to J.S. Mill.' In *James and John Stuart Mill: Papers of the Centenary Conference*. Ed. John M. Robson and Michael Laine. Toronto: University of Toronto Press, 1976, 55-66. (Chiefly concerns economics)

1720   Stillinger, Jack. 'The Text of John Stuart Mill's *Autobiography*,' *Bulletin of the John Rylands Library*, 43 (1960), 220-42

1721   ——, ed. *Autobiography by John Stuart Mill*. Boston: Houghton Mifflin, Riverside Editions, 1969

1722   ——, ed. *The Early Draft of John Stuart Mill's Autobiography*. Urbana: University of Illinois Press, 1961

1723   ——, ed. *J.S. Mill, Autobiography and Other Writings*. Boston: Houghton Mifflin, 1969. (Includes, in addition to the *Autobiography*, 'Thoughts on Poetry and Its Varieties,' 'Bentham,' 'Coleridge,' 'Nature,' and *On Liberty*)

1724   Stirling, James. 'Annotations and Supplementary Notes' to his trans. of Albert Schwegler's *Handbook of the History of Philosophy*. Edinburgh: Edmonston and Douglas, 1867. Frequently reprinted and corrected. (JSM and Comte in relation to Hegel)

1725   —— 'Mr Mill on Trades Unions: A Criticism.' In *Recess Studies*. Ed. Alexander Grant. Edinburgh: Edmonston and Douglas, 1870, 309-32. Trans. T.N. Bernard as 'De quelques opinions de M. Stuart Mill sur l'unionisme ouvrier,' *Journal des Economistes*, 3e sér, 20 (1870), 5-26

1726   Stocker, Michael. 'Consequentialism and Its Complexities,' *American Philosophical Quarterly*, 6 (1969), 276-89. (General discussion with some references to JSM)

1727   Stocks, John Leafric. 'The Empiricism of John Stuart Mill.' In his *Reason and Intuition, and Other Essays*. London: Oxford University Press, 1939, 208-17

1728   Stokes, Eric. *The English Utilitarians and India*. Oxford: Clarendon Press, 1959

1729 Stone, Donald David. *Novelists in a Changing World: Meredith, James, and the Transformation of English Fiction in the 1880's.* Cambridge: Harvard University Press, 1972. (Sketchy references to JSM, but clearly sees him as a strong influence. Lionel Stevenson, reviewing Stone [*Nineteenth-Century Fiction,* 27 (1972), 222]: 'The most potent new influences on fiction are defined as Nietzsche and Pater, with a runner-up [surprisingly] in John Stuart Mill.')

1730 Stork, C.A. 'Mr Mill's Autobiography as a Contribution to Christian Evidence,' *Quarterly Review of the Evangelical Lutheran Church,* 4 (1874), 258-77

1731 Storring, Gustav Wilhelm. *J. Stuart Mills Theorie über den psychologischen Ursprung des Vulgärglaubens an die Aussenwelt.* Halle: von Knoll and Wölbling, 1889

1732 Stout, George F. 'Belief,' *Mind,* 16 (1891), 449-69. (Includes discussion of James Mill and JSM on association of ideas. See also Baldwin and Pikler.)

1733 —— 'The Genesis of the Cognition of Physical Reality,' *Mind,* 15 (1890), 22-45. (Begins with an examination and rejection of JSM's theory. Discusses permanent possibilities of sensation, *Sir William Hamilton's Philosophy.* See also Baldwin and Pikler.)

1734 Strachey, A. 'J.S. Mill's Philosophy Tested by W.S. Jevons,' *Mind,* 3 (1878), 283-7. (See Jevons)

1735 Strachey, Ray [formerly Rachel Costelloe]. *'The Cause': History of the Women's Movement in Great Britain.* London: Bell, 1928. (Frequent references to JSM; photo)

1736 Strakhov, Nikolay Nikolayevich. *Zhensky vopros. Razbor sochineniya Dzhona Styuarta Millya 'O podchinenii zhenshchiny' [The Woman Question. An Analysis of John Stuart Mill's Work, 'On the Subjection of Women'].* St Petersburg, 1871

1737 Street, Charles Larrabee. *Individualism and Individuality in the Philosophy of John Stuart Mill.* Milwaukee: Moorehouse, 1926

1738 Stroll, A. 'Mill's Fallacy,' *Dialogue,* 3 (1965), 385-404

1739 Strong, Edward W. 'William Whewell and John Stuart Mill: Their Controversy about Scientific Knowledge,' *Journal of the History of Ideas,* 16 (1955), 209-31

1740 Struhl, P.R. 'Mill's Notion of Social Responsibility,' *Journal of the History of Ideas,* 37 (1976), 155-62

1741 Stuart-Glennie, J.S. 'James and John Stuart Mill: Traditional and Personal Memorials,' *Macmillan's Magazine*, 45 (1882), 490-8. Reprinted in *Eclectic Magazine*, ns 35 (1882), 74-82; and in *Littell's Living Age*, 153 (1882), 236-43

1742 —— 'The Principle of the Conservation of Force and Mr Mill's System of Logic,' *Nature*, 7 Apr. 1870, 583

1743 Sugihara, S., and S. Yamashita. 'J.S. Mill and Modern Japan,' *Mill News Letter*, XII, 2 (1977), 2-6

1744 [Sully, James.] 'Professor Grote and the Utilitarian Philosophy,' *Westminster Review*, ns 95 (1871), 41-55. (Review of Grote's *Examination of the Utilitarian Philosophy*)

1745 Summers, R. 'John Stuart Mill and Liberty,' *Adelphi*, ns 20 (1944), 39-45

1746 Sumner, L.W. 'Mill and the Death Penalty,' *Mill News Letter*, XI, 1 (1976), 2-7

1747 —— 'Mill and the Death Penalty: Some Addenda,' *Mill News Letter*, XIII, 2 (1978), 13-19

1748 —— 'More Light on the Later Mill,' *Philosophical Review*, 83 (1974), 504-27. (Review of *Later Letters of John Stuart Mill, 1849-1873*, ed. Francis E. Mineka and Dwight N. Lindley, *Collected Works*, XIV-XVII [Toronto: University of Toronto Press, 1972])

1749 Sutherland, J. 'An Alleged Gap in Mill's Utilitarianism,' *Mind*, 11 (1886), 597-9

1750 Swart, Koenraad. '"Individualism" in the Mid-Nineteenth Century,' *Journal of the History of Ideas*, 23 (1962), 77-90. (Brief reference to JSM)

1751 Syford, Ethel. 'Recent Letters of John Stuart Mill,' *New England Magazine*, ns 43 (1911), 643-8

1752 Sylvester, Robert P. 'Pleasures: Higher and Lower,' *Personalist*, 56 (1975), 129-37

1753 Szerer, Mieczyslaw. 'Zywot Czlowieka Madrego' ['The Life of a Scientist'], *Droga*, 5 (1930), 399-416. Cited in *Social Science Abstracts*, 4 (1932), 1732 (no 18119)

1754 T., L. 'Autobiography of John Stuart Mill,' *Southern Magazine*, 14 (1874), 667-72. (Review, signed L.T., concentrates on mental crisis. 'When Mr Mill talks of love we have a cold shiver. A man who took quite late in life to poetry to galvanise his heart, which had been killed by analysis and philosophy, could hardly have been capable of a very profound passion.')

1755 Tabanets, P. 'Mill', Dzhon Styuart' ['Mill, John Stuart']. In *Filosofskya entsiklopediya [Philosophical Encyclopedia]*. Moscow, 1964, III, 442-3

1756 Taine, Hippolyte Adolphe. 'John Stuart Mill et son système de logique,' *Revue des Deux Mondes*, 32 (1861), 44-82. Trans. as 'Sovremennaya angliyskaya filosofiya. Dzhon Styuart Mill' i yevo sistema logiki' ['Contemporary English Philosophy. John Stuart Mill and His System of Logic'], *Vremya [Time]*, 3 (1861), 356-93

1757 —— 'La Philosophie. Stuart Mill.' In his *Histoire de la littérature anglaise*. 4 vols. Paris: Hachette, 1863-64, IV, 339-429. Trans. H. van Laun as *History of English Literature*. 2 vols. Edinburgh: Edmonston and Douglas, 1871, II, 477-517. (Discussion of *Logic*)

1758 —— *Le Positivisme anglais: étude sur Stuart Mill*. Paris, 1864. Trans. T.D. Haye as *English Positivism: A Study on John Stuart Mill*. London: Simpkin, Marshall, 1870

1759 Tanesse, Georges. 'La Philosophie pratique de John Stuart Mill,' *Revue de l'Enseignement Philosophique*, 14 (1963), 12-24

1760 ——, introd. and trans. *L'Utilitarisme*. Toulouse: Pravat, 1964

1761 Tarozzi, Giuseppe. *Stuart Mill*. 2 vols. Milan: Athena, 1929-31

1762 Tatalovitch, Anne. 'John Stuart Mill - *The Subjection of Women*: An Analysis,' *Southern Quarterly*, 12 (1973), 87-105

1763 Tatarkiewicz, Wladyslaw. 'John Stuart Mill and Empiricism.' In his *Nineteenth Century Philosophy*. Belmont: Wadsworth, 1974, 32-44. Trans. from Vol. III of his *Historia filozofi*. Warsaw: Panstwowe Wydawnictwo Naukowe, 1970

1764 Tate, Allen. See Huntington Cairns

1765 Taussig, Frank William. 'John Stuart Mill.' In his *Wages and Capital*. London: Macmillan; New York: Appleton, 1896, 216-40

1766 —— 'Longe - Thornton - Mill - Cairnes.' In his *Wages and Capital*. London: Macmillan; New York: Appleton, 1896, 241-65

1767 Tawney, Guy Allan. *John Stuart Mill's Theory of Inductive Logic*. Cincinnati: Cincinnati University Press, 1909

1768 Taylor, Algernon. *Memories of a Student*. London: Simpkin, Marshall, Hamilton, Kent, 1895. (Taylor was Harriet Mill's son)

1769 Taylor, Henry. *Autobiography*. 2 vols. London: Longmans, Green, 1885. (Contains description of the young JSM at the London Debating Society)

1770 —— *Correspondence of Henry Taylor*. Ed. Edward Dowden. London: Longmans, Green, 1888. (Descriptions of JSM as a young man)

1771 —— 'Mr Mill on the Subjection of Women,' *Fraser's Magazine*, ns 1 (1870), 143-65

1772 Taylor, Mary. 'Mrs John Stuart Mill: A Vindication by Her Granddaughter,' *Nineteenth Century and After*, 71 (1912), 357-63. (Reply to Anon., 'Famous Autobiographies,' which see)

1773 —— 'Some Notes on the Private Life of John Stuart Mill.' In *The Letters of John Stuart Mill*. Ed. H.S.R. Elliot. 2 vols. London: Longmans, 1910, xxxix-xlvi

1774 Taylor, Richard. 'The Classical Defence of Liberty.' In his *Freedom, Anarchy and the Law*. Englewood Cliffs, NJ: Prentice-Hall, 1973, 55-61. (Argues that JSM's principle as formulated in *On Liberty* is 'a vague and meaningless exhortation' as no law really violates it)

1775 Taylor, Robert H. *Authors at Work*. New York: Grolier Club, 1957. (Address at opening of exhibition of MSS; catalogue and reproductions. Address refers to the loss by JSM of Carlyle's *French Revolution*. No JSM MS in exhibition.)

1776 Ten, C.L. 'Enforcing a Shared Morality,' *Ethics*, 82 (1972), 321-9. (Critical of attempts by Patrick Devlin in *The Enforcement of Morals* and Basil Mitchell in *Law, Morality and Religion in a Secular Society* to suggest that society may legislate against individuals in order to enforce a shared morality associated with certain important social structures and institutions in face of JSM's views in *On Liberty*)

1777 —— 'The Liberal Theory of the Open Society.' In *The Open Society in Theory and Practice*. Ed. Dante Germino and Klaus von Beyme. The Hague: Nijhoff, 1974, 142-63

1778 —— 'Mill and Liberty,' *Journal of the History of Ideas*, 30 (1969), 47-68

1779 —— 'Mill on Self-Regarding Actions,' *Philosophy*, 43 (1968), 29-37. Reprinted in *Mill: Utilitarianism*. Ed. S. Gorovitz.

Indianapolis and New York: Bobbs-Merrill, 1971, 345-51; and in *On Liberty*. Ed. David Spitz. New York: Norton, 1975, 238-46

1780 —— 'Mill's Stable Society,' *Mill News Letter*, VII, 1 (1971), 2-6

1781 —— 'Self-Regarding Conduct and Utilitarianism,' *Australasian Journal of Philosophy*, 55 (1977), 105-13

1782 [Tennant, Charles.] *Utilitarianism Explained and Exemplified in Moral and Political Government*. London: Longman, Green, Longman, Roberts, and Green, 1864

1783 Thayer, J.B. 'Mill's Dissertations and Discussions,' *North American Review*, 100 (1865), 259-66

1784 Thibaudeau, A.W. *Catalogue of the Collection of Autograph Letters and Historical Documents Formed between 1865 and 1882 by Alfred Morrison*. 6 vols. London: privately printed, 1883-92, IV, 252-7. (14 letters 1834-36, chiefly to A.M. Guilbert dealing with matters concerning the *London Review*)

1785 Thieme, Erich. *Die Sozialethik John Stuart Mills*. Leipzig: Wiegandt, 1910

1786 Thilly, Frank. 'The Individualism of John Stuart Mill,' *Philosophical Review*, 32 (1923), 1-17. (Deals chiefly with the implications of Bk VI of the *Logic*)

1787 Thirlwall, Connop. 'The Bishop of St David's on Mr Mill's Heresy,' *Spectator*, 38 (1865), 667-8. (Letter defending JSM against an anonymous attack in the *Record* [1865], which see. Refers to *Sir William Hamilton's Philosophy*, Chap. 7. See *Later Letters of John Stuart Mill, 1849-1873*, ed. Francis E. Mineka and Dwight N. Lindley, Vols. XIV-XVII of *Collected Works* [Toronto: University of Toronto Press, 1972], XVI, 1070, 1079; and Sangar above.)

1788 Thom, John H., ed. *The Life of the Rev Joseph Blanco White*. 3 vols. London: Chapman, 1845. (Contains letters to JSM in 1830s, mostly about the *London Review*)

1789 Thomas, William E.S. 'James Mill's Politics: A Rejoinder,' *Historical Journal*, 14 (1971), 735-50. (A reply to W.R. Carr, 'James Mill's Politics Reconsidered,' which see)

1790 —— 'James Mill's Politics: The "Essay on Government" and the Movement for Reform,' *Historical Journal*, 12 (1969), 249-84. (Presents a thesis contradicting Joseph Hamburger, 'James Mill on Universal Suffrage and the Middle Class,' *Journal of Politics*, 24

[1962], 167-90, who argues that James Mill advocates universal suffrage in the *Essay on Government*. Thomas refers to JSM's views on Catholic relief in Ireland and on suffrage. See Thomas, 'James Mill's Politics'; and Carr.)

1791 —— 'J.S. Mill and the Uses of Autobiography,' *History*, 56 (1971), 341-59

1792 —— 'The Philosophic Radicals.' In *Pressure from Without in Early Victorian England*. Ed. Patricia Hollis. London: Arnold, 1974, 52-79

1793 ——, and Francis E. Mineka, eds. 'New Letters of J.S. Mill to Sir William Molesworth,' *Mill News Letter*, VI, 1 (1970), 1-13

1794 Thompson, Daniel G. 'President Porter on Mill,' *National Quarterly Review*, 41 (1880), 377-414. (See Noah Porter)

1795 Thompson, Kenneth. *Auguste Comte: The Foundation of Sociology*. London: Nelson, 1976. (Includes selections from the Comte-Mill correspondence)

1796 Thompson, M.H., Jr. 'J.S. Mill's Theory of Truth: A Study in Metaphysics and Logic,' *Philosophical Review*, 56 (1947), 273-92

1797 Thorlby, Anthony. 'Liberty and Self-development: Goethe and John Stuart Mill,' *Neohelicon*, 1 (1973), 91-110

1798 Thornton, William Thomas. 'Anti-Utilitarianism,' *Fortnightly Review*, ns 8 (1870), 314-37

1799 —— 'John Stuart Mill: His Career in the India House,' *Examiner*, 17 May 1873, 506-8. Reprinted in *Popular Science Monthly*, 3 (1873), 371-3; and in *John Stuart Mill: Notices of His Life and Works*. Ed. H.R. Fox Bourne. London: Dallow, 1873, 30-7

1800 —— *Old-Fashioned Ethics and Common-Sense Metaphysics, with Some of Their Applications*. London: Macmillan, 1873. (An attack on Utilitarianism and on scientific atheism with special reference to JSM)

1801 Thouverez, Emile. *Stuart Mill*. Paris: Bloud, 1905

1802 Thwing, Charles Franklin. 'Education According to John Stuart Mill,' *School and Society*, 3 (1916), 1-8, 49-58

1803 —— 'The Grave of Mill,' *Nation*, 127 (1928), 201

1804 Tillotson, Geoffrey. 'A Mill-Lewes Item,' *Mill News Letter*, IV, 2 (1969), 17-18

1805 Tocqueville, Alexis de. *Oeuvres, papiers et correspondances.*
Vols. V and VI of *Oeuvres complètes.* Ed. J.-P. Mayer. Paris:
Gallimard, 1954. (Letters to and from JSM)

1806 Todhunter, Isaac. *William Whewell. An Account of His Writings, with
Selections from His Correspondence.* London: Macmillan, 1876.
(Contains discussions of JSM's work and of his criticism of Whewell)

1807 Tollemache, Lionel A. 'Mr Charles Austin,' *Fortnightly Review*, ns 17
(1875), 321-38. (Discusses differences between Austin and JSM.
Repeats anecdote which refers to JSM as 'Very like a melon. ...
There is a great spot in him, just as there is in the melon; and, just
as the melon owes all its richness to the spot, so it is with John Mill
also.')

1808 Tollison, Robert D. See Ekelund

1809 Tonsor, S.J. 'John Stuart Mill's Essays on Politics and Culture,'
National Review, 13 (1962), 396-8

1810 Torrens, Robert. *The Budget. On Commercial and Colonial Policy. With
an Introduction in Which the Deductive Method, as Presented in Mr Mill's
System of Logic, Is Applied to the Solution of Some Controverted
Questions in Political Economy.* London: Smith, Elder, 1844

1811 —— *The Principles and Practical Operation of Sir Robert Peel's
Bill of 1844, Explained and Defended Against the Objections of Tooke,
Fullarton, and Wilson. With Additional Chapters on Money, the Gold
Discoveries, and International Exchange; and a Critical Examination of
the Chapter 'On the Regulation of a Convertible Paper Currency,' in
J.S. Mill's 'Principles of Political Economy.'* 2nd ed. London:
Longmans, 1857. (1st ed. [1848] does not have additional chapters)

1812 Towers, [Robertson] C. Marion D. 'John Stuart Mill and the London and
Westminster Review,' *Atlantic Monthly*, 69 (1892), 58-74

1813 Towle, George M. 'John Stuart Mill,' *Appleton's Journal of Literature,
Science, and Art*, 3 (1870), 126-9. (Biographical sketch and portrait)

1814 Towry, M.H. 'On the Doctrine of Natural Kinds,' *Mind*, 12 (1887), 434-8.
(Replies by F. and C.L. Franklin, and by W.H.S. Monck, which see)

1815 Trakhtenberg, O.V. *Ocherki po istorii filosofii i sotsiologii Anglii
XIX veka* [*Essays in the History of Philosophy and Sociology in England
in the Nineteenth Century*]. Moscow, 1959

1816 Trevelyan, George Macaulay. *The Life of John Bright.* London:
Constable, 1913

1817   Tricerri, Carlo. *Il sistema filosofico-guiridico di John Stuart Mill.*
        Milan: Giuffrè, 1950

1818   Trilling, Diana. 'Mill's Intellectual Beacon,' *Partisan Review*, 19
        (1952), 115-16, 118-20. (Review of Hayek, *John Stuart Mill and Harriet
        Taylor*)

1819   Trilling, Lionel. *Matthew Arnold.* New York: Columbia University
        Press; London: Allen and Unwin, 1949, 259-65. (Relations between
        Culture and Anarchy and *On Liberty*)

1820   Trimen, Henry. 'John Stuart Mill: His Botanical Studies,' *Examiner*,
        17 May 1873, 509-10. Reprinted in *Popular Science Monthly*, 3 (1873),
        375-7; and in *John Stuart Mill: Notices of His Life and Works*. Ed.
        H.R. Fox Bourne. London: Dallow, 1873, 43-8

1821   Tuell, Anne Kimball. *John Sterling.* New York: Macmillan, 1941

1822   Tugan-Baranovsky, Mikhail Ivanovich. *Dzhon-Styuart Mill'. Yevo zhizn'
        i uchono-literaturnaya deyatel'nost'* [*John Stuart Mill. His Life and
        His Scholarly and Literary Activity*]. St Petersburg, 1892

1823   —— 'Mill', Dzhon-Styuart' ['Mill, John Stuart']. In
        Entsiklopedichesky slovar' [*Encyclopedic Dictionary*]. Ed. F.A.
        Brockhaus and I.A. Yefron. St Petersburg, 1896, XXXVII, 306-8

1824   Turgeon, Charles Marie Joseph. *La Valeur d'après les économistes
        anglais depuis Adam Smith jusqu' à nos jours.* Rennes, 1913. Published
        dissertation. Revised and completed by Charles Turgeon and Charles-Henri
        Turgeon as *La Valeur d'après les économistes anglais et français.*
        Paris: Société de Recueil Sirey, 1921

1825   Turin, Sergei Petrovich. 'Nicholas Chernyshevsky and John Stuart Mill,'
        Slavonic Revie, 9 (1930), 29-33. Reprinted London: Eyre and
        Spottiswoode, 1930

1826   Turner, Bryan.S. 'The Concept of Social Stationariness: Utilitarianism
        and Marxism,' *Science and Society*, 38 (1974), 3-18

1827   Turner, Frank Miller. *Between Science and Religion: The Reaction to
        Scientific Naturalism in Late Victorian England.* New Haven and London:
        Yale University Press, 1974

1828   Tyler, Moses Coit. 'Mr Mill in the House of Commons,' *Nation*, 2
        (1866), 598-9

1829   Ueberweg, Friedrich. *Das neunzehnte Jahrhundert.* Vol. IV of
        Grundriss der Geschichte der Philosophie. Berlin: Mittler, 1906,
        425-32. (Numerous printings)

1830 Ulam, Adam Bruno. *Philosophical Foundations of English Socialism.* Cambridge: Harvard University Press, 1951

1831 Upton, Charles Barnes. 'Mill's Essays on Religion,' *Theological Review*, 12 (1875), 127-45, 249-72

1832 Urmson, J.O. 'The Interpretation of the Moral Philosophy of J.S. Mill,' *Philosophical Quarterly*, 3 (1953), 33-9. Reprinted in *Mill: A Collection of Critical Essays.* Ed. J.B. Schneewind. Garden City, NY: Doubleday, 1968, 179-89; in *Mill's 'Utilitarianism.'* Ed. J.M. Smith and E. Sosa. Belmont: Wadsworth, 1969, 117-25; and in *Mill: Utilitarianism.* Ed. S. Gorovitz. Indianapolis and New York: Bobbs-Merrill, 1971, 168-74. (See also Mabbott, Mandelbaum, Smart)

1833 V., B. 'John Stuart Mill on Religion,' *National Reformer*, 24 (1874), 290-2, 309-10, 329-30, 345-7, 362-8, 377-9, 390-1, 403-4

1834 V., Ye. 'Zhizn' Dzhona Styuarta Millya' ['The Life of John Stuart Mill'], *Severny vestnik* [*Northern Herald*], 3 (1889), 195-222; 4:129-48; 5:73-101

1835 Van Arsdel, Rosemary T. 'The *Westminster Review*: Change of Editorship, 1840,' *Studies in Bibliography*, 25 (1972), 191-204. (Uses material from Cole's diary and Robertson's letters. Suggests alterations to Mineka's dating of JSM's letters concerning this matter.)

1836 Van Doren, Mark. See Huntington Cairns

1837 van Holthoon, F.L. 'Enkele opmerkingen over Mill's *On Liberty*,' *Wijsgerig perspectief op maatschappij en wetenschap*, 13e jaargang, no 5 (1972-73), 218-40

1838 —— *The Road to Utopia: A Study of John Stuart Mill's Social Thought.* Speculum historiale, 7. Assen: van Gorcum, 1971

1839 [Vasey, George.] *Individual Liberty, Legal, Moral, and Licentious; in Which the Political Fallacies of J.S. Mill's Essay 'On Liberty' Are Pointed Out.* 2nd ed. London: Burns, 1877. 1st ed., 1867, signed 'Index'

1840 Vaysset-Boutbien, R. *Stuart Mill et la sociologie française contemporaine.* Paris: Presses Universitaires, 1941

1841 Veblen, Thorstein. 'The Preconceptions of Economic Science: III,' *Quarterly Journal of Economics*, 14 (1900), 240-69. Reprinted in his *The Place of Science in Modern Civilization and Other Essays.* New York: Huebsch, 1919, 148-79; and in *Veblen on Marx, Race, Science and*

Economics (The Place of Science, etc.). New York: Capricorn, 1969. (Discusses the philosophical background referring especially to JSM and Cairnes)

1842 Venn, John. *The Principles of Empirical or Inductive Logic*. London and Cambridge: Macmillan, 1899. 2nd ed., 1907

1843 Véran, Jules. 'Le Souvenir de Stuart Mill à Avignon,' *Revue des Deux Mondes*, 41 (1937), 211-22

1844 Vesey, G.N.A. 'Sensations of Colour.' In *Mill: A Collection of Critical Essays*. Ed. J.B. Schneewind. Garden City, NY: Doubleday, 1963, 111-31

1845 [Villard, Henry.] 'John Stuart Mill Visited by an American,' *Chicago Tribune*, 16 Mar. 1868, 2. Reprinted, drastically abridged, in *Littell's Living Age*, 97 (1868), 447-8

1846 Villey, Daniel. 'Sur la traduction par Dupont-White de "La Liberté" de Stuart Mill,' *Revue d'Histoire Economique et Sociale*, 24 (1938), 193-231. (Relations between JSM and Dupont-White and his criticisms of *On Liberty*)

1847 Vincent, John. *The Formation of the Liberal Party, 1857-68*. London: Constable, 1966. (Contains extended comment on JSM, especially concerning his relations with workingmen)

1848 Viner, Jacob. 'Bentham and J.S. Mill: The Utilitarian Background,' *American Economic Review*, 39 (1949), 360-82. Reprinted in his *The Long View and the Short: Studies in Economic Theory and Policy*. Glencoe, Ill.: Free Press, 1958, 306-31

1849 —— 'J.S. Mill's Bibliography,' *Modern Philology*, 43 (1945), 149-50. (Review of MacMinn)

1850 Vissac, Marc de. John-Stuart Mill,' *Mémoires del'Académie de Vaucluse*, 2e sér, 5 (1905), 311-23. (Brief summary. Reproduces amusing conversation to illustrate associationism.)

1851 Vladislavlev, M. 'Dzhon Styuart Mill'' ['John Stuart Mill'], *Zhurnal ministerstva narodnovo prosveshcheniya* [*Journal of the Ministry of Public Education*], 175 (1874), 112-51

1852 Vogeler, Martha S. 'Comte and Mill: The Early Publishing History of Their Correspondence,' *Mill News Letter*, XI, 2 (1976), 17-22

1853 Wägner, Sven. *John Stuart Mills logiska System och dess kunskapsteoretiska förut sättninger*, *Lund Universitets Års-skligt*, 16 (1879-80), 1-45

1854 Walker, A.D.M. 'Negative Utilitarianism,' *Mind*, 83 (1974), 424-8. (Challenges the easy assumption that there is equal merit in causing pleasure and avoiding pain)

1855 Walker, Angus. 'Karl Marx, the Declining Rate of Profit and British Political Economy,' *Economica*, 38 (1971), 362-77. (JSM's influence on Marx, *inter alia*)

1856 Walker, Francis A. *The Wages Question*. New York: Holt, 1891

1857 Wallas, Graham. *The Life of Francis Place*. London, New York, and Bombay: Longmans, Green, 1898

1858 Waller, John Oscar. 'John Stuart Mill and the American Civil War,' *Bulletin of the New York Public Library*, 66 (1962), 505-18

1859 Walsh, H.T. 'Whewell and Mill on Induction,' *Philosophy of Science*, 29 (1962), 279-84

1860 Waltham, R.C. 'Modern Utilitarianism,' *Universalist Quarterly Review*, ns 9 (1872), 34-45

1861 Walton, Douglas. 'Mill and De Morgan on Whether the Syllogism Is a *Petitio*,' *International Logic Review*, 15 (1977), 57-67

1862 ——, and John Woods. 'Is the Syllogism a Petitio Principii?' *Mill News Letter*, X, 2 (1975), 13-15

1863 Ward, James. 'J.S. Mill's Science of Ethology,' *International Journal of Ethics*, 1 (1891), 446-59

1864 Ward, John W. 'Mill, Marx, and Modern Individualism,' *Virginia Quarterly Review*, 35 (1959), 527-39

1865 Ward, Julius H. 'John Stuart Mill,' *Boston Review*, 6 (1866), 104-20

1866 —— 'The Political Writings of John Stuart Mill,' *Boston Review*, 6 (1866), 567-90

1867 Ward, Wilfred. 'John Stuart Mill,' *Quarterly Review*, 213 (1910), 264-92. Reprinted in his *Men and Matters*. London: Longmans, 1914, 145-201

1868 —— 'John Stuart Mill and the Mandate of the People,' *Dublin Review*, 147 (1910), 85-96

1869 Ward, William George. *Essays on the Philosophy of Theism*. Ed. Wilfred Ward. 2 vols. London: Kegan Paul, Trench, 1884. (Vol. I contains the following essays reprinted from the *Dublin Review*: 'The Rule and Motive of Certitude' [1871], in part a review of the 3rd ed. of

An Examination of Sir William Hamilton's Philosophy; 'Mr Mill's
Denial of Necessary Truth' [1871], on the 3rd ed. of *Hamilton* and
the 7th ed. of the *Logic*; 'Mr Mill on the Foundation of Morality'
[1872], on *Dissertations and Discussions* and Utilitarianism; 'Mr
Mill's Reply to the "Dublin Review" ' [1873], on the 4th ed. of
Hamilton and the 8th ed. of the *Logic*; 'Mr Mill's Philosophical
Position' [1874], on the 4th ed. of *Hamilton*, the 8th ed. of the
Logic, and the *Autobiography*; 'Mr Mill's Denial of Freewill'
[1874], on the 4th ed. of *Hamilton* and the 8th ed. of the *Logic*;
'Mr Mill on Causation' [1876], on the *Logic*. Frequent discussion of
JSM in Vol. II. The entire work projected as an attempt to
'point out the fundamental fallacies in the Experience system of
philosophy as represented by the late Mr Stuart Mill.')

1870 [——] 'Inaugural Address ... By John Stuart Mill,' *Dublin Review*,
ns 8 (1867), 505-9. ('Address on its (ir)religious [*sic*] side is
remarkable for nothing so much as its singular godlessness. ... At the
same time it is bare justice to say, that no writer more carefully
abstains from indulgence in any kind of contemptuous or bitter
expression towards those who differ from him ever so fundamentally'
[505].)

1871 —— *On Nature and Grace. A Theological Treatise. Book I:
Philosophical Introduction*. London: Burns and Lambert, 1860.
(JSM's views are discussed, 25-9)

1872 Warnock, Mary. *Ethics since 1900*. London: Oxford University Press,
1960, 28-40, 49-50. Brief section reprinted as 'On Moore's Criticism of
Mill's "Proof." ' In *Mill: A Collection of Critical Essays*. Ed. J.B.
Schneewind. Garden City, NY: Doubleday, 1968, 199-203

1873 Warren, Alba H. 'John Stuart Mill.' In his *English Poetic Theory,
1825-1865*. Princeton: Princeton University Press, 1950, 66-78

1874 Warren, Howard C. *A History of the Association Psychology*. London:
Constable, 1921

1875 Watkins, J.W.N. 'John Stuart Mill and the Liberty of the Individual.'
In *Political Ideas*. Ed. D. Thomson. London: Watts, 1966, 161-75

1876 Watson, D.R. 'Clemenceau and Mill,' *Mill News Letter*, VI, 1
(1970), 13-19

1877 Watson, J. *Comte, Mill, and Spencer*. Glasgow: Maclehose, 1895

1878 Watts, Robert. *Utilitarianism, as Expounded by J. Stuart Mill, Alex.
Bain, and Others*. 2nd ed. rev., Belfast, 1868

1879 Wedar, Sven. 'Duty and Utility in Hedonistic Utilitarianism as Represented by Bentham and J.S. Mill.' In his *Duty and Utility: A Study in English Moral Philosophy*. Lund: Gleerup, 1952, 33-51

1880 Weinberg, Adelaide. *John Elliot Cairnes and the American Civil War*. London: Kingswood Press, [1970]. (References to JSM's attitude to slavery, and reactions to the Civil War)

1881 —— 'A Meeting of the Political Economy Club, on 7 May, 1857. From John Elliot Cairnes' Notebook,' *Mill News Letter*, I, 2 (1966), 11-16. (An account of a meeting of the Club of which JSM was a member, based on a letter and an unpublished notebook of Cairnes)

1882 —— 'Richard Hussey Walsh and Mill's Theory of International Values,' *Mill News Letter*, IV, 2 (1969), 9-14

1883 —— *Theodor Gomperz and John Stuart Mill*. Geneva: Librairie Droz, 1963

1884 Weinstein, W.L. 'The Concept of Liberty in Nineteenth-Century English Political Thought,' *Political Studies*, 13 (1965), 145-62

1885 Wellington, Samuel. 'John Stuart Mill, the Saint of Rationalism,' *Westminster Review*, 163 (1905), 11-30

1886 Wellman, Carl. 'A Reinterpretation of Mill's Proof,' *Ethics*, 69 (1959), 268-76

1887 Welty, Gordon A. 'Mill's Principle of Government as a Basis of Democracy,' *Monist*, 55 (1971), 51-60

1888 Wenger, C.N. 'Sources of Mill's Criticism of "Pauline,"' *Modern Language Notes*, 60 (1945), 338

1889 Wentscher, Else. 'John Stuart Mills Stellung zur Religion,' *Archiv für die gesamte Psychologie*, 77 (1930), 48-66

1890 —— *Das Problem des Empirismus dargestellt an John Stuart Mill*. Bonn: Marcus and Weber, 1922

1891 Wertz, S.K. 'Composition and Mill's Utilitarian Principle,' *Personalist*, 52 (1971), 417-31

1892 West, E.G. 'J.S. Mill's Redistribution Policy: New Political Economy or Old?' *Economic Inquiry*, 16 (1978), 570-86

1893 —— 'Liberty and Education: John Stuart Mill's Dilemma,' *Philosophy*, 40 (1965), 129-42

1894 —— 'The Role of Education in Nineteenth-Century Doctrines of

Political Economy,' *British Journal of Educational Studies*, 12
(1964), 161-72

1895 ——, and R. W. Hafer. 'J.S. Mill, Unions, and the Wages Fund
Recantation : A Reinterpretation,' *Quarterly Journal of Economics*,
92 (1978), 603-19

1896 West, Henry Robison. 'Mill's Qualitative Hedonism,' *Philosophy*, 51
(1976), 97-101. (Reply to Rex Martin, which see)

1897 —— 'Reconstructing Mill's Proof of the Principle of Utility,'
Mind, 81 (1972), 256-7

1898 West, Julius. *John Stuart Mill*. London: Fabian Society, 1913

1899 West, Mrs Max. 'A Boy's Education,' *Education*, 19 (1899), 434-5

1900 Westholm, Carl-Johan. *Ratio och universalitet: John Stuart Mill och
dagens demokratidebatt*. Skrifter utgivna av Statsventenskapliga
föreningen i Uppsala, nr 72. Np: Rabén and Sjögren, 1976. (With
summary in English)

1901 A Westminster Elector. *Mr John Stuart Mill and the Ballot. A Criticism
of His Opinions as Expressed in 'Thoughts on Parliamentary Reform.'*
London: Ridgway, 1869

1902 Wethered, Herbert Newton. *The Curious Art of Autobiography: From
Benvenuto Cellini to Rudyard Kipling*. London: Johnson, 1956

1903 Wharton, Nicholas. 'John Stuart Mill,' *Listener*, 74 (1965), 803.
(Letter to the editor on Alan Ryan's 'John Stuart Mill's Art of Living,'
which see)

1904 Whewell, William. 'Comte and Positivism,' *Macmillan's Magazine*, 13
(1866), 353-62

1905 —— *Elements of Morality*. 2 vols. 3rd ed. with supplement.
London: Parker, 1854. 1st ed. 1845. (Chap. 2 of supplement gives a
careful reply to JSM's review)

1906 —— *Of Induction with Especial Reference to Mr J. Stuart Mill's
System of Logic*. London: Parker, 1849. Reprinted, revised, in his *On
the Philosophy of Discovery*. London: Cambridge [printed], 1860

1907 —— *Six Lectures on Political Economy*. Cambridge: Cambridge
University Press, 1862. (Refers, *inter alia*, to JSM's *Principles
of Political Economy*)

1908 Whitaker, Albert Conser. *History and Criticism of the Labor Theory of*

Value in English Political Economy. New York: Columbia University Press, 1904

1909 Whitaker, J.K. 'John Stuart Mill's Methodology,' *Journal of Political Economy*, 83 (1975), 1033-49

1910 White, Carlos. *Ecce Femina: An Attempt to Solve the Woman Question. Being an Examination of Arguments in Favour of Female Suffrage by J. Stuart Mill, and Others, and a Presentation of Arguments against the Proposed Change in the Constitution of Society.* Hanover, NH: published by the author; Boston: Lee and Shepherd, 1870

1911 White, Richard Grant. 'John Stuart Mill's Autobiography,' *Galaxy*, 17 (1874), 332-43

1912 White, R.J. 'John Stuart Mill,' *Cambridge Journal*, 5 (1951), 86-96. (Criticism of JSM's interpretation of Bentham and Coleridge)

1913 White, William. *The Inner Life of the House of Commons.* Ed. with Preface by Justin McCarthy. 2 vols. London: T. Fisher Unwin, 1897, II, 30-3. Reprinted Freeport: Books for Libraries, 1970. (White was Assistant Door-Keeper and Principal Door-Keeper of the House of Commons, 1854-75. Journal entries 10 and 24 Feb. 1866 deal amusingly and approvingly with JSM's performance in the House.)

1914 [Whitehurst, E.C.] 'Caroline Fox, John Sterling, and John Stuart Mill,' *Westminster Review*, ns 62 (1882), 156-81. Reprinted in *Littell's Living Age*, 154 (1882), 667-81. (Review of *Memories of Old Friends.* 'In Caroline Fox's memories of him and in his own letter to Barclay Fox, JSM appears in a far more genial light than in his "Autobiography."....')

1915 Whitmore, C.E. 'Mill and Mathematics: An Historical Note,' *Journal of the History of Ideas*, 6 (1945), 109-12. (Note on the proposition that two and two might equal five, quoted by JSM from Fitzjames Stephen, in *Sir William Hamilton's Philosophy*)

1916 Whittaker, Thomas W. *Comte and Mill.* London: Constable, 1908. Reprinted in his *Reason: A Philosophical Essay with Historical Illustrations.* Cambridge: Cambridge University Press, 1934, 31-80

1917 Wilks, Sarah. 'The Mill-Roebuck Quarrel,' *Mill News Letter*, XIII, 2 (1978), 8-12

1918 Willcox, J.K. Hamilton. 'A Visit to John Stuart Mill at Avignon,' *Appleton's Journal*, 9 (1873), 785-8

1919 Willey, Basil. 'John Stuart Mill.' In his *Nineteenth Century Studies*. London: Chatto and Windus, 1949, 141-86

1920 Williams, G.L. 'Mill's Principle of Liberty,' *Political Studies*, 24 (1976), 132-40

1921 Williams, Raymond. 'Mill on Bentham and Coleridge.' In his *Culture and Society*. London: Chatto and Windus, 1958, 49-70. Reprinted Harmondsworth: Penguin, 1961

1922 Williams, Robert. 'A Few Words on Utilitarianism,' *Fraser's Magazine*, 80 (1869), 248-56

1923 Williams, Stanley Thomas. 'John Stuart Mill and Literature,' *London Mercury*, 19 (1929), 395-9

1924 —— 'Two Victorian Boyhoods,' *North American Review*, 213 (1921), 819-26. (Comparison of *Autobiography* with Gosse's *Father and Son*)

1925 Williams, Tom A. 'Intellectual Precocity: Comparison between John Stuart Mill and the Son of Dr Boris Sidis,' *Pedagogical Seminary*, 18 (1911), 85-103. (Argues that early commencement of education is not harmful)

1926 [Williamson, Emma Sara.] William Kirkus (pseud). 'Mr John Stuart Mill.' In her *Miscellaneous Essays*. 2nd ser. 2nd ed. London: Longmans, Green, Reader, and Dyer, 1869, 326-70

1927 [Wilson, H.B.] 'Examination of Sir William Hamilton's Philosophy,' *Westminster Review*, ns 28 (1865), 513-16. (Review)

1928 [Wilson, John.] '*Liberty, Equality, Fraternity*: John Stuart Mill,' *Quarterly Review*, 135 (1873), 178-201. (Review of James Fitzjames Stephen, *Liberty, Equality, Fraternity*; William Thomas Thornton, *Old-Fashioned Ethics and Common-Sense Metaphysics with Some of Their Applications*; W.R. Grey, *Enigmas of Life*; and H.R. Fox Bourne, ed., *John Stuart Mill: Notices of His Life and Works*)

1929 Wilson, John Matthias, and Thomas Fowler. *Principles of Morals. Pt I: Introductory Chapters; Pt II: Being the Body of the Work.* Oxford: Clarendon Press, 1886-87. (Sheets for Pt I originally printed, but not published, in 1875

1930 Wilson, Roland K., J.H. Levy, *et al. Individualism and the Land Question: A Discussion.* London: Personal Rights Association, [1912]. (JSM's position is central to much of the debate)

1931 Winch, Donald Norman. 'Classical Economics and the Case for Colonization,' *Economica*, ns 30 (1963), 387-99

1932 —— *James Mill: Selected Economic Writings*. Edinburgh and London: Oliver and Boyd, for the Scottish Economic Society; Toronto: Clarke, Irwin, 1966. (Biographical sketch and introductions, several references to JSM)

1933 ——, ed. *Principles of Political Economy. By J.S. Mill*. Harmondsworth: Penguin, 1970. (Not the full text, only Bks IV and V, with Chaps 1 and 2 of Bk II, reprinted from the 1871 edition, plus an introductory essay by Winch)

1934 Winch, Peter. *The Idea of a Social Science and Its Relation to Philosophy*. London: Routledge and Kegan Paul, 1958, 66-94

1935 Winkelman, P.H. *De vrijheid sedert John Stuart Mill*. Groningen: Walters, 1950

1936 Winsløw, Christian. *Stuart Mills Etik: et Forsog til en Fremstilling og Kritik*. Copenhagen: Gyldendal, 1909. (With short foreword by Harald Høffding)

1937 Wisniewski, Joseph. *Etude historique et critique de la théorie de la perception extérieure chez John Stuart Mill et Taine*. Paris: Jouve, 1925. (Published dissertation)

1938 Wolfe, Julian. 'Mill on Causality,' *Personalist*, 57 (1976), 96-7

1939 Wolfe, Willard. *From Radicalism to Socialism: Men and Ideas in the Formation of Fabian Socialist Doctrines, 1881-1889*. New Haven and London: Yale University Press, 1975. (Treats JSM's influence on the Fabians)

1940 Wolff, Robert Paul. 'Liberty.' In his *The Poverty of Liberalism*. Boston: Beacon, 1968, 30-50. (See also 138-50)

1941 —— 'On Tolerance and Freedom,' *Dissent*, 14 (1967), 95-8. (Continues the discussion engendered by Wolff, *et al.*, *A Critique of Pure Tolerance*. See Green, Spitz.)

1942 ——, Barrington Moore, Jr, and Herbert Marcuse. *A Critique of Pure Tolerance*. Boston: Beacon Hill, 1965. 2nd ed. with 'Postscript' by Marcuse, London: Cape, 1969. (An attack from the radical left on, *inter alia*, JSM's concept of liberty. See Green, Spitz.)

1943 Wolin, Sheldon S. 'Liberalism and the Decline of Political Philosophy.' In his *Politics and Vision*. Boston and Toronto: Little, Brown, 1960, 286-351

1944   Wollheim, Richard. 'Crime, Sin, and Mr Justice Devlin,' *Encounter*, 13 (1959), 34-40

1945   —— 'J.S. Mill and the Limits of State Action,' *Social Research*, 40 (1973), 1-30

1946   —— 'Without Doubt or Dogma: The Logic of Liberalism,' *Nation*, 183 (1956), 74-6

1947   Woods, John, and Douglas Walton. 'Is the Syllogism a Petitio Principii?' *Mill News Letter*, X, 2 (1975), 13-15

1948   Woods, Thomas. *Poetry and Philosophy. A Study in the Thought of John Stuart Mill*. London: Hutchinson, 1961

1949   Wordsworth, W. Letter to the editor, *Spectator*, 47 (1874), 1396-7. (Responding to a review of *Three Essays* defending JSM. Dated Rydall Mount, 1 Nov. 1874; probably by the poet's son William)

1950   Wright, Carroll D. *The Relation of Political Economy to the Labor Question*. Boston: Williams, 1882. (Cites *Essays on Some Unpublished Questions* [*sic*] and 'Chapters on Socialism')

1951   —— *Some Ethical Phases of the Labor Question*. Boston: American Unitarian Association, 1902. (Single citation as above, but corrected. A 'sociological' work.)

1952   Wright, Chauncey. 'John Stuart Mill - A Commemorative Notice,' *Proceedings of the American Academy of Arts and Sciences*, 9 (1873-74), 285-97. Published as a pamphlet Boston, 1873; reprinted in his *Philosophical Discussions*. New York: Holt, 1877, 414-28. (Appears untitled and unsigned in *Proceedings*)

1953   —— 'Mansel's Reply to Mill,' *Nation*, 4 (1867), 27-9. Reprinted in his *Philosophical Discussions*. New York, Holt, 1877, 350-9. (Review of *The Philosophy of the Conditioned*)

1954   —— 'Mill on Comte,' *Nation*, 2 (1866), 20-1

1955   —— 'Mill on Hamilton,' *Nation*, 1 (1865), 278-81

1956   —— 'Mill on Hamilton,' *North American Review*, 103 (1866), 250-60

1957   Wyrouboff, G. *Stuart Mill et la philosophie positive*. Printed with E. Littré's *Auguste Comte et Stuart Mill*. Paris: Germer Baillière, 1866

1958   Yake, J. Stanley. 'Mill's Mental Crisis Revisited,' *Mill News Letter*, IX, 1 (1973), 2-12

1959 Yamashita, S., and S. Sugihara. 'J.S. Mill and Modern Japan,' *Mill News Letter*, XII, 2 (1977), 2-6

1960 Youmans, E.L., ed. *The Culture Demanded by Modern Life.* New York: Appleton, 1867. (Sub-title cites JSM, but no article by him in collection; Introduction, 'Mental Discipline in Education,' refers to *Inaugural Address* and *Logic*)

1961 Zenger, A. *Dzh. St. Mill', yevo shizn' i proizvedeniya* [*J.S. Mill, His Life and Works*]. Trans. from the German by L. Ivanova under the editorship of Ye. Maksimova. St Petersburg, 1903

1962 Zimmer, Louis B. 'John Stuart Mill and Democracy, 1866-7,' *Mill News Letter*, XI, 2 (1976), 3-17

1963 —— 'The "Negative Argument" in J.S. Mill's Utilitarianism,' *Journal of British Studies*, 17 (1977), 119-37. (See also Himmelfarb)

1964 Zinkernagel, Peter. 'Revaluation of J.S. Mill's Ethical Proof,' *Theoria*, 18 (1952), 70-7

1965 Zuccante, Giuseppe. 'Alcune idee del Comte e dello Stuart Mille, intorno alla psicologia,' *Rendiconti*, ser 2, 30 (1897), 741-53

1966 —— 'Ancora genesi della dottrina: i precursori dello Mill in Inghilterra,' *Memorie del Reale Instituto Lombard di Scienze e Morale*, 20 (1899), 323-72. Reprinted in his *Giovanni Stuart Mill e l'utilitarismo*. Florence: Vallecci, 1922

1967 —— 'Del determinismo di John Stuart Mill,' *La filosofia delle scuole italiane*, 2 (1884), 60-84, 133-70

1968 —— *Giovanni Stuart Mill e l'utilitarismo.* Florence: Vallecci, 1922

1969 —— 'Intorno alle origini della morale utilitaria dello Stuart Mill,' *Rendiconti*, ser 2, 30 (1897), 1143-63. Reprinted in his *Giovanni Stuart Mill et l'utilitarismo*. Florence: Vallecci, 1922

1970 —— 'Intorno all'utilitarismo dello Stuart Mill,' *Rivista italiana di filosofia*, 13 (1898), 247-87

1971 —— *La morale utilitaria dello Stuart Mill: esposizione della dottrina. Memorie del Reale Instituto Lombardo di Scienze et Lettere*, 21 (12 ser, III). Milan: Hoepli, 1899. Reprinted in his *Giovanni Stuart Mill e l'utilitarismo*. Florence: Vallecci, 1922

APPENDICES

Verse

Abacus Politicus. Untitled, *Blackwood's*, 99 (1866), 648

Anon. 'Pegasus in Parliament,' *Fun*, ns 3 (1866), 248

—— 'Anacreontic,' *Fun*, ns 4 (1866), 142. ('But mark me, not all your philosophers up / From quaint Master Mill to antique Aristotle,/ Shall make me turn tail on the saucer and the cup')

—— 'Extension of the Franchise to Women: Notes of a Speech Delivered by J.S. Mill, Esq, MP, during the Debate on the New Reform Bill,' *Fun*, ns 4 (1867), 251

—— 'Double Acrostic No 6 Verse 51,' *Fun*, ns 5 (1867), 58. (Answer *ibid.*, 88)

—— 'A Mill-ody,' *Fun*, ns 5 (1867), 107

—— 'The Progress of Reform,' *Fun*, ns 5 (1867), 181

—— 'Dreams,' *Fun*, ns 5 (1867), 228

—— 'The Power of Speech,' *Fun*, ns 6 (1868), 218

—— 'Womanhood Suffrage,' *Fun*, ns 7 (1868), 173

—— 'The Female Franchise,' *Fun*, ns 8 (1868), 123. ('They'd make us all mere chattels, yet our Mill has fought our battles')

—— 'A Triple Hurrah for Mill,' William Gladstone Papers, British Library Add. MSS 44756, f. 55. (Privately printed and set to music)

—— '*Judy*'s Opening Speech, Women of England,' *Judy*, 1 (1867), 3

—— 'Potter to Beales,' *Judy*, 1 (1867), 281. (Regarding Reform League)

—— 'At Last!' *Judy*, 2 (1868), 240. (Disraeli becomes Prime Minister – he 'gets the best of every Mill')

—— 'No Thoroughfare: A Monologue Addressed by Mr Gladstone to Miss Mill,' *Judy*, 2 (1868), 275. (With cartoon between 276 and 281)

—— 'Raising the Wind; or, The Modern Iphigenia,' *Judy*, 2 (1868), 315. (With cartoon between 328 and 333)

—— 'Gladstone's Dream,' *Judy*, 3 (1868), 29. (With cartoon between 30 and 35)

—— 'The Hanging Committee,' *Judy*, 3 (1868), 59. (Gov. Eyre controversy. With cartoon between 60 and 65.)

—— 'To Mr Robertson Gladstone,' *Judy*, 3 (1868), 69. (With cartoon between 70 and 75)

—— 'The Drawbacks of Jamaica Ginger Beer,' *Judy*, 3 (1868), 75. (Regarding Governor Eyre controversy)

—— '"Wired"; or, Political Croquet,' *Judy*, 3 (1868), 89. (With cartoon between 90 and 95)

—— 'Female Patriotism,' *Judy*, 3 (1868), 202. ('And Mill has talk'd on the rights of our sex')

—— '"Overboard!" or, The "Liberal" Privateersman,' *Judy*, 3 (1868), 222. (With cartoon)

—— 'No Third Class!' *Judy*, 4 (1868), 32. (With cartoon)

—— 'Miss Mill Joins the Ladies,' *Judy*, 4 (1868), 43. (JSM defeat. With cartoon.)

—— 'Election Ballads, 3: Air - "The Mistletoe Bough,"' *Judy*, 4 (1868), 44. ('The "great modern thinker," Mr John Stuart Mill./ Where will he mizzle now?')

—— 'Rhymes of the Rejected Ones,' *Judy*, 4 (1868), 60

—— 'The Ladies in Parliament, a Fragment after the Manner of an Old Athenian Comedy,' *Macmillan's Magazine*, 15 (1866), 1-14

—— 'John Stuart Mill,' *Owl*, 18 Mar. 1868, 4

—— 'Mr J.S. Mill's Debut,' *Press*, 14 (1866), 205

—— 'Lush against Mill,' *Punch*, 49 (1865), 2

—— 'The Tribulation of the "Tizer,"' *Punch*, 49 (1865), 24

—— 'Philosophy and *Punch*,' *Punch*, 49 (1865), 32

—— 'The Power of the Pens. By a Westminster Boy,' *Punch*, 49 (1865), 51

—— 'The Leading Members ...,' *Punch*, 50 (1866), 53. (With drawing by C.H. Bennet)

—— 'What Lord Russell May Be Saying,' *Punch*, 50 (1866), 103

—— 'The Gladiators' Muster,' *Punch*, 52 (1867), 44. (With cartoon)

—— 'Song of Head Centre,' *Punch*, 52 (1867), 109

—— 'Why, at Last, I Believe in Reform. By a Sceptic,' *Punch*, 52 (1867), 212. ('Or think John Mill can ne'er make a blunder')

—— 'A Vision of the Future,' *Punch*, 52 (1867), 217

—— 'A Fenian on His Friends,' *Punch*, 54 (1868), 107

—— 'The Revolt League against Eyre,' *Punch*, 54 (1868), 237. (Supports Eyre against the Jamaica Committee; does not mention JSM by name)

—— 'Robinson's Reverie,' *Punch*, 54 (1868), 250

—— 'Election Amenities,' *Punch*, 55 (1868), 171

—— 'Cox for Finsbury!' *Punch*, 55 (1868), 191. ('Why should Lockes of Southwork creak?/ Why should Rats of Lambeth squeak?/ Chaff and flower of speech at will / Why should grind Westminster's Mill?')

—— 'After the Mêlée,' *Punch*, 55 (1868), 226

—— 'Black and White,' *Tomahawk*, 2 (1868), 240. (Refers to the Governor Eyre controversy)

—— 'Elections' Eve: A Song of the Future(?),' *Tomahawk*, 3 (1868), 250

—— 'The Ballad of the Beaten,' *Tomahawk*, 5 (1868), 247. ('And back to calm Avignon / Had Despot Mill to go')

B., E. 'John Stuart Mill,' *Examiner*, 13 (1873), 518

[Bentley, Edmund Clerihew.] 'John Stuart Mill.' In his *Biography for Beginners*. Ed. E. Clerihew, BA. London: T. Warner Laurie, 1905, np. Reprinted in his *Clerihews Complete*. London: T. Warner Laurie, 1951, np. (A clerihew, illustrated by G.K. Chesterton: 'John Stuart Mill / By a mighty effort of will,/ Overcame his bonhomie / And wrote "Principles of Political Economy"')

C., F.W. 'Mill-iania,' *Press*, 14 (1866), 366

Elder, W. 'Acrostic,' *National Reformer*, 21 (1873), 359

G., E. 'John Stuart Mill,' *Examiner*, 13 (1873), 518

Moore, Thomas. 'Ode to the Goddess Ceres.' In *Poetical Works of Thomas Moore*. Oxford: Oxford University Press, 1924, 570-2

—— 'Ode to the Sublime Porte.' In *Poetical Works of Thomas Moore*. Oxford: Oxford University Press, 1924, 587. Reprinted in *Mill News Letter*, VIII, 1 (1972), 1

Murphy, Joseph John. 'John Stuart Mill,' *Macmillan's Magazine*, 28 (1873), 348-9

Neaves, Charles. 'Buridan's Ass; or, Liberty and Necessity,' *Blackwood's*, 99 (1866), 246. Reprinted in *Littell's Living Age*, 89 (1866), 637. (Lord Neaves was a Scots judge)

—— 'Stuart Mill on Mind and Matter,' *Blackwood's*, 99 (1866), 257-9. Reprinted in *National Reformer*, 7 (1866), 108. (Poem refers to *Sir William Hamilton's Philosophy*)

—— 'Stuart Mill Again; or, The Examiner Examined,' *Blackwood's*, 100 (1866), 246

R. 'To Mr Mill,' *Spectator*, 45 (1872), 1397-8. 'Whom shall we follow? The flame-haired daughter / Of Chaos and Change ...?/ Or Thee, with the brows that know not trouble./ ... For the good, the better, - Whom shall we follow?')

Shore, A. 'To John Stuart Mill,' *Examiner*, 13 (1873), 518

Smith, E.G. 'Written in Commemoration of the Great Reform Demonstration Held August 27th, 1866,' *Commonwealth*, 15 Sept. 1866, 5

Weston, J. 'A Whit-Monday Political Poem,' *Commonwealth*, 19 May 1866, 5

—— Untitled, *Commonwealth*, 28 Apr. 1866, 5

Cartoons

'A New "King of the Castle,"' *Fun*, ns 4 (1867), between 232 and 235.
(Disraeli, challenged by Gladstone, stands on rock(?) labelled 'Treasury
Bench,' JSM and Bright, among others, in background)

'The "Mill"-ennium,' *Fun*, ns 5 (1867), [82]. (JSM proposes a toast to the
ladies)

'Dishing the Whigs,' *Fun*, ns 5 (1867), between 250 and 253. (Head of JSM,
among others, in dish labelled 'Reform Bill')

'Poor Ireland!' *Fun*, ns 7 (1868), between 29 and 33. (JSM, among consulting
physicians, offering 'Heroic Remedies' from a box)

'The Tug of War; or, An Old Game with New Players,' *Fun*, ns 7 (1868),
between 177 and 181. (JSM pulling with the Liberals)

'The New House: A Great Squeeze at the Doors,' *Fun*, ns 8 (1868), between
86 and 91. (JSM among others trying to get in)

'An Election in Outline: Polling Day,' *Fun*, ns 8 (1868), between 117 and 121.
(Line drawing showing JSM at Trafalgar Square)

'Out in the Cold,' *Fun*, ns 8 (1868), 129. (JSM among the defeated
candidates)

'The Lucky Boy: Who Got Such a Large Hamper from the Country,' *Fun*, ns 8
(1868), between 148 and 151. (Members preparing to cut cake labelled
Cabinet. JSM looking on through window,)

'Parliamentary,' *Judy*, 1 (1867), 156. (JSM in skirt and cap, carrying parasol)

'"Deep" Sea Voices,' *Judy*, 1 (1867), 227. (JSM swimming with reformers -
complaints by Derby, Disraeli, Gladstone)

'The St Stephen's Meet,' *Judy*, 2 (1868), between 202 and 207. (JSM mounted
in woman's habit)

'No Thoroughfare,' *Judy*, 2 (1868), between 276 and 281. (Gladstone, Bright,
Russell and JSM, dressed as a woman, halted by Conservative policy)

'Raising the Wind; or, The Modern Iphigenia,' *Judy*, 2 (1868), between 328 and
333. (JSM participates as Irish Church is sacrificed. With verse, 315)

'Gladstone's Dream!' *Judy*, 3 (1868), between 30 and 35. (Maynooth and the
Irish Question. Gladstone dreams that JSM along with Bright and others are
going to burn Trench and Beresford at the stake)

'The Hanging Committee,' *Judy*, 3 (1868), between 60 and 65. (JSM with others attempting to hang Eyre's portraits. Pro-Eyre. With verse, 59.)

'Beautiful for Ever,' *Judy*, 3 (1868), between 70 and 75. (Gladstone being barbered by his brother with JSM and Bright looking on. With verse, 69.)

'"Wired"; or, Political Croquet!' *Judy*, 3 (1868), between 90 and 95. (JSM dressed as a lady at game which Gladstone is losing to Disraeli. With verse, 89.)

['All About Everything,'] *Judy*, 3 (1868), 181. (JSM in skirt and cap along with Bright)

'Lightening the Ship,' *Judy*, 3 (1868), between 222 and 227. (JSM and others being tossed overboard from the 'Liberal' as frigate 'Constitution' closes fast. With verse, 222.)

'No Third Class!' *Judy*, 4 (1868), between 24 and 29. (Odger and Bradlaugh kept off Liberal Parliamentary train; JSM in first-class carriage. With verse, 32.)

['All About Everything,'] *Judy*, 4 (1868), 43. (JSM as a baby. With text.)

'Miss Mill Joins the Ladies,' *Judy*, 4 (1868), between 44 and 49. (JSM as a lady defeated by Smith. With verse, 43.)

['All About Everything,'] *Judy*, 4 (1869), 189. (JSM in skirt and cap ripping down Smith's poster)

'The Leading Members of the British Senate,' *Punch*, 50 (1866), 53. (JSM chained to Bright who is labelled 'Reform')

'Gladiators Preparing for the Arena,' *Punch*, 52 (1867), 46-7. (JSM among them drinking from a cup labelled 'Logic.' With verse, 44.)

'Mill's Logic; or, Franchise for Females,' *Punch*, 52 (1867), 129

'The Lady's Advocate,' *Punch*, 52 (1867), 225. (JSM in barrister's wig consoled by large female)

'D'Israel-i in Triumph; or, The Modern Sphynx,' *Punch*, 52 (1867), 246-7. (JSM one of group pulling triumphal car)

Initial for '*Punch*'s Essence of Parliament,' *Punch*, 54 (1868), 122. (JSM holding baby)

'Before the Tournament,' *Punch*, 55 (1868), 216-17. (JSM on foot)

'Rotten Row,' *Tomahawk*, 2 (1868), 251-2. (Composite drawing with short sketch, 253)

'Not for Jo(hn Stuart Mill); or, A Smith for Westminster,' *Tomahawk*, 3 (1868), 203. (JSM, among others, fishing for votes)

Portraits and Other Representations

Portraits
   E. Goodwyn Lewis. 1869. In the possession of Dr Graham Hutton. Reproduced
   in *Later Letters*. Ed. Francis E. Mineka and Dwight N. Lindley. Vols. XIV-
   XVII of *The Collected Works of John Stuart Mill*. Toronto: University of
   Toronto Press, 1972, XVI, facing 985. (Perhaps after 1865 engraving.)
   G.F. Watts. 1873. National Portrait Gallery. Reproduced in:
   —— *Art Annual*. 3 vols. London: Virtue, 1892-96, III, 26
   —— *Das neunzehnte Jahrhundert in Bildmissen*. Ed. Karl Werckmeister.
   5 vols. Berlin: Photog. Gesellschaft, 1898-1901, II, plate 172
   —— *National Portrait Gallery*. Ed. Lionel Cast. 2 vols. London: Cassell,
   1901-2, II, 303
   —— *Bookman*, 12 (1901), 478
   —— Garnett, Richard, and Edwin Gosse. *History of English Literature*.
   4 vols. London: Heinemann, 1903, IV, 296
   —— Hamerton, Phillip Gilbert. 'Portrait of John Stuart Mill. Etched by
   Rajon, from the Painting by G.F. Watts,' *Portfolio*, 6 (1875), 11
   —— Wickenden, R.J. 'Paul Adolphe Rajon,' *Print Collector's Quarterly*,
   6 (1916), 411-34

Painting
   'An Incident in Connection with the Presentation of the First Women's
   Suffrage Petition to Parliament in 1866. Miss Emily Davies and Miss
   Elizabeth Garrett hide the roll with 1499 signatures under the apple-
   woman's stall in Westminster Hall until Mr John Stuart Mill, MP, comes to
   collect the petition.' Bertha Newcombe, 1910. Fawcett Society, London

Daguerreotype
   Reproduced in *Letters of John Stuart Mill*. Ed. Hugh Elliot. 2 vols. London:
   Longmans, Green, 1910, I, frontis.
Photographs
   3 poses. London Stereoscopic Co. 1865. Single pose Berlin: Photo. Verl.
   Sophus Williams, 1884. (Private sitting in 1865 subsequently passed to
   London Stereoscopic Company. See *Later Letters*. Ed. Francis E. Mineka

and Dwight N. Lindley. Vols. xiv-xvii of *The Collected Works of John Stuart Mill*. Toronto: University of Toronto Press, 1972, xvi, 1078, 1082, 1091-2.)

John Stuart Mill and Helen Taylor. Reproduced in Michael St John Packe. *The Life of John Stuart Mill*. London: Secker and Warburg, 1954, facing 480; and in Eugene August. *John Stuart Mill: A Mind at Large*. New York: Scribners, 1975, 161

Engravings (after photographs)

I

Plummer, John. 'Remarkable Men: Members of the New Parliament. No 1. John Stuart Mill,' *Cassell's Illustrated Family Papers*, 3rd ser, 16 Sept. 1865, 87-8. (Summary of career by Plummer with pen and ink sketch)

Harper's Weekly, 9 (1865), 677. (With short summary of career complimenting JSM on his election)

Toule, George M. 'John Stuart Mill,' *Appleton's Journal of Literature, Science and Art*, 3 (1870), 126-9. (Biographical sketch with engraving)

Harper's Weekly, 17 (1873), 436. (With obit.)

Popular Science Monthly, 3 (1873), 528

II

Illustrated London News, 48 (1867), 280. (With summary of career and suitability as an MP)

National Reformer, 7 (1866), 195-6. Reprinted from Illustrated London News, 48 (1867)

Eclectic Magazine, 67 (1866), frontis. (Short summary of career [120-1] quotes *Illustrated London News*, 48 [1867])

Galaxy, 12 (1871), facing 149

Illustrated London News, 62 (1873), 456. (With obit.)

Outlook, 56 (1897), 569

III

Harper's Magazine, 47 (1873), 528. (With obit.)

Independent, 68 (1910), 297

Life, 22 (24 Mar. 1947), 101. (With short text)

Caricatures

[Ward, Leslie.] Spy (pseud). 'A Feminine Philosopher,' *Vanity Fair*, 9 (1873), 102. (With text, 103-4. Original sketch in National Portrait Gallery.)

Beerbohm, Max. 'Mr Morley of Blackburn, on an Afternoon in the Spring of '69 Introduces Mr John Stuart Mill.' In his *Rossetti and His Circle*. London: Heinemann, 1922, plate 18

Poster

'The Westminster Guy.' Hambleden Archives. (W.H. Smith setting effigy of JSM alight. Refers to 1868 election.)

Cameo

Ca. 1840. Reproduced in *Letters of John Stuart Mill*. Ed. Hugh Elliot. 2 vols. London: Longmans, Green, 1910, II, facing 233; and in Michael St John Packe. *The Life of John Stuart Mill*. London: Secker and Warburg, 1954, facing 128

Statue

Thomas Woolner. 1878. Victorian Embankment Gardens east of Temple Station. Photographs in Paul William White and Richard Gloucester. *On Public View*. London: Hutchingson, 1971, 153; and in Eugene August. John Stuart Mill: A Mind at Large. New York: Scribners, 1975, 226

Medal

Alphonse Legros. 1883. City of Manchester Art Gallery. Photograph in *International Studies*, 20 (1903), 16. Reproduced on dust jackets of *The Collected Works of John Stuart Mill*. Ed. J.M. Robson. Toronto: University of Toronto Press, 1965

INDEX

John Stuart Mill

Other Writers